Strangers
to the Tribe

§

STRANGERS
TO THE TRIBE

*Portraits of
Interfaith Marriage*

GABRIELLE GLASER

A Marc Jaffe Book
HOUGHTON MIFFLIN COMPANY
Boston · New York   1997

For information about permission to reproduce selections from
this book, write to Permissions, Houghton Mifflin Company,
215 Park Avenue South, New York, New York 10003.

Library of Congress Cataloging-in-Publication Data
Glaser, Gabrielle.
Strangers to the tribe : portraits of interfaith
marriage / Gabrielle Glaser.
"A Marc Jaffe book."
p. cm.
Includes bibliographical references.
ISBN 0-395-72776-6
1. Interfaith marriage — United States. 2. Marriage — Religious
aspects — Judaism. 3. Marriage — Religious aspects —
Christianity. I. Title.
HQ1031.G5   1997
306.84'3 — dc21   97-18827   CIP

Printed in the United States of America

QUM 10 9 8 7 6 5 4 3 2 1

FOR STEPHEN

Acknowledgments

❦

This book is the result of many trips and conversations across the United States. I drew enormously on the experience of those who counsel and study intermarried families. To that end, I would like to thank Dr. Arthur Blecher, Dr. Egon Mayer, Rabbi Jack Moline, Rabbi Mindy Portnoy, the Reverend Joe Russell, Lisa Shapero, and Rabbi Harold White. Many people identified families whose stories were compelling, and gave insight on the topic of intermarriage: David Alston, Jennifer Alston, Leslie Mitchel Bond, Blanca Espinoza, Vera Glasberg, Vic Glasberg, Adam Glenn, Howard Goldberg, Cristina Leckie, Helen Lichtenstein, Robin Long, Michele Gottlieb Nemschoff, Mrinalini Rajwar, Pat Reynolds, Steve Roberts, Maura Burke Weiner, and Ed Weiner. Of course, I am indebted to the families I interviewed for the book. More than anything, I thank them for their trust and their willingness to lay bare their relationships with God and with each other. I hope they find their stories accurately represented.

I had the luck to have as my editor Marc Jaffe, who gave sage advice and encouragement along the way. Thanks are also due to Glen Hartley, my agent, and Frances Apt, my manuscript editor. I am grateful to those who read chapters and gave helpful suggestions: Karen Breslau, Edward Engelberg, Elaine Engelberg, Steve Glaser, Virginia Glaser, Michelle Glaser Jackson, John Keitel, Mindy Keskinen, Tara McKelvey Kott, Martha Ann Overland, Rivka Raffel, Miriam Reinharth, Diane Solway, and Joyce Weatherford. I am most indebted, of course, to my husband, Stephen, who patiently read and improved the book in its various drafts, and whose enthusiasm for this project helped bolster my own.

Contents

Preface

In the easy suburban evenings our parents waited
for our American disaster. We were schooled in the
talk of fires. We knew what should be grabbed . . .
"You are not American," our father said. He said it to
us the way we heard other fathers tell their children
not to play in the street.[1]

§

JEWS WHO CAME to America in the late nineteenth and early
twentieth centuries succeeded beyond their wildest imaginings.
Still, there was a sense of foreboding, an underlying assumption
that chaos lurked just over the horizon. It was only a matter of
time, they believed, before the Christian majority of the United
States turned on the strangers in their midst. Over the centuries,
after all, the cycle of terror, flight, and temporary refuge had always
repeated itself: in Spain, in Russia, in Poland, and in Germany. It
was the inevitable cost of living in the Diaspora, a reality as familiar to Jews as the rhythms of Hebrew prayer.

But in America, a different history unfolded. The fears of an
American disaster gave way to the American dream. In a single
generation, sometimes even within a few years of arrival, Jewish
immigrants moved from the edges of American life to its center.
By the 1960s, Jews had vaulted past the quotas and restrictions
placed on their parents and reached every sector of American society — the arts and literature, science and technology, even politics.
They also met, and fell in love with, non-Jews. Within decades, intermarriage, forbidden by Jewish law, had been transformed from

scandal to commonplace. In many senses, it was a measure of the acceptance of Jews in America.

In the 1940s and 1950s, it was plausible for a Jewish family to sit shiva for that rare child who strayed from the tribe in choosing a mate. By the 1970s, in all but the most Orthodox families, such a response would have been as anachronistic as it was pointless. Hundreds of thousands of young Jewish men and women married Catholics, Protestants, Hindus, even Muslims. They raised their children to appreciate both parents' faiths, or ceded Judaism to the prevailing Christian culture. Ornamental Stars of David rested atop Christmas trees. Priests stood alongside rabbis beneath the sacred Jewish wedding canopy, the chuppah. As the trend widened, so too did the panic among the Jewish community's elders. Silent Holocaust. Finishing Hitler's work. Self-loathing Jews. These were just a few of the epithets used to dismiss the phenomenon and its practitioners. In 1977, the Harvard demographer Elihu Bergman went so far as to predict that the number of American Jews could shrink from nearly six million to fewer than a million — even as low as 10,420 — by the year 2076.[2]

While Bergman's dire prognosis appears unlikely, the uproar over intermarriage stems from some undeniable statistics. The National Jewish Population Survey in 1990, the most extensive study in the history of the American Jewish community, inflamed passions on the subject. It found that 52 percent of Jews who married since 1985 had chosen a Gentile mate. That news alone reverberated among the leaders of the nation's 5.5 million Jews, who, according to the survey, made up 2.5 percent of the U.S. population. But perhaps even more alarming was the news that little more than a quarter of intermarried couples — 28 percent — said they were raising their children as Jews. Thirty percent said they were raising their children with no religion, and another 41 percent said they were raising their children in a religion other than Judaism.[3]

Numbers like those came as a stunning blow to the immigrant generation and their children. They had aspired to success in America, of course, but had always expected that it could be accomplished without sacrificing much, if any, of the Jewish identity they had enjoyed while living in tightly knit Jewish communities in and around major cities. Meanwhile, more than any other religious group in America, the Jews became a largely secular people.

Intermarriage — and how to address it — has roiled intellectuals and put the two largest branches of American Judaism, the Reform and Conservative movements, at odds. When the numbers of Jews intermarrying began rising steadily twenty years ago, Reform leaders resigned themselves to the inevitability of these unions. They began, tentatively, to welcome intermarried Jews and their families into the fold of Jewish community life. In fact, in 1983 the American Reform movement declared that it would recognize as Jews the children of Jewish fathers and Gentile mothers, provided that the children were raised as Jews. It was a step away from centuries of Jewish tradition, which considers anyone born of a Jewish mother a Jew, since one could always determine the mother at the time of birth. Jews can also be made, by the formal process of conversion. (Paradoxically, if you are born a Jew and practice another religion, you are still Jewish under Jewish law.)

Among Jewish lay leaders, the trend is met with great consternation. Most lament the rapid decline of a culture so nearly extinguished during World War II. Others, though they are few, see the non-Jewish influx into Jewish America as new breath in the community, and even an opportunity to expand its ranks, if approached properly.

This is not a book about statistics or the questions about the methodology used to make the most dire projections. The debate over the accuracy of the surveys and what intermarriage means to American Judaism is a real one — and one I leave to social scientists. But journalists have a separate, and important, role to play in mapping the emotional landscape behind the numbers. Like snapshots, they freeze a moment in time. The reality, of course, is far more fluid. I am convinced that the complexities of merging two cultures can hardly be understood by learning, as surveys ask, whether a family lights candles on Friday nights, or has a Christmas tree.

And so I set out to explore the spiritual and emotional lives of different families throughout the United States. I interviewed dozens of interfaith couples, met rabbis, priests, and ministers, and heard up close the raging debate that intermarriage has provoked in the Jewish community. It is a topic that has changed dramatically in the 1990s alone, spawning its own chat rooms on the Internet, its own newsletters, greeting cards, and children's books.

I leave to others more trained in Jewish learning the historic and vexing question, "Who is a Jew?" But I can report from my journey along the spiritual frontlines that couples are confecting their own mixtures of religions. Are these intermarried Jews, whose children celebrate Passover, Hanukkah, and Christmas, real or ersatz Jews? It is not for me to say. In my travels, I heard from time to time that intermarriage would be the end of Judaism in America. My evidence is anecdotal but suggestive. And what it suggests is that, beyond the reach of the surveys and synagogues, a significant number of Jews who marry outside their faith are making serious efforts to pass on the religion and culture of their forefathers. Judaism survived the travails of exile in Egypt, forced conversion in Spain, and the Holocaust. If the interfaith couples I met over the past three years are any measure — and I think they are — it will surely survive modern intermarriage.

I recognize that the eleven families portrayed do not reflect the statistical profile of interfaith couples. For instance, I have included three converts to Judaism, more than a third of the book, while in reality fewer than 15 percent of non-Jewish spouses convert to Judaism. In addition, I chose two couples from Hawaii; the Jewish partners in those marriages help illustrate the broad differences in what it means to grow up Jewish in America.

Indeed, the marriages depicted in this book cast a wide net. Trudy Schandler-Wong was raised in an Orthodox Jewish home in rural North Carolina; she married a Chinese-American convert to Judaism. As a child in Brooklyn, Morris Rabinko had no idea that Jews were a minority in the world. The son of Holocaust survivors and a gifted linguist, he speaks Japanese to his half-Japanese daughters, along with Yiddish and Russian. Maura Fitzsimmons, a granddaughter of Ireland, learned of forgiveness and tolerance from her parents and her parish priest. Yet those lessons were difficult to put into practice as she struggled with her future in-laws, Jews from Cleveland; for years, they referred to her not by name but simply as "the Catholic." Joe Gold, the son of Jewish immigrants who settled in San Francisco, converted to the Lutheranism of his wife, Barbara.

I chose my subjects according to a simple criterion: I found the people and their decisions captivating. I did not set out to make judgments about the multiplicity of choices couples make. My intent was to write about their lives, their reflections on their decisions, the long-term influence of angry or even dead relatives on adult children, their spouses, their grandchildren. No matter how much people insisted they were ordinary people, with ordinary lives, I found quite the opposite.

Often, the Christian partners in interfaith marriages voiced objections to the terms used to describe them. One Catholic woman bristled at the term "non-Jew." "You might as well say 'non-person,' " she said. "That's what it sounds like." Another woman disliked the word "Gentile." "It sounds like 'goy' to me," she said, "and that's pretty much what it means — anybody who's not Jewish."[4] I apologize to anyone who is offended by these terms, but I had to include them, since, in addition to Christians, I spoke to Hindus, Buddhists, Muslims, and atheists.

These couples are not composites, although many have chosen to use pseudonyms and to change slight details of their identities. Friends, therapists who work with interfaith couples, Christian clergy, and rabbis who knew I was working on the book led me to many of these people. Others I knew myself, from long ago.

I talked to dozens of couples and their extended families, rabbis and ministers, priests and therapists, from Honolulu to Chicago to New York. For this book, I chose the stories that illustrate larger issues, the seamless compromises that some people are able to reach, the heartache that others endure.

Strangers to the Tribe

❦

ONE

That's a Jewish Name, Isn't It?

❧

T HE POLISH VILLAGE of Swiebodzice is notable only for its
ugliness. It sits, trapped, in a dirty valley surrounded by coal
mines. The industry has left its mark — on blackened windowsills,
on soot-stained buildings, and in the lungs of the people who live
there. Few inhabitants survive beyond their sixtieth birthday; few,
it seems, would want to. It is a bleak place, its only spots of beauty
the gnarled apple trees and wild lilacs that have somehow defied
their poisoned elements, and line the road into town.

In 1884, my great-grandparents, Ernst and Louise Glaser, left
Swiebodzice for a better life in the New World. A little more than a
century later, my parents and I arrived there to take a look, on a
cold, rainy day in May. My father got out of the car, a beat-up
yellow Mercedes we had hired in Cracow. He drew a deep breath
and glanced at the dreary store that passed as a grocer's, a thick
block of beige cheese, drying at the edges, its only window display.
My father squinted, as if to get a better view where none was to be
had. And how could there be? We had spent the morning at Auschwitz. In the afternoon, we drove through Europe's most decimated
land, the polluted sprawl of Silesia. At our hotel, my mother and I
were mistaken for prostitutes, simply because I spoke Polish and
because we were unaccompanied women waiting in the lobby. It
was impossible, it seemed, to go downhill. But Swiebodzice was
hardly the idyllic village of family lore. I watched my father's blue-

gray eyes search the streets, the trees, the sky, and waited for him to say something. An eyebrow shot above his glasses. "Well," he said, "I'm glad Grandpa Glaser left."

It is a sentiment expressed by thousands of American Jews when they finally visit the East European shtetls that loom large in family legends. But though the emotions may be much the same, my story is a good bit more complicated. When Ernst Glaser set out from Swiebodzice, then the German village of Freiburg, he was a tailor, the youngest of his family's four sons. From Hamburg, Ernst sailed with his young bride, Louise Reichter, to Baltimore. They traveled to Kansas, where — mysteriously, for an impoverished couple who had never grown so much as turnips — they tried their hand at raising wheat and cattle. Their attempts brought one failure after another. Kind strangers paid for the family's passage to Oregon, where, once again, they set up a farm. This one was a success, fueled by the labor of a dozen hardworking children. Each Sunday, the family climbed into a horse-drawn wagon to attend services at the Sandridge Community Church, the local Protestant church.

This was the story committed to memory and retold at family reunions each year by a talkative aunt who stood on a chair so that everyone could hear. Almost all my relatives, including my parents, were farmers. As far as most of them were concerned, our history began when the farm did. They had settled in Sandridge; that was what there was to know of my great-grandparents. A century later, however, I found myself living near Ernst and Louise's hometown, which had become Polish territory at the end of World War II. As a journalist, I began to wonder about their lives and my distant links to them. Soon enough, I found parts of their story that didn't quite fit.

Freiburg, according to an 1880 German census, was a largely Jewish town, a shtetl. Seventy-seven percent of its inhabitants were Jews. The other 23 percent were Catholic. In America, Ernst and Louise said they were Lutheran. But in Freiburg, in 1880, there were no Lutheran churches, nor were there any for miles around. The more I delved, the more the questions mounted. Glaser, meaning "glassworker," is often, but not always, a Jewish surname. Some of Ernst's relatives had borne decidedly Old Testament first names — Isak and Lea. On the other hand, his brothers were Gustav, Wilhelm, and Karl. Good Germans? Or Jews trying desperately to assimilate in the hostile terrain of nineteenth-century Prussia? Many of Freiburg's records were destroyed in a turn-of-the century fire. The few surviving photos shed little light on Ernst's origins: one, snapped at a studio the year before he left, shows a small dark man with crinkly eyes, a wary smile, and a long black biblical beard. Louise Christine Reichter had an undeniably Christian middle name, but Reichter could as easily be Jewish as Christian. They were sketchy clues, but they made me wonder. Were she and Ernst pioneers of intermarriage?

Ernst and Louise followed the same path as many poor Jews who emigrated at the turn of the century. More than 1.5 million Central and Eastern European Jews swarmed to the United States between 1881 and 1910, fleeing pogroms and poverty. Philanthropic Jewish organizations were eager to see Jews fan out from crowded Eastern cities; nationwide depressions in the 1890s had prompted high unemployment, not to mention resentment of immigrants competing for jobs. German Jews, who had been in the United States for decades, were not eager to welcome these reminders of their humble origins. Partly out of altruism, partly out of embarrassment, they funded westward passage for many new immigrants. Some Jews became tradesmen, opening shops in growing towns and cities. Others became farmers, inspired by the belief that Jewish renewal depended on returning to the land. Farming, essential as it was to survival, was off-limits to Jews in most European countries, who were relegated to more marginal work. Thousands of Jews settled in the Dakotas, Kansas, Missouri, even Texas. Still others went farther West. Petaluma, California, a small town south of San Francisco, was home to a small Jewish farming community. A group of young Jewish immigrants from Odessa founded a utopian community called New Odessa, in southern Oregon, in 1882.[1] New Odessa lies a few miles from Roseburg, Oregon, a town founded by Aaron Rose, a Jewish pioneer and farmer who welcomed Jews to the West as early as 1854.[2] Coincidentally — or perhaps not — Roseburg was Ernst and Louise's first stop in Oregon before they started their own farm.

My great-aunts and uncles recall candles at the dinner table, special fish balls, and prayers said over bread. My own grandfather rested his hands on our heads when we were young, moving his lips in an inaudible prayer. Then, I thought it was weird. As an adult, I see links to the Sabbath blessings elders say for their children, hands placed on their heads. If Ernst and Louise were Jewish — and I am convinced that at least Ernst was — one thing is certain. The Glasers, in America, left Judaism at the frontier.

I arrived in Swiebodzice that day with far more modern reasons to be pondering the quandaries of intermarriage, spirituality, and family history. A hundred years after the union of Ernst and Louise I had stood under a chuppah with Stephen Engelberg and repeated the words of the Hebrew wedding ceremony. Our immediate roots were radically different, Swiebodzice aside. My mother's family were French Canadian Catholics on her father's side, Protestant pioneers who had been in Oregon since Lewis and Clark on her mother's. (One great-great-grandmother who was born in Oregon in 1870 passed herself off as half "Gypsy." There were few non-Indian women in the state at that time, let alone any Romany. Her high cheekbones, olive skin, straight black hair, and piercing dark eyes make my family think she was at least part Native American, and loath to admit it.) The Glaser side had its own obscure past, but my grandfather, John Glaser, married a woman who claimed centuries of American forebears. Grammie was fiercely proud of her membership in the local chapter of the Daughters of the American Revolution and insisted that we were related to Daniel Boone. (She envied my mother's very clear ties to Betsy Ross, an even greater figure in the Revolution.) Stephen's mother's family were Russian Jews, transplanted to Brooklyn. His paternal grandfather, Jakob, was a Polish Jew who had migrated to Germany after World War I, married a German-Jewish woman, and started a family of his own in southeastern Germany — not far, coincidentally, from today's Swiebodzice. Jakob was arrested during the Nazis' Kristallnacht rampage and interned at Dachau, where he suffered repeated truncheon blows to the head. The family escaped to America before the outbreak of World War II, but Jakob died soon after, of a cerebral hemorrhage. Doctors attributed his death to the beatings at Dachau.

Stephen and I had agreed to raise our children as Jews. But I wondered what would become of me. My own family was in something of a spiritual flux. My father, an only child, had been raised a Methodist. The parents of my mother, also an only child, had attended no church. My grandfather, raised by a Presbyterian father and a Catholic mother, left religion behind when his dad and brother died of tuberculosis within a few weeks of each other. My grandmother, Nana, was raised without an organized faith, and seemed to like it that way. But my mother sought a spiritual niche. As a young girl, she walked to the stone Presbyterian church not far from her house; she married my father there in 1958.

My parents started their family early, and within a decade, four kids — three girls and a boy — filled my mother's station wagon. Each of us was baptized a Methodist, in a modern church with huge panes of colored glass, stuck in their frames like square Sucrets. I have few memories of the place, except that the building was always chilly. I understood years later that it was just as unwelcoming to my parents spiritually. When I was nine, we switched to a modest Episcopal church a few blocks away.

I liked the church, and the people were friendly. The priest, Father Joe Russell, became a figure in the life of all of us. A tall, slender man with an unwavering voice and a generous smile, Father Joe delivered sermons with his arms outstretched in welcome. He and his wife, Jane, threw parties with biblical themes and set up religious classes in the form of theater, where we were Old and New Testament actors. I liked Sunday school for a time; I loved the stage. Some prayers — for the needy, the sick, the grieving, the lonely — stay with me still. But I often struggled with others. One recitation particularly stung: "Forgive us, O Lord, for we are not fit to pick up the crumbs beneath your table." Even then I was uncomfortable with the notion that I was born a sinner, that Christ had died for my transgressions. I especially resented having to ask God constantly for his forgiveness. God was a loving father, I was told, but somehow I understood that, like Santa, he always watched and always remembered. Young as I was, it struck me as odd: was I really such a bad person? Still, I was convinced that some slip-up — tattling on my older sisters, not sharing with my little brother — would land me in hell. In fact, my paternal grandmother, Grammie, warned me as much. "Be a good girl," she would admonish, "and you will go to the kingdom of heaven." From everything I'd heard, it sounded like a nice place. I imagined people wandering around on clouds, in soft, flowing robes, wearing Frisbee-sized haloes. God — with a white beard, of course — presided from a golden throne.

Hell was as scary as heaven was serene: a goateed devil, complete with a tail and pitchfork, ran around tormenting the dreadful souls whose misdeeds had landed them there. Orange flames leaped in the background, and caldrons bubbled with their sinister potions, straight out of a scene from *Snow White*. Snakes, rats, and other vermin ran amuck. These images came partly from Sunday school, partly from Grammie, but my rich fantasy life fueled them, too. They came to me early, and for a long time they stuck. Still, even as a child, I had a hard time believing the other stories: the Virgin birth, Jesus being the son of God. I knew early how reproduction worked — I was in 4-H.

In fact, my hometown of Tangent — "Population 540, Please Drive Carefully," the sign read — had more sheep than people. Yet Tangent, narrow as it was, opened up to a much broader world. From the two-hundred-acre plot Ernst and Louise Glaser had bought, the many Glaser grandchildren had developed diversified farms. Some grew wheat, some corn, others cherries and walnuts. My father, Stephen, had chosen a single crop for his farm: grass seed. When I was growing up, the rainy green valley where we lived provided 70 percent of the world's seed — for lawns, golf courses, soccer and football fields. My father farmed in the summer and sewed up business for his seed company in the spring. We went along wherever sports took him: Italian soccer fields, English cricket greens, Virginia horse country, lush Hawaiian valleys where the wealthy played golf.

My mother, a voracious reader, saw to it that we learned about these far-off places and others beyond them. During the Munich Olympics of 1972, when the Palestinian group Black September killed eleven Israeli athletes, I bombarded her with questions. At eight, I had only a dim impression of the news, but this struck me as very serious indeed. What happened, and why? I asked her. With a measured voice, she described the events of the night before. I knew about the Holy Land from Sunday school, but not about modern-day Jews. My mother sat at the kitchen table and pointed to Israel in the atlas. From that followed a long discussion of the Second World War, an event I had heard of before, since I knew people who had been wounded fighting in it. But it now seemed more clearly defined: a battle between good and evil. The more questions I asked, the more horrors she revealed: the indignities suffered, the laws passed, the concentration camps, the children wrested from their parents. Six million dead had little meaning until my mother bought me *The Diary of Anne Frank*. This could happen to someone scarcely older than I? How?

Three years later, on a family trip to Europe, we shuffled through the Franks' hiding space in Amsterdam; the following week, we went to Dachau. For months afterward, I thought about Jews and the Holocaust incessantly. I looked under "Jews" in the card catalog at the public library. I thumbed through books about the war, and saw pictures of the emaciated bodies. I read Elie Weisel's *Night*. In high school, I had a history teacher, an army veteran, whose obsession with World War II matched my own. I watched with grim resignation the newsreels he showed of goose-stepping Nazis and burning synagogues. By that time, it was a familiar story.

I'm not sure why I became interested in lives so far from my own. My first obsessions were ordinary: Bigfoot, the Loch Ness monster, the Bermuda Triangle. Later, I fastened on Sacagawea, the Native American woman who had helped guide Lewis and Clark. On bright autumn days, my siblings and I would search my dad's newly plowed fields for arrowheads. If you looked carefully, you could find tiny pieces of flint and obsidian in these sacred burial grounds — Indian mounds, we called them.

My favorite time of year was Christmas. The day after Thanksgiving, we drove to the nearest Boy Scout lot to pick out a tree and boxes of greens. My mother taught us how to coax pine boughs and juniper berries into fragrant wreaths. We painstakingly iced homemade gingerbread men and hung them on the tree as ornaments. On Christmas Eve, we visited my mother's parents, Nana and Poppy, and opened their presents to us after a ham dinner. Later, we went to midnight mass. Poppy always accompanied us to church; Nana never did. She would plead fatigue, saying she needed to be energetic for the next day, at our house, which began very early. No one stayed in bed long on Christmas morning.

I should have liked Easter — we dyed dozens of eggs and had huge baskets full of candy on Easter morning — but I didn't. The year I turned ten, my birthday fell on Good Friday. My mother planned a party for the following Monday; Good Friday was too solemn a day, she said, for celebration. I hadn't paid much attention to the holiday until then; for me, it meant nothing more than the Easter bunny. But anything that made me miss my birthday also made me sit up and take notice. Maybe at ten a child's sense of mortality is naturally awakened. And for me, it all came crashing down that weekend. I saw a passion play at our church, and weeks later still dreamed of the bloody holes in Christ's hands, of his unquenchable thirst, of the masses crying, "Crucify him! Crucify him!" After that year, I couldn't put these images behind me for the joy that others took in the day. I couldn't understand why, if Christ had departed so cruelly, anyone should celebrate. To me, redemption seemed a distant consolation for watching a beloved son and friend die in agony on the cross. And the guilt. Everyone said Christ died because he loved us, and for our sins. But we still did bad things, didn't we? I didn't understand.

When I got to junior high, I asked Nana why she didn't go to church. She often mentioned prayers. I wondered whether God heard her the same way if she recited them only at home. Services were non-negotiable at our house. You got up on Sunday mornings and you went. Period. But Nana, ever an iconoclast (for forty-five years she has told people she is thirty-five), had her own ideas. Of course she believed in God, she said. I pressed for details. She saw Christ differently from the way others did. She respected him as a teacher, as a man of good deeds, as a wise and noble soul who cared about everyone, but she didn't see him as God's son. It was God she spoke to when she prayed, she said, and she could speak to him anywhere. I felt so relieved: she had put words to the ideas already percolating in my head. Nevertheless, I continued to go to church, though I more and more resented sitting there, reciting things I did not believe.

My religious ideas were among the things that set me apart from my classmates in Albany, Oregon, the farm-and-mill town of thirty-five thousand where I attended school after the sixth grade. In a small town, it is difficult to be different, not to be rooted in the mores of those around you. Many of my friends belonged to after-school Bible study groups, and they found my beliefs outlandish indeed. I became a nerd and spent a lot of time reading at home.

I was glad to leave for college in California. I came across Judaism again, almost immediately, when the name G. Glaser in the student registry prompted invitations to Hillel functions, Shabbat dinners, Israeli dance performances. Friends who lived near campus asked me home for Passover, Rosh Hashanah, and break fasts at Yom Kippur. I had many Jewish friends, including one who shared my last name. Her father once interrogated me on Glaser history. "Darling, there's no way your family wasn't Jewish in the old country." I didn't know what to think, but the assumptions persisted. I had a crush on a Jewish classmate from L.A. who asked me out for a date. Over drinks, his first question was, "So how did a nice Jewish girl like you get to Oregon?" "I'm not Jewish," I responded. He looked at me, astonished. "Don't let my mother know." At a dinner with his parents two weeks later, I kept my mouth shut.

By the time my father, mother, and I had reached Swiebodzice in 1991, our family priest had moved on, and so had all of us. My father, mother, and oldest sister, Stephanie, had converted to Catholicism. My middle sister, Michelle, had married a Jewish man and joined a synagogue. My brother Mitchell and I no longer attended services anywhere. My own marriage only added to the questions I already had about religion. What are the spiritual legacies parents and grandparents give to their children? I believed in God. I prayed. But beyond the obvious — the Golden Rule and the Ten Commandments — I couldn't have said what religious values I wanted to pass on.

When I started dating Stephen in the late 1980s, I didn't think twice about his Jewishness. I knew many intermarried couples — not just my sister and brother-in-law, but colleagues, friends, and cousins. They hardly seemed remarkable in my nominally religious world. Church, for me, had gone by the wayside as soon as I hit college. Before we married, religion seemed to touch Stephen's life as sporadically as it did mine; he attended Rosh Hashanah and Yom Kippur services at a nearby university and participated in a cousin's Passover seder. When we went to Jewish weddings, he helped hoist the bride or groom up on a chair for the hora, the circle dance.

When we were first together, our only strained moments came at Christmastime. We never fought about a tree, but its presence was always awkward. "Put one up if it makes you happy," Steve would say when the topic arose. It hardly seemed like Christmas cheer to me. The first year we were together I dragged a small fir into the house after work and put it up alone. I had envisioned replicating the resplendent tree of my childhood. But this looked pitiful. It tilted to one side, and the lights I had wrapped around it made it look garish, like a fifteen-year-old girl wearing too much make-up. I took it down on Christmas night.

The next year, 1989, Steve and I avoided the topic by going on vacation. If I didn't believe in Christ as my savior, why should I participate in Christmas at all, I wondered. So we planned a trip to the Middle East. Our last stop was Israel, where we arrived on December 21. Eager to avoid huge crowds, we went to Bethlehem early that morning. Hordes of people rushed through the Church of the Nativity, led by tour guides who shouted through megaphones in their respective languages. I strained to see what everyone was snapping pictures of and stood on my toes to peer over shoulders. Resting on the star where Christ is said to have been born was a plastic baby doll, swaddled in a dirty blue flannel blanket, with a shiny aluminum halo affixed to its head. Postcards of the scene were for sale outside the chapel. I could feel myself wince as I passed them. It was hardly the holy scene that "Away in a Manger" had left in my head.

I insisted that we spend December 25 at the Israel museum. That evening, though, I was sad when we ordered kung pao chicken from a kosher Chinese restaurant in Jerusalem. Men were removing their ties after work, drinking beer at the bar. There, the hours had passed like those of any day. I thought of my family together in Oregon, eating turkey and pecan pie. Unlike Ebenezer Scrooge, I didn't have the chance to relive the day.

We weren't married yet, but it was clear we were going to be. With the exception of Christmas Day, when would there be any conflict? I liked Jewish holidays more than my own. I felt a little clumsy at my first seder, making the obvious mistake of reading the Haggadah from left to right. But I loved the warmth of Jewish gatherings and the pride Jews took in their stories, their history. As far as I could see it, our kids would be raised as Jews but would have a Christmas tree in December. That was the agreement, and it seemed simple enough. When we married, in 1990, a rabbi conducted a Jewish ceremony, and my childhood priest, Father Joe, delivered a homily. There was no mention of Christ and no cross — the wedding was in an eighteenth-century art gallery. The rabbi, Harold White, was the son of a Russian Jew and a Connecticut Protestant who had converted to Judaism. He had his own ideas on intermarriage — mainly that Jews could, and should, make Judaism hospitable to Christian partners. Rabbi White, the only Washington rabbi who performed interfaith ceremonies at the time, had several weddings to perform that September day, and we planned ours around his schedule. Father Joe, delighted to be part of the service, had also presided at mixed ceremonies before. So our wedding seemed no big deal, nothing extraordinary. In the requisite counseling session before the wedding, Father Joe and Rabbi White warned of the necessity of understanding each other, each other's family. We nodded in polite agreement. Days after our wedding, we left for Warsaw, where Stephen was to cover Eastern Europe for his newspaper. I would trade my job as a reporter in Baltimore to free-lance for magazines and newspapers.

In Poland, I suddenly saw a new dimension of intermarriage: history. Poland had been home to nearly 40 percent of the world's Jewish population, 3.3 million, before the Second World War. Many of those Jews had integrated into urban society, but the awkward symbiosis in which they lived with Poles was evident even fifty years after most of them had vanished. Indeed, Poles seemed acutely aware of any links I might have to Judaism. Everyone from my postman to dockworkers I interviewed would study my face, stare at my written name, and ask: "Are you Jewish?" The first few months I was there, I struggled along with the story of my complicated family tree, invariably to knowing nods. "I thought so," people would say.

Our time in Warsaw coincided with the fall of communism, and with it, the eruption of nationalism. Poland for the Poles, we heard at political rallies. Once, a man pounded his fist on the hood of my red Russian Lada and shouted: "Ugly, dirty Jew! Out of Poland! Poland for the Poles!" So after a while, when anyone asked about my religious affiliation, I said I was Jewish. Out of solidarity. And association.

This guessing about my religion had darker implications in a Poland marked by a growing anti-Semitism, even one without Jews. For the first time I began to feel what it was like to be a curiosity, different. Each drunken slur, each raised eyebrow, each bit of scrawled graffiti about Jews and gas chambers had a deeper meaning. It was during those years in Eastern Europe, as I visited Jewish cemeteries, that I began to understand my husband's sense of growing up an outsider in America, his painful stories of singing "Silent Night" as an elementary school student, his reluctance to have a Christmas tree in our home, his ability to make friends with almost any Jewish person he met — even if their faith was the only thing they seemed to have in common.

In Poland, where I met dozens of Holocaust survivors, where I traveled frequently to Auschwitz to cover stories, and where the ghosts of Jews seemed to haunt even everyday expressions, it all began to make sense. Poles, unlike any people I had ever met, seemed to have a historical perspective on their nation and on themselves. Cab drivers recited the dates and details of battles fought by valiant Polish soldiers hundreds of years earlier. Yet for all their historical insight, there was a glaring omission. Jews had flourished in Poland for five hundred years, but when I heard mention of Jews, it often came in the form of stereotypes or of Hitler "not finishing his work." Indeed, the Nazis constructed dozens of death camps in Poland, and in time the country became the epicenter of the Holocaust. Kielce, in southern Poland, was the site of Europe's only postwar pogrom, in 1946. The Polish government organized an anti-Semitic campaign in 1968; a distant relative of Stephen's who had survived the war lost his job as a diplomat. Even Lech Walesa, hero of anticommunism, declared when he ran for president that "hidden Jews" in Polish life should show themselves. Poles scrutinized the few remaining Jews, real or imagined. In the wider world, Jews scrutinized the Poles.

It was a painful time for both Jews and Poles. In covering these seemingly ceaseless struggles, I came to see this tangled relationship in sharp focus, not only with the lens of history, but with my own. Poles and Jews, in their bitter struggle to make the other listen, struck me as people in a curious kind of marriage, one born of the intimacy of sharing close quarters but not necessarily of understanding. Each group had a passionate allegiance to its identity, to its own history. It was their most admirable quality, and it had allowed them to preserve their cultures against enormous odds. But their vision of what it meant to be a Pole or a Jew was quite different from my own childhood identity as an Oregonian, an American, or a Christian. For Poles, Eastern European Jews, or their offspring in America, all history was personal.

It was a lesson I quickly learned in my own family. When I was pregnant in 1992 with our first child, we (foolishly, it turned out, as any expectant parent can attest) divulged the names we were mulling over. I had spent a lot of time reading about Jewish ritual and tradition and considered myself sensitive to them. We tentatively agreed on a boy's name — Jacob, for Stephen's grandfather, the one who had died during the war. Everyone seemed pleased with that except me. I thought it was scary to give a child the name of someone who had died so tragically, so prematurely, so violently. Wasn't it bad luck, I wondered secretly. The name seemed sacred, not up for discussion. Stephen was set on it. He wanted to honor the tradition of naming a Jewish child after a dead relative, he said. I guessed that his parents shared my thoughts; Grandfather Jakob had died long before Stephen and his brother were born, yet neither carried on the name. "Too painful, probably," Steve said. Why was it our responsibility, I wondered. I hoped for a girl.

That was an easy choice. We loved the name Ilana — tree, in Hebrew. But when we told the Engelbergs about it, my father-in-law, Ed, took me aside and told me it was out of the question. I was stunned. Of course I knew about the Ashkenazic (European Jewish) superstition never to name a baby after a living relative, based on the belief that giving the child the name of the loved one would rob the elder of his or her full life. I also knew that Sephardic (North African and Middle Eastern) Jews freely bestow on their babies the names of their living parents and grandparents. The Sephardim consider it an honor to have a child or grandchild named after them, much as Christians do.

But Ed was insistent. Ilana was too close to Elaine, my mother-in-law's name, he said. I had foreseen this difficulty, and explained that Elaine was the Old English form of the Greek "Eleni," or "light." The two names bore no resemblance in meaning, and to us only remotely in sound. Still, Ed shook his head. It's just not done, he said. I was indignant, and felt my face flush as the conversation veered toward intransigence. I could feel tears stinging my nose, and I left the room. "They think I'm a stupid shiksa," I said to Stephen. "No, they don't," he said. "It's our baby. Don't worry." I wanted him to stick up for me, stick up for our choices. I cooled off, and left the Hebrew name book out on the dining room table.

My mother loved the name Ilana, but jokingly asked when someone would name a child after her. This would be her fourth grandchild, after all, and her own name, Virginia Helen, was a tribute to her parents' sisters. Virginia was out as a middle name: too many syllables, too Christian. What about Helen or Helene? Ilana Helene, she wondered aloud. I liked the sound of it, too. But Helen, in fact, is another version of "Eleni" — the same meaning as Elaine. That certainly wouldn't work. My mother understood the status of the name Jacob, but what about something from our side for a middle name, she asked. She floated Mitchell, my brother's name. Nice name, and of course I love my brother. But such a choice would no doubt upset the Engelbergs, since he is very much alive.

What to do? How to settle this problem of naming a child? When she was born, we called our daughter Ilana Suzanne: Ilana for the meaning and the sound, and Suzanne after a great-grandmother on my mother's side. If there was any disappointment over it, no one let on.

But the incident was revealing. In honoring one side's traditions, one could easily offend the other. The totemic value of a grandchild's name can be touchy in any family, but for us it was explosive. My parents-in-law were not-so-subtly voicing their concerns that their first grandchild, born of a non-Jew, would be lost to Jewish tradition forever — on her very arrival into the world. And for my mother, the stakes seemed just as high. Ilana Engelberg, while a beautiful name, identified the child as a Jew: different from my family. Distant.

When we planned a naming ceremony, I asked Elaine what the family tradition of godparents was. I knew that a sandek — Hebrew for godfather — held a baby boy for his bris, and I thought I was asking a good question, one that demonstrated my understanding of Jewish tradition. It came across as just the opposite. "What are you trying to tell me?" Elaine asked, hurt. "Godparents are a Catholic tradition. [The tradition of godparents has its roots in the Jewish bris, or circumcision ceremony. During the bris, the sandek holds the infant during the procedure. The honor is reserved for a close friend or relative, just as it is for Christian godparents, who hold godchildren during baptisms.] Are you going to baptize her?" Deep down, I'm sure the Engelbergs knew nothing could be further from our thoughts. But theirs was the fear of a generation of Jewish parents whose children have married outside the faith. That their son's decision to marry a non-Jew meant he had forgotten where he came from. Who he was. What his ancestors had lived through.

Women in my family, who had had their sons circumcised in the hospital, were clearly uncomfortable at the ceremonial bris of my sister Michelle's son. The whole family gathered, made merry over the beautiful baby boy, and sat anxiously during the unfamiliar ritual. Although the baby had been circumcised in the hospital, for the occasion the rabbi drew a drop of blood from his penis. In speaking of the event later, some referred to it as that "day when they hurt him." To them, undertaking the procedure once was fine; to inflict pain — however minor — a second time seemed unnecessary.

Such quandaries made me wonder just what it was we were doing. Was there something I could read, something that would point out the inevitable pitfalls of raising children in a household with two very different backgrounds? There were books and magazine articles, but they didn't delve into the lives of the people who made these decisions and lived by them. How did the children turn out, I wondered. How did people work out their lives, even when, on the surface, everything seemed to be fine? Steve and I had a lot in common: our jobs, our education — we had both majored in history and toyed with becoming professors. Even our families, dissimilar as they were, shared many things.

There were no answers for my family and me the day we visited Swiebodzice. No gravestones with the name Glaser in Hebrew letters. No real sign of who we had been or where we came from. But the questions about spirituality and religion continued to deepen for me when we returned to the United States with our infant daughter. I set out to write this book to find out what others were doing. I remained uncertain about my own spiritual plans, and our plans as a family. I thought about conversion from time to time. But how did it work out, in the end? How did converts feel? Were they taken seriously by either side? Weren't they suspect in the Jewish community, looked upon as having jumped through hoops only to please a spouse or parents-in-law? What about children raised in two faiths? What happened to them as adults? Were their loyalties divided? Did they, as I had read, end up feeling that they had "chosen" between parents if they ended up as Jews, or as Christians? And what about children with Jewish fathers and non-Jewish mothers who are raised as Jews? The Reform movement recognized them as Jews, but did they "feel" Jewish? I didn't have strong roots in Christianity, but other non-Jewish partners in interfaith marriages did. What about their spirituality? Somehow, in the emphasis the Jewish community places on intermarriage, the faith of Gentiles seemed overlooked. What about believers, those who felt the need to baptize their children, to raise them in the church? And what about those who came from two strong cultural backgrounds? The permutations seemed endless.

I began with a couple who were just starting their marriage, but whose courtship and wedding forced them to confront the quandaries of interfaith marriage.

TWO

Good Catholic, Good Jew

§

M AURA FITZSIMMONS and Joshua Steinberg have been
married only months, and speak of their wedding as a
romantic idyll. Sitting on their spotless white couch, Josh weaves
his fingers through Maura's as he speaks; her diamond catches
the winter sun. Their townhouse in suburban Washington, built
two years ago, smells unused, like a car just driven off the lot.
Its fresh yellow paint, gleaming hardwood floors, and starched
draperies make it look like a page from a Crate and Barrel catalog.

Both in their late twenties, Maura, a Catholic, and Josh, who is
Jewish, view their life together very much as people of their generation do: they share just about everything. Each has a demanding
job, Maura as the publicist of a newsmagazine and Josh as a
spokesman for a Republican United States senator. Their domestic
responsibilities are pretty evenly split: they take turns doing the
laundry, and, when they are both in town, alternate the cooking.
Whoever makes dinner gets a pass on the dishes. Josh vacuums;
Maura dusts. On weekend mornings, Maura walks the dog while
Josh drives to get a dozen bagels from their favorite shop. On the
way home, he swings by a 7–Eleven to get a six-pack of Diet Coke;
Maura can't start her day without it.

Maura and Josh almost never interrupt each other or correct
the other's telling of joint memories. They sit side by side and refer
to the other as "my wife" or "my husband," as if trying on the

phrase. Their politeness is remarkable; maybe it's because they are new to each other and to marriage.

Their wedding photographs — and the event itself — testify to their commitment to equality. A rabbi joined a monsignor in conducting the ceremony; draped over the chuppah was a sheath of Irish linen. The priest offered a benediction in English; the rabbi closed the ceremony in Hebrew. As soon as the rabbi had finished, Maura's uncle, clad in a kilt, wet the reed of his bagpipe and began to play. As the melancholy wail filtered into the tent, Maura and Josh turned to follow him out into the cool evening, their guests trailing behind them.

But their domestic harmony was hard won. Josh and Maura's path to the altar was strewn with guilt, heartbreak, and quiet despair.

Maura Fitzsimmons's roots lay firmly in Ireland. Two grandparents had left the island for the United States as youngsters; the other two were born to Irish immigrants in New York City. Her grandfathers — an elevator inspector and an engineer at Radio City Music Hall — were union employees whose lives were expanded by their union membership. Protective as they were of their Irishness and the struggles of the Irish people, they learned that neither had a monopoly on suffering. In the unions, they realized that other immigrants — the Italians, the Greeks, and the Jews who worked alongside them — had their share of hardships, too.

Soon, her grandparents prospered. They bought cars, their own houses. Their children moved to the suburbs, and on to successful careers in business or civil service. Still, two generations later, as Maura grew up comfortably in Fairfield County, Connecticut, she was aware of the injustices her people had endured when they came to this country, when they looked for work or an apartment. She heard the stories time and again: no Irish need apply.

"I knew my history, my ancestry, from the Irish potato famine to the discrimination against the Irish here. I learned about it early.

I heard about it from my grandparents and in school. But it always extended broadly, to the suffering of others."

Maura describes herself as looking like her name: "really Irish Catholic." And indeed, she was easy to spot, blocks away, on a sunny autumn day. Tall and graceful, her bright copper hair glinting in the sun, she stood out among the somber tones of a busy Washington street. Almost always in green, she turns heads, a fact of which she seems remarkably unaware.

When Maura becomes angry, a patch of red appears on her neck, a stark contrast to her white skin, dotted with tiny freckles, and her pale lime eyes. It is easy to know when she is about to mention something that bothers her: the blotch lets on before she says a word. Thoughtful and kind, soft-spoken and determined, she is cautious, without so much as a speeding ticket to her name.

The second child of four, and an only daughter, Maura grew up in a small, close-knit town. About half the population worshiped at the nineteenth-century Catholic church, St. Mary's, just off the picturesque main street lined with Revolutionary clapboard buildings. Maura, like a number of her friends, attended a parochial middle school. After Vatican II, the uniforms and corporal punishment common in Catholic schools gave way to a more liberal atmosphere. At Maura's school, even the nuns wore street clothes.

Maura's parents, Catherine and John, had been raised in Irish neighborhoods in Queens and Brooklyn. Their families moved to the rhythms of the Catholic church: honoring each saint's day, eating fish or spaghetti on Fridays, and stopping by a confession booth every week. When Catherine was a small girl in parochial school, she went home at noon for lunch. On warm days, as she returned to school, neighbors on their stoops would clip roses from their bushes and pass them through the fence. "Give this to the Virgin," they would tell her.

For the Fitzsimmonses, church was a focal point, at least for Catherine and her children. "My grandfather died when my dad was young, so at that point my dad kind of checked out of the church," Maura says. But Catherine, a striking redhead in her early fifties, instilled in her children her love of God, of her church, and of her Irish-Catholic traditions. The Fitzsimmonses boarded an AerLingus jet every few summers for a trip to Ireland, where they rode their bikes through the rocky countryside of County Mayo, visited relatives, and learned, to their surprise, that the house in which Catherine's mother was born had become a barn. They spent evenings in Galway pubs, listening to the haunting tunes of Irish singers over their tall glasses of Guinness. With these trips, the family celebrated its heritage. And back home in Connecticut, Ireland was never far away. The Irish blessing, resting beneath a wooden frame, greeted visitors. The stereo, more often than not, played recordings of the Clancy Brothers or the Wolf Tones. Catherine prepared a St. Patrick's Day feast each March, with boiled potatoes, corned beef, and cabbage. Maura even took a brief stab at step-dancing lessons. "Those didn't take too well," she says.

The Fitzsimmonses wanted to make sure they instilled a sense of Irish pride in their children, but Catherine was particularly careful not to foster Irish chauvinism, as her mother had done with her. She laughs when she recalls her upbringing. Catherine didn't dare even look at a boy who came from a different background. "If your last name wasn't Irish, for my mother you could forget it," she says. A leader of Bible study groups and a believer in healing through prayer, Catherine considers her spirituality her bedrock.

So does her daughter. "I loved church," Maura says, "and I loved it more and more as I got older." Her admiration was due in part to the parish priest, Father Ryan, who established an ecumenical retreat that drew children of all denominations. Everyone was involved, Maura says, even teachers at her public high school. "The retreats pulled kids together and pulled them into church. It was wonderful. It was fun. Christianity was a part of my life that started early and grew as I got older. It was strengthened by Father Ryan's love of us all, and by his love of God. My friends and I prayed together; we went to mass together. It was part of the way we looked at the world."

In church, Maura felt a quiet peace she experienced nowhere else. She listened to the sermon, of course, but sometimes her mind would wander. Her eyes would dart around the sanctuary, looking to see which of her friends were there. She went every weekend, partly because she liked Father Ryan and being in church, but also because she and her young friends had formed something of a congregation for themselves. Church, Maura says, "felt like home."

In fact, the draw of St. Mary's was so great that even Maura's father, John, became involved again, after a hiatus of some twenty years. With the rest of his family so active in the parish, he had begun to feel isolated. He even served, along with Catherine, as a sponsor for one of the church's youth retreats.

The Fitzsimmonses' house was home not only to their four children; school friends often lingered into the evening for dinner. "Come in, take off your shoes," they'd say. "Just take your plate to the kitchen when you're done."

In the 1980s, teenage girls all over America idolized the pop singer Madonna and her flagrant disrespect for authority — particularly for the Catholic church. They infuriated their parents with their torn jeans, ratted hair, and gaudy jewelry. Maura, however, shied away from such trends. She took pride in other matters, namely, a rough wooden cross she had made by hand during one of her youth retreats. She wore it to church, she wore it to school, she wore it everywhere. It made her think about what it meant to be a Christian and to lead a Christian life.

As a teenager, whenever Maura had a problem, she talked with her friends, her mother, or her priest. She could always find solace through her faith. "We talked a lot about the love Jesus had for all people. That's what it centered on, as opposed to a lot of the doctrine of the Catholic church. That's how I was raised, and that's what I brought with me when I went to college."

Away from home, Maura thrived as a student at George Washington University in Washington, D.C. She excelled in her classes, even studied in Ireland for a year, at the University of St. Aquinas in Galway. She studied Irish history and politics, and tried, unsuccessfully, to learn Gaelic. "Even though I was pure Irish, I discovered there was a huge difference between being Irish American and Irish."

Back in Washington, she concentrated on her major, political communication. Among her classmates was Josh Steinberg, a lively and vocal Republican who was never shy about expressing his views. "I didn't actually like him at first," she says. "He always tried to have the last word. So at first I thought, 'Who is he? And who does he think he is?'"

Like Maura Fitzsimmons, Josh Steinberg had never had any doubt about who he was. He was a Jew. So was everyone who populated his life. His neighbors were Jewish, his teachers were Jewish, his doctors were Jewish. Affable, with a cheerful round face, warm brown eyes, and closely cropped dark hair, Josh says that three quarters of his childhood friends were Jewish. "Those who weren't were Jewish by association. After you go to a dozen bar mitzvahs, you pretty much get the picture," he says.

The second of Lillian and Richard Steinberg's two sons, Josh grew up in a Cleveland suburb. As he remembers it, the Steinbergs moved there because it was a predominantly Jewish neighborhood, close to the Jewish community center. "By the time I was sixteen, we didn't go there anymore. But, by God, the joke was always that we were fifteen minutes away from the JCC."

The Steinbergs' ties to other Jews, both near and far, were strong. The fact that they attended their Conservative synagogue only for the High Holidays and bar and bat mitzvahs seemed of little importance. Religious practice was hardly a focal point; it was the community that mattered. A ceramic mezuzah marks their doorway, and Israeli art is displayed just beyond the foyer. A silver menorah occupies a place of pride in the center of the living room bookshelves. "No question," Josh says, "it's a Jewish home." As children, Josh and his older brother, Jason, went to Hebrew school three times a week. An uncle and his family lived in Israel. The Steinbergs visited them when Josh was in high school, deepening the family connection to the Jewish state.

Friday nights were reserved for dinners together. Lillian often lit candles, but even when she didn't, it was always understood that the evening was the Steinbergs' time as a family. "We didn't make a big deal out of its being Shabbat," Josh says. "It was more like dinner together, just us."

Because Lillian and Richard lived far from their own families, they relied on a group of Jewish friends as stand-ins for aunts, uncles, and cousins. "They were our family away from family," Josh says. Every Passover, every Rosh Hashanah, every break fast, was spent together. Each year the Steinbergs were hosts of at least one seder. Lillian would begin cooking days in advance, and the tantalizing smells of chicken soup and kugel flooded the house. She set an elegant table and cleaned the house from top to bottom. "We had a deep sense of identity, as a family and who we are as a people," Josh says. "We were very, very culturally Jewish."

Jewish summer camp was a defining experience; Josh went every year from the time he was eight to eighteen. He slept in tents. He swam, played basketball. He had Jewish history lessons and saw slides of Israel. He learned songs, both ancient and modern. "Camp made me prouder and prouder of my Judaism. Not in the go-to-synagogue-and-pray sense," he says. "What I really learned is what it meant to be Jewish."

The second summer at camp, Josh and some friends gathered for a movie in a conference room, giggling as their counselor threaded the tape through the projector. When the film finally appeared on the screen, Josh sat up and paid attention. The subject was intermarriage. "It was really serious stuff," Josh says. "If you married someone who wasn't Jewish, your parents would cover the mirrors, they'd sit on low chairs, the whole works. 'If you do this, you're dead.' I was scared to death. It was like seeing that film about drugs in sixth grade, *Scared Straight*, I think it was. It was exactly the same philosophy. That scared the hell out of me, too!"

The message was emphasized at home, as well. Among the Steinbergs' friends, hardly anyone intermarried. But when the subject arose, his parents would shake their heads in dismay. "Every intermarriage that had ever been pointed out to me was either a complete debacle or had ended in divorce," Josh says. He mimics an authoritarian voice and knits his brow into a deep frown. "There are certain things that Jews do, certain things they don't," he says. "Like 'Jews go to the movies on Christmas Eve, and then out for Chinese food.' Or 'Jews don't drink.' 'Marry someone not Jewish? Jews just don't do that.'" He looks out the window of the Thai restaurant and onto the frozen street.

He pauses. "When I was growing up, and even to a degree today, a lot of the focus of the Jewish community was on coming up with ways to get Jews to marry other Jews. And I bought it," he says. "I was brought up to believe that if you married out, it was a tremendous tragedy. Not just a disappointment. A tragedy."

When Josh was a teenager, he served as president of his synagogue's chapter of the B'nai B'rith Youth Organization. "If I heard of someone intermarrying, I was very critical," he says. "It wasn't, like, 'How could you?' But I did say things like 'Are you sure you're doing the right thing?' And I would write them off in my mind. I thought, 'Well, Judaism just isn't that important to you.' I felt bad that the religion was losing a good person. Because how could anybody who marries someone who isn't Jewish have any kind of commitment to raising his kids as Jews? You marry a non-Jew, you're out of the fold. I never had an ambition to be the president of the synagogue or anything like that, but at the same time, I always wondered, 'How can I make my contribution?' And I definitely thought that if you married someone who wasn't Jewish, you'd be taken out of play. That's what I'd been brought up to think. You're out. You're still a Jew, but only marginally. You don't really get to vote any more. It bothered me that people would do that. I believed it was true. And I repeated the message myself, to people I knew."

At eighteen, Josh decided to go to George Washington University, in part because its student population was largely Jewish. "I think it appeared on the B'nai B'rith's list of top campuses where your kid could go to meet a Jewish mate," he says. The Steinbergs could not have been more pleased.

Once in college, Josh thrived on life in Washington. He loved the city, the intrigue of Capitol Hill, and the proximity of the downtown campus to the White House. Josh is a funny guy, eager to draw laughs, and he wasted no time in doing so in class. He spoke his mind, too, in small courses and seminars, whenever he got the chance. He couldn't help noticing a tall redhead who seemed a bit on the serious side. She wasn't as talkative as Josh himself, but her calm and intelligence were striking.

Little by little, Josh became friends with Maura Fitzsimmons, who had chosen the same major. One day after class, he noticed her struggling on crutches to get down the steps with her books. "Let me help you," he said, and raced down the stairwell. Once outside, they lingered in the winter evening for an hour, chatting in the harsh light of a streetlamp.

Soon after, they began dating. Religion, not surprisingly, came up immediately. "Ever since I was twelve or so, and capable of making decisions by myself, I knew I was going to marry a Jew. So I kept telling myself, 'Wow, I really like this girl, but how do I square this with what I want to do and what I'm supposed to do?' But the relationship kept developing, and I kept thinking, 'Well, I'll deal with that later.'"

It wasn't so simple. Although by graduation Maura and Josh had been close for some months, Josh omitted mentioning that to his parents, preferring to introduce Maura as a "friend." The Steinbergs were mildly interested but had no idea their son was dating Maura. "It didn't hurt that he didn't tell them the whole story, because we hadn't been together that long," Maura says, "and I was really more focused on my girlfriends." The Fitzsimmonses, however, did know, and they took a shine to Josh.

After graduation, Maura traveled in Europe for the summer, returning to Washington in the fall. She and Josh corresponded frequently and began to tell themselves, "This is serious." They found jobs and got apartments near each other in the hippest part of town, Dupont Circle. Soon enough, they were spending most of their free time together and were enough of a couple to answer each other's phone. One evening, Maura picked up the receiver and heard Lillian's voice. Although she had been dating Josh for more than a year, she felt as anonymous as a hotel operator. "She just asked, 'Is Joshua there?'" Maura says. "No 'Hi, this is Lillian Steinberg. How are you?' No niceties, no nothing. They knew who I was, because they had met me. And they suspected we were dating, although they didn't know any details. What I'm able to see now, but what I couldn't see then, is that they didn't want to show interest, because it might be interpreted as approval. So they just ignored me."

Almost a year had passed. Josh and Maura were living together, essentially, although they kept separate apartments. Yet Josh had still not mentioned the arrangement to his parents. Of course they knew something was going on, and the iciness on the phone got worse.

"It was very —" Maura falters here. The red spot on her neck glows crimson, and her eyes water. "The emotions are really hard to put in words." She takes a deep breath. "Josh was always the kid who did good things, the kid who did what his parents wanted. He was a good son. He was good in school. His parents were always proud of how well he did, always telling their friends. And then suddenly they weren't doing that anymore. They didn't completely cut him off, but they weren't involved with him the way they had been. And he was just heartbroken."

Josh was torn. "Maura was upset with me because I wouldn't confront them, and my parents were upset because I was doing something they didn't agree with. At the same time I was upset because I figured, 'I'm the one to blame.' I also knew I was in love with her" — he corrects himself — "we were in love, and it was a question of 'How do we make this work? Let's try.' I just didn't know how we were going to make it happen."

Finally Josh summoned the courage to tell his parents, on the Steinbergs' yearly winter trip to Puerto Rico. It was a hot, muggy day, and Josh lingered by the pool for the morning. At lunch, he went alone with Lillian to a pizzeria. He ordered a Coke and fiddled nervously with his straw. His felt his pulse quicken. Even though he was hungry, lunch suddenly seemed a bad idea. He cleared his throat. "Mom, I've got something to tell you," he said.

"What?" Lillian replied, a horrified look on her face. "Maura and I are getting pretty serious," he told her. "I kind of sensed that," she said. Her face crumpled, and she began to cry.

"It'll never work," Lillian said between sobs. "You'll end up divorced. Your kids will never be Jewish." She drew out her entire arsenal. "You're going to kill us," she said. "This will kill your father. He'll never make it through this."

Josh looks up, as if anticipating a question. "My father's perfectly healthy! He's fine!"

"But there were threats that he was going to have a heart attack," Maura says.

"No, there weren't," Josh says. "But she kept on: 'The family will never be the same.' And I said, 'No, Mom, it won't be. You're right. But families are never the same. Families are always one day older, and whenever you add one person, regardless of who it is, the family is not the same.'" His parents' idea, Josh says, was to pay no attention. It wouldn't work out anyway, so why bother? Josh and his father never spoke about it; there was no reason to. Josh knew he would hear the lines he had heard since he was a kid. From his parents' point of view, he thought, he was just a twenty-three-year-old kid, totally unqualified to make a rational decision. Sooner or later he would come to his senses.

"When I was growing up, the worst thing I could ever do was disappoint my parents. And this was the worst kind of disappointment I could think of. It caused a lot of problems between Maura and me because I understood my parents, and I was siding with them, in a way, by not speaking out. But I also sided with Maura. I was trying to play the middle ground. Everybody was right. My parents were right; Maura was right."

"And it really hurt me," Maura says. "How could he let them treat me this way?"

Other family members were also disapproving. Lillian's sister told her young sons that Josh could no longer be their role model, now that he had a Christian girlfriend. She instructed them to be polite to Maura during any encounters with her, but only because

Josh was still family. Unpleasant as this was, Lillian made sure that Josh knew, hoping perhaps that he would rethink his decision.

Maura and Josh decided to take a new tack. "We never wanted to let things get ugly, to respond to all this negativity in a negative way. We told ourselves we'd take the high road," she says. During family gatherings or phone calls, Maura and Josh vowed never to waver, never to be impolite, never to raise their voices. It was not easy.

The Steinbergs, meanwhile, were beside themselves. A year passed, and things had still not calmed down. In the late autumn, they asked Josh to join them on their trip to Puerto Rico but did not extend an invitation to Maura. "I'm not going," Josh said flatly. "But it's my birthday," Lillian pleaded, crying into the phone. "You have to come." "Sorry, Mom," Josh said. "I just couldn't back down," he explains. "I knew I had to stand up. I felt terrible. But I had to deal with the burden. This was nobody's problem but mine."

That December, Maura and Josh decided to drive to Connecticut and spend Christmas with the Fitzsimmonses. The eighth night of Hanukkah preceded Christmas by just a few days. On one of the last nights of the holiday, Josh and Maura decided to stop in on his aunt, Lillian's sister, during the drive. She and her family lived just minutes from the highway. When Josh and Maura arrived, Josh's aunt and her husband began to explain Hanukkah in an elementary way, as if they were speaking to preschoolers. Maura, piqued, responded by reciting an obscure fact about the battle fought by the Maccabees. They seemed surprised, she says, that she knew anything at all. "But it was really Josh who was upset. He was, like, 'I am a Jew. Who do you think I am here? I am Jewish, and this is my girlfriend, who happens not to be Jewish. Of course we've talked about this. Of course we've been celebrating it the last five nights. Don't belittle me, as a Jew.' We didn't actually have this conversation with his aunt outright. But it was hard not to. We had to keep telling ourselves, 'Don't respond on their level.'"

As Maura says this, her hands tremble as she squirts lime into her seltzer. She stares at it, eyes glistening with tears. Her voice breaks, and she takes a deep breath. "My parents are so wonderful and loving," she says, choking out the words. Although the Fitzsimmonses had met Josh many times, it was his first Christmas with them. For months Maura had waxed nostalgic about the holiday: how she loved to decorate the tree with special family ornaments, go to midnight mass after her parents' open house. Catherine greeted Josh with a hug, John with his customary firm handshake. Resting on the table was a pile of dreidels, the four-sided tops used to play a game of chance during Hanukkah.

"My mother is a woman of incredible reason and is very thoughtful," says Maura. "She was a good sounding board, and would try to put it all into perspective for me. Sometimes when I had terrible thoughts, or said a terrible thing, or wanted to give the cold shoulder right back, she would say, 'But that's not who you are.' And through all this I realized more and more who I was, and who I was as a Christian. Aspects of my upbringing and faith are important to me. And forgiveness is one of them. As a Christian, I hold that as a very important value."

That seems a lesson drawn from her mother. The Fitzsimmonses were deeply troubled by the pain their daughter was enduring. "What, my daughter's not good enough?" was John Fitzsimmons's response. Maura's three brothers were furious and fiercely protective of her. "I tried to shield Maura from their anger," Catherine says. "She was dealing with enough." She sighs. "I have been constantly supportive of the direction they've taken. They've lived through a lot of turmoil and anger and sadness for such young people starting out." She chooses her words carefully. "My biggest concern for Maura has been and always will be her happiness." She pauses, then drops her guard for a moment. "The hardest part for me was that someone would reject another person on the basis of religion, without knowing them. It seemed predetermined, how they reacted. I wished I could understand, but it was difficult. Maybe I'll be wise enough someday." Quietly, she adds, "I have a lot of love and a lot of prayers for Josh's family."

The Steinbergs, for their part, didn't ease up. "My mom would start in on how hard it was going to be on the family. She'd say stuff like 'It's hard enough to introduce a spouse into a family, let alone a Catholic!'" Josh laughs. "Let's face it; in our world families don't pick your spouse. Which is something I had to remind them of. Finally I said, 'Look, I'm not asking you to approve of my relationship. But I am asking you, because you love me, to continue to be my parents and to have us as part of your lives.' I knew as long as they were in our lives, they would finally come around."

Guilt never lurks far from Josh. As troubled as things with his parents became, he found ways to rationalize his relationship. He loved Maura. They had been together for three years and had begun living with each other just months before. But when he saw *Schindler's List* late one winter evening, Maura at his side, he found himself wondering once again whether he was really doing the right thing.

"I expected the movie to be powerful, but I didn't expect it to be as powerful as it was," Josh says. For years, he had ruminated on how much he was disappointing his family, how he was letting them down. And as he watched the movie, tears poured freely down his face. All those corpses piled up on the truck beds, all those elderly Jews at Schindler's grave — Josh couldn't get the images out of his mind. When he walked out of the theater, his head was pounding. "I couldn't help thinking I had betrayed my whole people, my whole life, and that all those Jews had died in vain. On the other hand I thought that we've persevered as a people through this terrible thing, and we have the obligation to tell others about it. I was so proud that Steven Spielberg was a Jew. Here he made this film, what a mensch.

"I thought, here's a person who's really making contributions. That was one of the things that was bothering me at the time. I wasn't sure how I could do that if I wasn't married to a Jew."

Maura felt that her relationship with Josh was far too concerned with religion and culture. Josh couldn't seem to get past the anguish of disappointing his parents, of letting his community down. At that very time the Holocaust Museum was opening in Washington, and the story dominated the news. Newspaper articles described architectural details designed to evoke concentration camps — the barred windows, cramped elevators, the cattle car visitors could walk through. With the painful history of the Jews a public focal point, Josh got tickets within a few months of the museum's opening.

For Maura, this was all a bit too much. "You know what? I got really angry," Maura says. "I said, 'Yeah, it's been really shitty, everything that's happened to the Jews. But guess what: you're not the only ones bad things have happened to in the world.' It was a big thing for us. *My* people have suffered, too. And not just them; millions and millions of others."

At the time, in fact, the war in Bosnia held little of the world's attention but much of Maura's. "Over and over again, I tried to expand any conversation beyond the suffering of Jews to the Cambodians, to the Irish potato famine, to Rwanda, to Bosnia. I did this for probably a few months, whenever anything came up about the Holocaust. It wasn't to take anything away from the Holocaust; it was just to say, 'Hey, you're not alone here.' For the sake of conversation, I felt obliged to point these things out.

"That was one of my first observations when I started attending Jewish functions with Josh. I thought, 'Well, you guys really get down on all these negative things that have happened in the past.' Understandably, to a certain extent. But that evolved into some of the more philosophical conversations we've had about interfaith marriage. What does it do to children in their understanding of their religion? Of their identity, and who they are becoming? And how does that contribute to intermarriage? As an outsider, I'm able to say that if children and adults are learning and concentrating on the oppression and the hardship and all the terrible things of the past, and parents encourage their kids to marry other Jews and set up teen tours to Israel, what does that do? You've got kids who are learning about all the terrible things that have happened to their ancestors, but they're not celebrating any of the holidays, any of the joyful aspects of their heritage. They're not reading, they're not learning about the great things. *That's* what keeps people in their religion. That's what makes people proud. That's what makes them want to continue things. That's why they want to pass things on."

The first autumn the couple lived together, Rosh Hashanah fell in the middle of the week. Because Josh had just begun a new job, he felt awkward about taking the time off to fly to Cleveland, as he had always done. He began moping. It was one of his favorite holidays, but it just wouldn't be the same without his family.

Maura listened sympathetically. "Why don't we have Rosh Hashanah here?" she suggested. They didn't have a dinner table, he replied. What were they to do, have a holiday meal on the floor? Nonsense, Maura replied. She would borrow a table from work. She would rent dishes, glasses, and silver. She and Josh went to a bookstore and bought some Jewish cookbooks. First, one couple said they would come. Then another. The guest list grew to eighteen. Lillian faxed Josh some recipes — he didn't tell her of their plans, only that he wanted the recipes. With Josh's help, Maura prepared a traditional feast: gefilte fish, tzimmes, a roast chicken, apples with honey. She bought loaves of challah and fresh flowers. Friends crowded around folding tables, artfully concealed with rented linens. Before dinner, Josh toasted to a healthy, happy new year for everyone. "L'chaim," he said, "To life." As he raised his glass, Josh Steinberg felt like an adult Jew.

"All I needed was that push. The fact that Maura cared enough to do this was such a mitzvah. We had all these Jewish friends and their girlfriends and boyfriends, whether they were Jewish or not. I don't know if anyone could be as loving, as understanding about me, about Judaism, and also my family. It made me realize we could create our traditions in our own home. It didn't have to be at my parents'. I could do these things, too, and I could do them with her."

The holiday meal was a milestone for Josh. He had never imagined that the transition from his childhood in a circumscribed Jewish world to the adult apartment he shared with his Catholic girlfriend could be so seamless. Maybe it was going to be possible, after all. Maybe he wouldn't be isolated from his community.

Maura knew it could work. Others had done it before her, in an age when intermarriage was almost unheard of. One of her colleagues and mentors was a Jew, married to a Catholic woman; they had grappled with the difficulties of an interfaith relationship for more than thirty years. They had raised their two children with both religions; they celebrated every holiday, and emphasized the similarities between Judaism and Catholicism. "Instead of bargaining down to find the lowest common denominator, bargain up," her mentor told them. "You can celebrate both religions, one, or neither — there's no one formula that works without fail for every couple. You've got to supply your own answers. The main thing is not to allow outsiders — parents *or* clergy — dictate how you deal with each other. Outsiders have a vested interest in stressing the differences. They're kind of like unions in that way — they're into their turf."

For the first time, Josh realized that marrying Maura didn't have to mean a loss to the Jewish community. After all, Maura's mentor identified himself as a Jew, attended synagogue, and was respected so much by Jewish groups that he was frequently asked to give speeches at their conventions around the United States. Josh could still celebrate his Jewishness and marry the woman he loved, despite their different faiths.

"It never occurred to me that you could make it work in a positive way. That you could have Jewish children, that you could still be very proud of your religion, your people, and be a positive force in Judaism. That you could still make a contribution to your religion. That you could even learn more about it, because you were forced to evaluate it in ways you never had before."

Maura hoped that things would change once she and Josh got engaged, but instead of improving, their relations with Josh's parents seemed to worsen. The Steinbergs invited Maura and Josh to Cleveland for Passover, but it was a tense affair. When they arrived at the airport, Maura and Josh stepped off the jetway, straining to see the Steinbergs. Lillian and Richard kissed their son warmly and extended a cool greeting to Maura. "Hi," they said.

At home, the table was set, and dozens were to gather later for the seder. Maura, overwhelmed and nervous, went upstairs to nap. "They probably thought I slept more than any human being on earth," she says. "That's all I did that weekend."

Among the guests that evening were a number of young men and women, college students who weren't able to travel home for the holiday. Maura seethed; it seemed as though Lillian had gone out of her way to seek pretty young Jewish women as a foil for Maura. "I was the Catholic," she says. "I didn't have a name, I wasn't a person; I was just the Catholic, the shiksa. If I became Maura, I couldn't be the Catholic anymore. The argument was always 'It's not about Maura; she's a nice girl.'" Her voice becomes petulant. "But you know what? At some point it was about me. I was the Catholic for a long time."

At the seder, no one asked Maura any questions. "I think giving the cold shoulder to someone is worse than standing up and screaming at her. They'd made their home welcoming to people they didn't know — these students — but not to me, their son's girlfriend."

To Josh, the holiday was a modest success; it passed without an eruption. But he soon saw that navigating this line between his family and Maura, even now that they were engaged, was more difficult than ever. "Everything was put under a magnifying glass," Josh says. Maura scrutinized all interactions with Josh's relatives. She was offended that there were no photographs of her and Josh in the Steinbergs' home, although they had been together for three years. Several pictures of Josh's brother and his new Jewish girl-friend, however, were on prominent display. Maura's name was often misspelled on envelopes mailed to their apartment in Washington. That was bad enough, but when an invitation to a bar mitz-vah arrived, addressed to "Joshua Steinberg and Fiancée," Maura was crushed. "That broke my heart," she says. "It was a very subconscious jab. Or maybe even a conscious jab: 'You're not worthy of having your name on an envelope.' I put my foot down on that one. I had met his aunt — the one who thought Josh was no longer a role model for her sons — a number of times. So I said, 'We're calling her on this. Please bring it to her attention that I am not 'fiancée.' My name is Maura Fitzsimmons, and if she doesn't know how to spell it, here's my work number. I'll be more than happy to go over it with her.'"

Josh worried that, no matter what, someone was bound to get angry. "Who knows why these things occurred? There was an environment in which any of these things could be misconstrued by either side, by anybody. I was afraid to do or say anything. It was just eggshells all the time. There was a lot of soul searching, all around. From my dad, I'd hear, 'How can I make your mother feel better?' And from my mom, I'd hear, 'How can I make your dad feel better?' And I wondered, 'How can I make Maura feel better?'"

Planning the wedding was a logistical disaster. Lillian called Maura the day after she and Josh became engaged to declare that if a priest was present, she and Richard wouldn't be. Maura calmly replied that a rabbi would officiate together with a priest. "She was hysterical," Maura says. "She told me, 'If you're going to have a priest there, don't have him wearing a collar or a cross.'" Maura shakes her head.

The Steinbergs insisted that Josh and Maura speak to the rabbi in their Conservative congregation, who, as Maura and Josh expected, dryly recited the reasons they should not marry. "First of all, you'll never find a rabbi to do it," the rabbi warned. Josh and Maura replied that they had already spoken to several who had agreed to marry them. Finally, he told Josh, "But you won't be able to join a synagogue."

"Of course I knew we could join a Reform congregation," Josh says. "What did he think, that we hadn't thought about this? That we hadn't done any research of our own?"

His family also warned Josh that knowledge of his Catholic fiancée would kill his grandmother. Yet when he introduced Maura, she gave the couple her blessing. And in the midst of the

Days of Awe, on a warm September evening, a rabbi joined the Fitzsimmons family priest — now a monsignor — to officiate at Maura and Josh's wedding. The day, in the end, went off without a hitch.

Josh seems determined to make a contribution of his own to Judaism, somewhere between Steven Spielberg's and the local synagogue president's. Maura, for her part, wants to instill her kids with the comfort she finds in faith and her relationship with God. "It is something of which my husband does not know," she says. When Josh and Maura speak of children, they say readily that their blueprint is still in the drawing. How can they know before they are born?

They plan to give their children a Jewish education and to raise them as Jews. "I want them to feel the links to their people, to the community, to history, that I feel, to feel the link to Israel," Josh says. "That's what I want to pass on the most. I want them to have their mother's spirituality, their mother's comfort with praying to God, and her comfort with God, yet have my links to my culture, to my people."

He sighs and draws a long sip on his second Coke. He speaks, wistfully, of becoming a Reform Jew. "It's not what I'm used to," he says. "I have to get used to saying it. I'm a Reform Jew. Maura doesn't want to be a part of a synagogue that won't welcome her fully. And until the Conservative movement does that, I'll be a Reform Jew. They'll recognize our children as Jews, so it's as simple as that."

He pauses. "I'm not asking Judaism to change the rules." He glances at his wedding band. "Jews marrying Jews — that's still the law. Kashrut is still the law. Keeping Shabbos is still the law." He raises his eyebrows. "Could I be a better Jew? Yes." Skilled in the art of sound bites, he offers this: "Hell, Moses could have been a better Jew."

Joshua Steinberg, only twenty-six, speaks of his marriage and his faith with a single-minded focus. "You can send your kids to college where a lot of other Jews go, but you can't control who your children fall in love with. I just happened to meet a fantastic woman who's Catholic. Obviously that's not the answer to what Jewish people need to do to survive. The reality is that you need to give your kids a sense of identity. I explained this to my parents. I said, 'I'm not ever not going to be a Jew. It may be hard. And it may be different. But I'm not ever going to stop being Jewish.' They didn't understand that for the longest time. They thought that because I was marrying someone who was Catholic, they were losing me as a Jew. I don't agree. We do not have a Christmas tree and call it a 'Hanukkah bush.' I knew going into this that Maura came with a Christmas tree, and that's what we have. We have Hanukkah. They are separate holidays, not related. We have seders. We have Rosh Hashanah dinners. We fast on Yom Kippur. Maura goes to church on Easter. I'm sure we'll dye eggs someday. I also wear a big Irish sweater on St. Patrick's Day. But this is not 'Judianity.' I'm still a Jew. And I'm proud of who I am. I can still have a connection to other Jews. Some may not want to have a connection to me, but that's their business."

When Maura discusses the future, she sounds equally confident that she and Josh can combine their approach to religion for the sake of their marriage, their children, and themselves. "I ask myself, what do I want to pass on? What is most important to me about being Catholic, being Christian? The things I most want to pass on to my children? Well, it's not an association with the church. A lot of things the church does — as an educated woman, I can't be a part of, or want to teach my daughter or my son."

She lists a number of things that trouble her about her church: the lack of voice and leadership allowed women, the ban on birth control and the repercussions that has on Catholics in the developing world. On a trip to Rome, she says, she was disturbed by the vast wealth of the Vatican. "I thought of how many poor, hungry Catholics there are in the world and it really troubled my heart and soul," she says. She mocks a gasp. "I'm going to be kicked out of the church for saying these things!" Yet Maura considers herself a Roman Catholic. "I'm still a Catholic because of the parish I grew up in, and because of the spirituality that it's given me. The teachings of Christ are important to me but are not embedded in all the rules and doctrine of Catholicism.

"We can incorporate those two things, by raising kids as Jews in synagogue and giving them a formal Jewish education. But they can learn about Christianity at home." She pauses, then clarifies. "Learn about it, but not necessarily make it their own. All I know is who I am. And the spirituality I grew up with. Our children will know that whether I want to teach it to them or not. They're going to learn what I've learned through the church because it's made me who I am, and I'm going to pass it on. It will be how they live. That's what will be in our home.

"Josh" — she falters here, for a moment — "loves Christianity, because it's made me. I have an even stronger connection to Judaism than that. I embrace it.

"People ask me, 'Are you going to baptize your children?' Why do people baptize their children? To wash away original sin. Well, what do I really think about original sin? If I look at it that way, it's really not important to me that I do. But it *is* important to my mother. She says she's going to do it whether I like it or not. I said, 'Okay, do what you want to do, Mom.' But I asked her, 'Do you really believe that, Mom? Do you really believe that if someone's not baptized, they're not going to heaven?' She said, 'No.' I asked, 'Well, why?' She said, 'I don't know.' So I said, 'Do what you want in the bathtub.'

On a warm April evening, Josh and Maura attend an outdoor seder. Maura has just learned that she is pregnant, but no one is supposed to know. Guests take turns at the pages of their shared Haggadahs, weaving through the wonderful tale of Moses, past the locusts and the frogs, the matzoh and maror. When it is Josh's turn to read, he recites his passages in English, then in flawless Hebrew. He puts others at the table to such shame that he quickly becomes the anointed Hebrew-reader. Near the end of the meal, he passes the book to Maura; the night has grown so dark that readers must put their pages directly to the candles if they are to see correctly.

When she comes to a prayer, she reads it with a perfect Hebrew accent. Most others — including those who were born Jewish — choose to recite the English versions. Hers seems a deliberate move, one born of stubbornness, perhaps, but also determination. She is Catholic, but on this night she rejoices in this story of freedom just as Jews do. It is her way of taking, as she would call it, the high road. It is a path she is prepared to take, with or without the support of her in-laws.

"If they're going to be my family — and they are my family, now — the Jewishness that I'm going to learn, the Jewish home that I'm going to provide, and I *am* going to provide one — who am I going to learn it from? From *them*. When you want something passed on, it's not through lectures and threats and looking down on others. Why not celebrate the beauty of the tradition? If you want us to have a Jewish home, teach me *why* I should have a Jewish home. I've tried to make a point, and Josh has, as well. And the point is that I have a lot to offer Judaism. I'm not taking Josh away from Judaism, or taking our children away from Judaism, or taking our children's children away from Judaism. I have so much to offer Judaism when it allows me to offer what I have to offer."

THREE

Evolution

&

IT WAS a warm spring day in Richmond, Virginia, and twelve-
year-old Aaron Green was playing with friends in his neighbor's backyard. The afternoon, he recalls, came at that awkward
but exciting time in an adolescent's life when the opposite sex is
beginning the metamorphosis from pest to object of interest. "We
were all out there being flirtatious," he says. Suddenly, the girl's
mother appeared. It was well past lunchtime, and she was surprised
to learn that the children had not yet eaten. "Y'all just sit tight," she
said, and disappeared into the kitchen. A few moments later she
returned with a tray loaded high with ham sandwiches and tall
glasses of milk.

Aaron looked on, mortified. What should he do? It was Passover, and his family abstained from eating chametz — leavened
products — during the holiday. But as the only Jew among his
peers that day, Aaron was afraid to speak up. So, like the other kids,
he wolfed down his sandwich and went back out to play. Almost
thirty years later, the memory is painful still; he recounts the story
in vivid detail, as if he is being forced to watch and narrate a home
movie of the incident. He winces as he recalls it, his gentle face
contorted with discomfort. "I'll never forget how bad I felt that,
number one, I ate it, and number two, I didn't have the courage to
say something. Because I was certain, knowing these particular
people, that they wouldn't understand and would probably hurt
my feelings with some sort of anti-Semitic remark."

He was, after all, used to such comments. Bigotry was a given fact in Aaron's Southern childhood. "I was at times ashamed of my religion because I didn't know how else to react," he says. "Anti-Semitism was a natural corollary to the racism around me." He remembers unspoken alliances with Catholics and blacks, even if they weren't friends. It was part of getting along in a world that was white, Anglo-Saxon, and Protestant. Other children called him a "bastard Jew," he says, but he is quick to add that African-American children around him had it much, much worse. In the seat of the Confederacy, he says, what would you expect? Besides, as the father of three, he realizes how natural it is for children to fight, and to do so unfairly. "Kids argue with each other and say things." He shrugs. "But the thing that would get to me the most was when they'd say, 'You're just a Jew.'" He sighs. "I experienced that from time to time, and I'm sure my two brothers and sister and the few Jewish friends I had did, too. But I internalized them." He drums his fingers lightly on the table, and comes back to the ham sandwich he ate nearly thirty years ago. "We all have recurring visions of certain things, and that one pops into my head every once in a while." He rises from the kitchen table in his spacious Long Island home to get a bottle of wine, then pours himself a glass. "I had a real sense of being different growing up. To this day, the kids I still think about, the kids I dream about at night, are my Jewish friends. In the long run, they were my closest friends. The years move on, and you end up picking the people you stay in touch with. But them — I keep up with them."

The experience of growing up as one among few Jews in a place where he felt unwelcome shaped Aaron Green in myriad ways. He never renounced Judaism. But when pushed, he felt more comfortable blending in with the majority. His parents, Stanley and Irene, both the offspring of Lithuanian Jews, were not particularly observant. They did not keep a kosher home, although they lit candles on Friday nights and recited the kiddush, the prayer that sanctifies the Sabbath. Irene had grown up in an Orthodox home, where rules were rules, down to the ritual slaughter of chickens. Yet Irene and Stanley only rarely attended their Conservative synagogue. Once, Aaron recalls, he even cajoled his parents into letting him sit on Santa's lap in a Richmond department store. And he remembers wandering down the street on Christmas to look at his friends' presents. He knew there there was no Santa, he says, but he longed to experience the magical morning his neighbors talked about so excitedly. "They had gifts galore," he says. "I mean, gifts galore. The grass was always greener on the other side." Indeed, one year he saved up his allowance and bought gifts for each of his family members. He hid them in his parents' bedroom, and slipped the wrapped packages into the living room on Christmas Eve. "We had a little Christmas," he says, shyly. "Just us. No tree, just presents. That was the only time it ever happened. Nobody was upset about it. They just let me do it."

Meanwhile, Aaron was preparing for his bar mitzvah. As one of the best students in his Hebrew class, he was proud of his facility with the language, and especially looked up to the cantor who helped teach him. He also served as president of his synagogue's junior congregation, the youngest ever to hold the title. "I liked leadership roles, and felt comfortable in them early on," he says. Aaron Green was seemingly eager to accept the mantle of Judaism. "Even as a child I wanted to respond to the challenge of certain restrictions that were imposed on me as a Jew." And so, even before his bar mitzvah — *especially* before his bar mitzvah — Aaron fasted on Yom Kippur and donated his time to Jewish causes. (Jewish adolescents are expected to fulfill their obligations as Jews once they have become a bat or bar mitzvah.)

But all was not as it seemed. Aaron had a gnawing lack of faith, a void that seemed to widen as his knowledge of Judaism deepened. It is a dilemma he wrestles with still. "Faith has always eluded me. I think I'll be very old when I fully understand what I need to understand about religion and God," he says, the sonorous cadences of Virginia impervious to his twenty years in New York.

Doubts or not, his decision to marry a non-Jew was a struggle. He knew with piercing clarity that he loved Helen Khoury, yet wondered how they would work things out. And she couldn't understand why, if he called himself a Jew, he never went to synagogue, and he never prayed. Maybe he could convert to Catholicism, she suggested. It would be so much easier. He considered it, briefly. Impossible, he decided. "I am Jewish to the core," he says. "There is something distinctly Jewish in my soul."

Even so, Aaron reluctantly agreed, first to a Christmas tree, then to his children's baptisms and weekly Sunday school lessons. These decisions remain at times a source of psychic conflict and pain. His family goes to church while he stays home on Sunday mornings. He practices Jewish rituals: he lights candles with his family and celebrates Hanukkah. On the High Holidays, he, Helen, and the children attend services at the Reform congregation to which they belong. Aaron fasts on Yom Kippur. The family holds a seder every year, which both sets of grandparents enjoy. When each son was a few days old, he was circumcised at home by a mohel (someone who is specially trained in the procedure). His daughter was blessed and named by a rabbi in a similar ceremony at home. In the secular realm, he serves on the board of directors at his local Jewish community center.

And Aaron Green has hopes. One day, perhaps when his children are older and ask the same questions about God that began surfacing in his youth, they will walk into his library filled with books about Jewish history, philosophy, and religion and pick one up. Perhaps they will find the faith that has escaped their father. Perhaps they will be drawn to their Jewish heritage after all. These are, Aaron Green quietly realizes, daydreams. But he keeps them, even as his family continues to be among that 41 percent of inter-married couples who raise their children as Christians. He says it was as much evolution as decision, mirroring the changes in his relationship with Helen, a vivacious New Yorker with whom he fell in love and married nearly two decades ago.

Helen Khoury Green has no conflicts about religion, her spirituality, or her identity as a Lebanese Catholic. She grew up in a Lebanese neighborhood in Brooklyn, the fourth of five children. Her parents, Albert and Marie, were first-generation Americans. As a child, Helen believed the world mirrored the concentric circles of her family, home, church, and school. "I just thought everybody had brown eyes, black hair, and tan skin," she says. Helen was six, she says, before she realized the rest of the world wasn't Lebanese. Sitting in a diner for breakfast with her family, she ordered eggs with bread. When the waitress plopped a basket of white bread on the table, Helen looked at her mother and said, "That's not bread. Where's the bread?" So accustomed was she to pita — "Syrian bread," she calls it — her hunger turned to disappointment, and she didn't eat. "Not a bite," she says. "A strike."

Helen was enrolled, as her sister and brothers had been before her, in a parochial school. By then, of course, she knew that not everyone was Lebanese. But in Helen's world, until she was in college, they certainly were Catholic. Like her classmates, she learned the prayers, the novenas, the recitations necessary to pass to the next grade. Unlike her husband, Helen found that faith flowed from ritual. The prayers were soothing, even if she didn't know exactly what they meant. "You just memorize this stuff," she says. "Nobody tells you what it means, and you're not exactly encouraged to ask." Still, Helen reveled in Catholicism; like the hummus and kibbe her mother prepared for family meals, it was part of her identity, who she was, and she was proud of it. She loved going to church with her family, where her father was a pivotal figure. He was a Knight of Malta and had received papal distinctions for his charitable work. In all ways, hers was the experience of a member of the prevailing culture, comfortably walking the path followed by everyone else she knew. Aaron Green's painful choice of eating a ham sandwich or unmasking himself as a Jew was as distant to the childhood of Helen Khoury as the civil wars of Lebanon.

After high school, she attended Cornell University. Her roommate was a blond, blue-eyed woman who shocked Helen one day when she announced that she was Jewish. "I was surprised, and I said something I realized I shouldn't have said. But it was my first reaction. I said, 'Well, you don't look Jewish.' I thought all Jews looked like *me*. All of the sudden I joined a sorority that was thirty percent Jewish. That was when I started meeting Jewish people." Her years at Cornell gave her other insights. She continued to attend mass, but her relationships with others stemmed from cultural rather than religious affinities. In some ways, she felt more comfortable with her Jewish friends. She understood their attitudes toward their families, the pressures they felt about academic achievements, their passionate arguments punctuated by flashing arms and hands, and, above all, the essential importance of food, copious trays of it.

Aaron Green arrived at Cornell the same year. His gangly adolescence had given way to a grown-up confidence. He had a slender tennis-player's build with striking features, light blue eyes, and brown wavy hair. Aaron had no shortage of dates, Christian or Jewish; religion was never an issue. But in his sophomore year, he met Helen, whose enormous soft brown eyes, bright smile, and throaty laugh struck him instantly. They began dating, but the courtship faltered almost immediately. Aaron aspired to become a neurologist and realized, with a maturity rare among college students, that he would never relinquish enough of his social life to succeed in his demanding premed course. He left Cornell for the University of Virginia. In a school where he knew hardly anyone, he figured he would be less tempted to forsake organic chemistry for kegs of beer. The couple began their long-distance romance two months later. "It was clear from the time we met that this was it. We didn't date other people," recalls Helen. "And we were hundreds of miles apart. It was obviously very serious." Soon, Aaron and Helen began to discuss getting married.

Their parents had other ideas. Helen recalls her father's reaction the day she told him that Aaron, the boyfriend he had recently met, was Jewish. "The way I broke it to my father was this. I said, 'Dad, does it bother you that Aaron's Jewish?' He was flabbergasted. He had just met Aaron. We'd gone to dinner with him and about five of my girlfriends. Aaron was shy and didn't talk. He just ate like a pig, which of course made my father love him. My dad said, 'Well, if it doesn't bother you, it doesn't bother me.'"

It was not that simple. Although it was literally true that one of. Albert Khoury's best friends was a Jew, that did not mean he necessarily wanted his youngest daughter to marry one. Both Albert and Marie worried about how their daughter would raise children in an interfaith home. Catholic dogma was clear on this point. You were either in the church or out of it. No halfway. No compromises. They liked Aaron, they were kind to him, and they knew he was a good man. But still, they worried. Helen's brothers were not quite so generous. They never said anything outright, but their behavior made it clear they thought their little sister was making a big mistake. "They were kind of into this Lebanese mafia mentality — let's keep it all in the family," she says.

In Aaron's family, the doubts were even more emphatic. When he told his parents of his plans to marry, Stanley Green started up on the history of the Jews. "But the Jewish people!" he said, time and again. "It was pretty neck and neck as to who was loudest," Helen says. "It was tough for each of them. They had gotten to know each of us and generally liked us, yet felt it was their duty to break us up. His mom took me aside and said, 'Look, I know my son, and I can see he loves you. I'm sure you could live together forever. But what are you going to do with your children?' And I didn't know."

She was, of course, telling the truth. Helen and Aaron had no earthly idea how they were going to raise a family. All they really knew was that they were in love and wanted to be together, regardless of their families' objections. In contrast to many interfaith couples, neither Helen nor Aaron took their parents' qualms to heart. "I didn't take the rejection by Aaron's parents personally," Helen says. "It had nothing at all to do with me. I knew they liked me as a person. And I certainly couldn't change myself. Nor did I want to. But I did feel bad for Aaron. He got it coming and going."

Aaron reflects on this for a moment, then fairly whispers, "I think the real difficulty with my parents was not the dramatic effect my marriage to Helen would have on the Jewish people, but their own sense of failure. It's not that they were being rejected, although maybe they were. But it was too painful for them to realize that my willingness to marry Helen was a failure on their part to instill

Jewishness in me. And if that's what they felt, to some extent they were probably right."

Helen recalls their wedding animatedly. Aaron was finished with medical school, and she was about to take the reins, with her siblings, of the advertising agency her father founded. She and Aaron had been together for years, and she looked forward not so much to the wedding, but the celebration afterward. She describes their chuppah, their flowers, then retrieves the photo album to reveal the day itself. Her family priest, a Lebanese Maronite, stood alongside a rabbi. When the rabbi read the ketubah, the Jewish wedding contract, he recited its words aloud in the language of the document, Aramaic, the vernacular during the period it was first recorded, the fourth century B.C.E. When the priest gave blessings unique to the Maronite order, he too spoke Aramaic. Helen, when describing this scene, wraps her arms around her husband's waist and peers up into his face — he stands a full head taller than she. "That made it easier for you, didn't it, honey?"

"No," he replies, and they burst out laughing.

Now, they can find humor in their differences. But a decade ago, there was a lot less laughter in the family.

When the Greens' first child, Zachary, was born, Aaron knew what was in store. He knew that Helen wanted him baptized. It pained him to envision it, but what was he to do? He wanted his son to have a bris, a ritual circumcision. Jewish law calls for a baby boy to be circumcised eight days after his birth. It does not specify that the surgery be done at home or by a mohel; any Jew proficient in the surgery and able to recite the appropriate blessings may do it. But Aaron wanted tradition, even if they would pass the mandate of the eighth day. He tracked down a mohel — "some ninety-year-old Brises-R-Us kind of guy," Helen recalls — who agreed to circumcise Zachary, despite the facts that Helen wasn't Jewish and the baby was ten days old.

Helen had never been to a bris or, for that matter, had ever had the opportunity. All of their Jewish friends had had their sons circumcised in the hospital. She didn't object to the procedure at all

— it was just the ritual performed at home, by this strange old man, which puzzled her. "It's extremely weird, any way you look at it. It was weird for me and weird for my family, but everyone hung in there," she says. "Even my mother-in-law took me into the kitchen while they were doing it. I kept asking her, 'Why are they doing this?' And she'd say, 'I don't know, but they do. Have some more wine, Helen. Here, have some more wine.' And I said, 'But they're out there cutting my son's penis off!' You know, I was a new mother, I wasn't getting any sleep, my hormones were completely whacked out, I was still sore from delivery, and then I go out into the living room, and everyone is clapping and hugging me and slapping me on the back."

To top it off, Marie Khoury, Helen's mother, herself hesitant about the event, tried to help in her usual way — by cooking mounds of food. She brought Lebanese dishes and pita, olives, wine, seltzer, even a huge tray of shrimp. "Aaron thought that was just great," Helen recalls. "He said, 'Wow, look at all this shrimp.' Nobody in his family is kosher, but even Aaron's mom said later, 'Gee, maybe the shrimp wasn't such a great idea.'" (Under Jewish law, shellfish is considered unclean, or treyf.)

Aaron insists the religious aspects of circumcision had little consequence to him. In fact, he knew Zachary would soon be baptized. Still, he wanted to welcome his son into the world as a Jew, with his parents and siblings. "It was an opportunity to share this life cycle event with members of my family," he says. "It was important to me, that's all. What does it mean to a child? Nothing. It's for the parents, the same as a baptism."

Weeks later, Helen and Aaron dressed for church. Helen put Zachary in the long white christening gown handed down to her, and they drove off to Helen's Lebanese church, where just her immediate family had gathered. Helen was nervous — she knew Aaron was uncomfortable about the whole idea. But how could he complain? "I felt I had stepped up to the plate for the bris," she says. Besides, she was a churchgoing Catholic, and this was a crucial element of her faith. It had to be done. She couldn't even say why.

"Why do we have to do it now?" Aaron asked. "Can't we wait until he gets older and chooses to do it?" "No," Helen responded. "Why?" Aaron asked. "I don't know why," Helen said. "It just has to be now." It wasn't as if she subscribed to the biblical verse that warned: "Except ye be converted, and become as little children, ye shall not enter into the kingdom of heaven" (Matthew, 18:3). If she believed that, she believed that Aaron wasn't going to heaven, either, and that wasn't how she saw things. Still, she would feel better once it was done.

It was a disastrous morning. Aaron sat in the pew, alone, while Helen and her family walked down the aisle. As he watched the priest anoint his son, he felt his mood grow dark and darker behind the sunglasses he was wearing inside the church. The glasses, he says years later, were not to hide tears; they were simply an outward expression of his bad humor. One of his sisters-in-law approached Aaron as the family was filing out. "I know this must have been really difficult for you," she told him. For a moment, he felt better. Less alone. At least someone understood this wasn't such a merry occasion.

At their house later, relatives poured in to meet the baby. Helen had sent out discreet invitations to family members, requesting their presence at a brunch. The cards did not mention the baptism, in deference to Aaron. Helen, in fact, felt she was playing down the event. Compared to the christenings of her nieces and nephews, Zachary's was a low-key affair, a stealth baptism. Still, Aaron could barely keep up a front. People hugged him and said congratulations, just as they had hugged Helen at Zachary's bris. He struggled to contain his unhappiness, but he didn't appear to fool anybody.

After everyone left, Helen started to cry. "Why did you act that way?" she asked. They began to fight. "How could you?" Helen asked. Aaron responded truthfully. He could hardly stand to see his wife and child at the baptismal font, he said. "When I saw you up there, I felt all the love I had for you and Zachary drain out of me," Aaron said. Helen was crushed, almost too stunned to breathe. She had anticipated Aaron's being unhappy, but never this. In fact, she was relieved that the baptism was over, and also that it had been done. She had had to do it. But she was also angry: Catholicism was her religion, and she took it seriously. Yet she participated willingly in the rituals of her agnostic Jewish husband — even ones she found baffling. But this? It was the worst day of her life.

Two years later, when their daughter, Danielle, was born, a Reform rabbi came to the Greens' house for her naming ceremony, and a baptism followed a few weeks later. This time, however, Helen planned things differently. The priest performed a simple outdoor christening in her parents' backyard, with only a few family members present. Aaron, for his part, went golfing. Or did he just stay home? Neither seems to remember. Aaron had agreed to Danielle's baptism, but he felt it best that he not attend. When Helen told her parents, Albert Khoury replied, "Well, Aaron's absence is his statement." Helen was sad that Aaron wasn't with her. She cried as she faced the priest alone, flanked by her parents and Danielle's godparents. "But I appreciated the fact that he just couldn't do it. I preferred that he not be there. It was simpler for everyone." And at least the occasion passed without a huge fight.

Five years after Danielle's birth, another son, Joseph, was born. His arrival was radically different from Zack's, seven years earlier. A hip young rabbi with a Jerry Garcia tie came to perform the circumcision, which he did on the kitchen table. He recited a poem — a Frank Sinatra song, actually — and put everyone, Catholic and Jewish alike, at ease. Aaron was so relaxed and comforted by the whole occasion he even attended Joseph's baptism, again held in the Khourys' backyard. "Both of us realized that these were ridiculous things to fight over," Helen says. "We kind of looked at each other and said, 'We've got a beautiful baby, he's healthy, and our lives are good.'"

Indeed, Aaron was beginning to see how things were turning out. Other friends were raising their children in both the Jewish and Christian faiths. There were support groups for interfaith couples at local churches and synagogues. He and Helen subscribed to a newsletter devoted to the solutions of couples like themselves. There was even a greeting card company catering to interfaith families and their holiday dilemmas. "It wasn't such a big mystery anymore," he says. "I could see how the older kids were turning out. And I could also see that the baptism ceremony itself was fairly meaningless to the children — it was something I just had to live through. The same was true for Helen about the bris." The isolation Aaron had felt at Zack's christening was long past. Although Zack and Danielle go to Sunday school, and love Christmas and Easter, they also light candles with Aaron on Friday nights. They delight in Hanukkah, and count the days until it begins. They love to find the afikomen at Passover. They attend Jewish summer camp. They belong to a Reform congregation full of other mixed families. Once, in line for a Disney movie one evening, Danielle broke into song. "Shabbat Shalom," she belted out, to the amazement of her father.

Aaron has even felt more welcomed by Helen's brothers. Albert and Marie Khoury had always extended their warmth and generosity to him — Albert counted many Jews among his friends and acquaintances, and even gave money to Jewish causes. From the start, Aaron says, Albert made clear that he realized Catholicism "wasn't the only game in town." Helen's brothers, however, were another story. Conservative and firmly ensconced in an all-Catholic world — their wives were Catholic, and their children attended parochial school — they had never so much as expressed interest in anything to do with Judaism. "It was always 'Merry Christmas' in December — never 'Happy Hanukkah' or even 'Happy Holidays.' It was as if they didn't even realize Jews had observances of their own." Aaron suspects that at some point Albert took his sons aside and insisted they treat Aaron with the respect he deserved, as Helen's husband and as a member of the family. The lesson seemed to stick. Helen says that recently one of her brothers spoke up indignantly to an acquaintance who used an anti-Semitic slur. "My brother-in-law is Jewish, and I take offense at that," he declared, and left the room.

Though time has smoothed many of the conflicts, the Greens still have their tensions. At Christmastime, Helen tries to minimize exuberance for the holiday. When she and Aaron commissioned the design of their new house several years ago, they asked the architect to draw a spacious living area perfect for entertaining guests. And it is spectacular. Enormous plate glass windows look out onto the Long Island Sound, and a giant stone fireplace stands majestically in a corner. In her mind, Helen can see a towering Christmas tree there, in the center of the room, its top brushing the cathedral ceiling. In reality, though, she and the children pick out a small tree each year and adorn it with a few modest decorations. Even that pushes the outer limits of comfort for Aaron. But to Helen, it looks almost as if she's forgotten to decorate. "You should see my Italian sister-in-law's home," she says wistfully. Every inch of that house is decorated. There are lights inside and out. Bing Crosby warbles from the speakers. The table is even set with Christmas plates.

While Helen's spirits soar as December spirals toward its twenty-fifth day, Aaron's deflate. Christmastime reminds him of everything he had hated about growing up in Richmond, where his house was the darkest on the block. He likes buying gifts for his wife and children, but loathes having to do it in crowds, and for an occasion that means virtually nothing to him. "We battle this out year after year," he says. "It could be a lot more fun if it weren't pushed down my throat. I've been exposed to its prevalence in our society all my life. I'm fairly laid back about most things. But with Christmas, it's just everywhere you go. And as the season goes on, I get progressively morose."

He realizes that Helen takes a minimalist approach to Christmas — she bakes without making a big fuss and trudges home empty-handed from the craft shows she frequents with her friends. He can't always manage, but he does try to muster up some cheer. Last year, he went shopping in early November, before the malls were swarming. He marched through Saks Fifth Avenue, snatching up everything he thought his wife could want: a leather jacket, a lamb's wool coat, a designer suit, a sweater in one of her favorite colors, maroon. He felt like the Pied Piper, the way saleswomen were trailing after him. He knew it would make Helen happy; he even knew that she would interpret the shopping spree as his warming up to the holiday. Nothing could have been further from the truth, frankly — he felt generous, and his actions happened to coincide with the Christmas season. He gave some of the packages to her for Hanukkah, and some for Christmas.

"I was shocked," she says. "Didn't all that shopping get you in the spirit?" she asks, hopefully.

"No," he answers dryly, and she rolls her eyes. "It did make it more comfortable. But it's still a rough time of year."

Helen feels the strain in a different way. The restraint she must display about an evocative holiday she loves wears on her after a while. And she is especially careful to make sure that Hanukkah and Christmas get equal time, so if a Santa decoration goes up, a basket of dreidels and gold-covered chocolate Hanukkah gelt get put out, too. "It's very clear what's going on in our home each December," Helen says. She sighs. The first doubts about Santa Claus have begun to appear, and she knows that as soon as Zack tells Danielle, Joseph will learn the truth too. "It's such a special time," she says. "I really want to share it with the children. It'll be over so soon."

Aaron is always glad when Hanukkah and Christmas overlap; when the stars are aligned that way, he doesn't feel so left out. "That way I don't have to get revved up twice." He is grateful, too, that America has changed since he was in grade school and had to sing along with every verse of religious Christmas carols. Now, though, as he watches Zack and Danielle at their public school plays — holiday recitals, he is quick to point out, not Christmas pageants, like the one he had — youngsters touch on everything. They sing a dreidel song, and they learn about Hanukkah in school. The secular Rudolph the red-nosed reindeer is more likely to appear than a nativity scene. "It shows how much things have evolved," he says. It is a word he uses often.

Indeed, when Hanukkah and Christmas intersect, the Khoury clan and the Greens make a point of marking the event together. Zack, Danielle, and Joseph light the candles in the menorah, and Aaron tells the story of Judah and the Maccabees. Albert follows with the tale of the night before Christmas. "It's just wonderful," Helen says. "It all blends together."

If that is the hope — the blending of two religions — it seems that Aaron and Helen Green have come a long way toward achieving it. Their older children, Zack and Danielle, call themselves "half-Catholic, half-Jewish," although their parents doubt they really know what that means. Zack, nine, just had his first communion, an event for which he mustered little enthusiasm. It's all a bore at the moment, something he does for his mom. Who is to say whether he would take to Judaism any differently? Aaron holds no dear memories of his own Jewish education. "It was a real turn-off," he says. And so he tries to answer his kids' questions about spirituality in ways that invite discourse, that provoke thought. When they asked, some years back, the meaning of the Hebrew blessings over the candles and the challah, Aaron was taken aback. "You know what? I didn't know what they meant," he says. "I'd never learned. No one ever said."

And so, as his family grows, and as he and Helen evolve, they wonder about who their children will become, the rites they will initiate, and how — or whether — faith will inspire them. (At the moment, Zack seems most moved by his living idol, Michael Jordan.) The children ask questions, sure. Danielle asks Helen about God from time to time — what does God look like? Is God a man or a woman? Helen does her best, she says, stumbling through incomprehensible and unsatisfactory answers: "God doesn't really look like anything. God is what you feel when you love someone, God is everywhere, God is both a man and a woman." And Danielle will look up with the huge brown eyes she inherited from her mother and shake her head. Helen laughs. "I just want to say, 'I have no idea, honey.'"

Aaron tries, too. He has talked to Zack and Danielle about the different beliefs people have all over the world, not just the two ways of thinking that coexist in their home. "There are many different ways of looking at God," he tells them.

Helen tells her children that even though there are different ways of looking at God, God loves everyone. That God made everyone. That striving to be a good person will lead everyone to God. And that even though Daddy and Mommy have different ways of looking at God, the end is the same.

Even to an adult, however, these concepts are hard to grasp. What Zack, Danielle, and Joseph will make of them as time goes on is hard to say. Zack has expressed no interest in a bar mitzvah, and Aaron is loath to put him through Hebrew school. Instead, they'll do something they read about in their interfaith newsletter: he and Helen will throw a party for Zack when he turns thirteen, as a celebration of his life. Danielle, who is already after her father to teach her Hebrew, wants to know about everything: the life of Jesus Christ, what prayers Jews say for certain things, and why, if Jesus was Jewish, Jews don't think of him as the Messiah.

How can anyone in Judaism know what is the right thing, Aaron wonders, when for centuries even the sages have been trying to puzzle it out? He reads and reads, trying to find the answer. "I continue to learn about the Jewish past, and I've learned that, hey, there's been at least a hundred brands of Judaism. There's Reform, there's Conservatism, there's Orthodox. There are Hasids. There are Lubavitchers and Reconstructionists. There are messianic Jews and kabbalistic Jews. And what I'm witnessing now is perhaps there's so much intermarriage in American culture that there's an evolution toward something unique that historians will write about two hundred years from now; at the moment we can't fully understand it right now. Maybe someday Judaism will touch my kids' souls, just as it does mine. For me, one of the most important things about being Jewish is the ability to identify with five thousand years of Jewish history and understanding. I hope my kids will take the time to learn, and I hope we can help them do it."

FOUR

Double Exposure

§

I T WAS THE PEAK of the rainy season, but the morning of
December 24, 1994, dawned bright and clear. The storm that
had drenched Oahu earlier in the week had finally blown out
to sea. Even so, Shaaroni Leesha Sun Lin Wong arose from bed a
nervous wreck. She had turned to her sleeping parents for comfort just before dawn, but their solace somehow worked only in
the dark.

She turned on the shower, her stomach in knots. Under the
warm stream of water, she took deep breaths to calm herself.

"Shaaroni, the time," called her father, Alvin, from the Wongs'
blue and white kitchen, where he was preparing his daughter's
breakfast. He poured a glass of guava juice and put it at her place.
His wife, Trudy, was out making last-minute preparations; it was
his job to drive their daughter.

"I'm not hungry, Daddy," she said. Even the cream doughnut
he had bought — Shaaroni's favorite — didn't entice her. "Take a
few bites," he commanded. "You'll be hungry later." He tapped his
wristwatch. Shaaroni was dawdling. She was late. Of all mornings.

Shaaroni took one last look at her things to make sure all
was ready: the violet muumuu, tailored especially for her slender
frame, hung on her door. Grandma Wong's pearl sweater clip from
Hong Kong rested in its pouch on her bureau. At last ready,
Shaaroni and Alvin climbed into Trudy's dark green minivan and
set out for the hairdresser. To stave off nervousness, Shaaroni
imagined herself doing the hula dance she was set to perform later

that day, and traced the delicate lavender roses painted on her gown. It didn't seem to work.

"I'm gonna die, I'm gonna die, I'm gonna die," she thought to herself. It had become her morning mantra. She felt sick. Four hundred and fifty people had congregated in Honolulu from as far away as New Jersey, Massachusetts, even Argentina. The occasion? Shaaroni's bat mitzvah, a vivid celebration of her passage to womanhood as a Jew and a tribute to her heritage as a third-generation Hawaiian-born Wong.

Hours later, draped in a purple and white tallis woven by a member of her grandmother's synagogue in Asheville, North Carolina, held fast with Grandma Wong's clip, Shaaroni took her place on the bimah. She read her portion of the prophets flawlessly, her jaw set in a straight line. "Shaaroni," relatives admonished later, "you looked so serious up there." "If I smiled, I would have broken my concentration," she said.

Shaaroni Wong's bat mitzvah is a colorful and exotic example of Jews reinterpreting their traditions, just as they have for millennia. Trudy Schandler-Wong, who was raised in Asheville in a traditional Jewish home, Alvin, a Chinese American who converted to Judaism, and their two children have taken a bit from here and there. They have woven Jewish, Chinese, and Hawaiian cultures into their home like a bird building a nest from twigs, mud, and foil. The Wongs' blend stands out, of course, from what most American Jews would recognize as their own Ashkenazic rituals.

But it is not radically different from those of other Jews of the Diaspora, who melded their unique customs, art, and diet with prevailing cultures from Holland to India. Jews in Morocco use the figs and dates plentiful in North Africa to make their Passover haroseth. Nineteenth-century Russian Jews fashioned gold medallions in Moses' likeness, borrowing a tradition from their Christian neighbors, who wore pendants of Christ and the saints. Jewish silversmiths in Poland crafted menorahs and mezuzahs with the eighteenth-century Baroque arches favored by Catholic Poles.

Indeed, the upbringing of Shaaroni and her older brother, Ari, as extraordinary as it has been, is not so unusual in Hawaii. The intermarriage rate among the state's Jews and the Asian Americans who make up the islands' majority is well over 50 percent, according to authoritative estimates. And because things Asian are so much a part of the Hawaiian fabric — particularly in Honolulu, where most of the state's Jews live — it is only natural that the offspring of such unions combine what is close to home with Judaism. To be sure, the Wongs, and scores of other families like them in Hawaii, are no more typical of interfaith marriage than Hawaii is typical of the United States. But in many ways the fusion of cultures in their household represents one of the most positive outcomes of intermarriage.

Trudy assumed that her Gentile mate was also attracted to Jewish culture and tradition. She, after all, was as interested in integrating Alvin's history into their family as Alvin was in participating in Trudy's faith and rituals. "They're not mutually exclusive," she says. Indeed, the Wongs show that couples can make choices resulting in a richer cultural life as a family than either member had alone. Trudy has nurtured her Judaism, and Alvin has, with Trudy's help, rediscovered his Chinese roots. For the Wongs, Judaism is more than lighting Hanukkah candles in December, or eating an occasional bialy sent by Federal Express from the East Coast. So, too, does their Chinese heritage extend beyond their last name or Sunday night dinners in Cantonese restaurants.

When Trudy and Alvin became engaged in the early 1970s, they were pelted with questions about the children they would have. In the Wongs' case, the preoccupation was alleviated by Alvin's conversion — done by a Reform rabbi, but under some Orthodox strictures, in part to please Trudy's Orthodox father. This ensured, of course, that any of Trudy and Alvin's offspring would be uncompromisingly Jewish. But Alvin's conversion did not obliterate Alvin's past and the fact that Shaaroni and Ari would always have Christian cousins.

Distant as Hawaii is from Asheville, a small city near the Appalachian Mountains, there are parallels between Trudy Schandler-

Wong's childhood and her life as a wife and mother. At the turn of the century, Trudy's Latvian-born grandfather settled in Asheville as one of the town's first Jews. Trudy and her two sisters had great pride in their heritage; along with their parents, Aaron and Lee, they took place among Asheville's small Jewish community as descendants of its founders. The kosher deli and store Trudy's grandfather established, the Pickle Barrel, was a city landmark.

Her recollections are rich, a blend of passionate Judaism and Southern protocol. Manners, gracious smiles, thank-you notes: all were as important as keeping kosher. As Trudy speaks, she leans back on a blue and white couch in her airy family room. Generous and warm, with a rich, deep voice, she has gentle lines around her mouth that reveal a life spent smiling. With graceful, manicured hands, she occasionally reaches up to push her blond bangs out of her eyes. Around her neck are several gold chains, each a testament to something: one is an heirloom, and two support the Star of David, one of gold, the other of pearls. "I've always worn my identity on my sleeve," she says.

That wasn't always easy in a small town, despite the closeness with which the Schandlers were integrated into Asheville society. The Ku Klux Klan concerned itself mostly with frightening blacks, torching crosses in nearby backyards. But swastikas appeared on the city's synagogue doors, too. And occasionally townspeople wandered into the Pickle Barrel to see if they could catch a glimpse of the notorious Jewish horns; Trudy's grandfather, a devout Jew, was never without his hat, fueling rumors that he was hiding something.

Once, when Trudy was in elementary school, she invited a classmate over to play. The girl, however, lingered outside in the yard. When Trudy's mother, Lee, urged her to come inside, the child refused. "I can't," she called to Lee in the doorway. "Well, why not, honey?" Lee Schandler recalls asking. "Because you're Jewish, and the Jews killed Jesus," the child said.

With her life in North Carolina as a backdrop, Trudy thought nothing of raising her children steadfastly as Jews, fully realizing that their faith would set them apart from their peers. The Jewish

Wongs? Trudy hardly thought twice about the circumstances. Having grown up in the Bible belt, she found nothing new in being an outsider.

Trudy and Alvin met in Honolulu, where Trudy was posted as a United Airlines flight attendant. Based in Washington, D.C., she had jumped at the chance to leave the capital's summer heat for a few months in Hawaii. "I just wanted a good suntan," she says. Her apartment was a dream, steps from the beach in one of Waikiki's most glamorous new buildings. "I was having a ball," she says. Her gregariousness quickly attracted friends. At a party in her building one night, she was introduced to Alvin Wong, a tall, slender, elegant man with a promising job as a hospital administrator. "He was so *nice*," she says. The pair quickly became friends, ate dinner together, and watched movies.

Through it all, Trudy explained her devotion to her faith and told stories of her family and traditions; Alvin listened attentively. He accompanied Trudy to dinner when Lee and one of her sisters came to visit, patiently answering their questions.

But Trudy didn't think of her relationship with Alvin as anything promising. She was headed back to Washington at the end of the summer, and Alvin, well, he was nice, but he wasn't Jewish. Besides, Trudy could tell that he wasn't ready to settle down. But his consideration of her family and his genuine interest in her religion left an impression. He was an old-fashioned gentleman in an age of rogues.

Surprisingly, once Trudy got back to the East Coast, her friendship with Alvin flourished. They called each other frequently; Alvin was especially solicitous when Trudy had surgery and was recuperating at her parents' home in North Carolina. "Here I was, twenty-eight years old, and my mother was waiting on me hand and foot. It was driving me crazy," she recalls. "I was complaining to Alvin and he said, 'Why don't you come back to Hawaii?'"

She sits up and declares in a stage whisper: "And then I tricked him into proposing. I said, 'I don't go anywhere without a commitment.' And he said, 'Well, consider yourself committed.' I figured that was a proposal." She winks. "So I called friends in L.A., I told my parents, I told everybody." An hour or so later, the phone rang again. It was Alvin. "Just what did you think I meant by commitment?" he asked. Trudy panicked. "I had to save face! I had told all these people we were getting married. I said, 'Well, I thought it meant we were getting married. Doesn't it?'"

And so, more or less, wedding plans were on. Indeed, even before their fateful conversation, Alvin had been making preparations to marry; he had met with a Reform rabbi to arrange his conversion in accordance with many of the Orthodox requirements. An acquaintance of the Schandlers, the Honolulu rabbi knew that a Reform conversion would not elicit Aaron Schandler's approval. Already circumcised, Alvin underwent a symbolic circumcision, in which the mohel drew a drop of blood from his penis. He immersed himself in the mikvah, the ritual bath (at the time there was no mikvah in Hawaii, so Alvin made do with the Pacific Ocean), and learned to read Hebrew.

Trudy soon realized she had to reconstruct many of the rituals that had seemed to her like second nature. "The hardest part of being Jewish and being married to Alvin, at the beginning, were my customs," Trudy says. "We had to establish observances that worked for both of us, not just for me."

Indeed, tradition was a strong undercurrent for both Trudy and Alvin. He even found much of what he covered in his eight-month conversion course somewhat familiar. Although kosher laws seemed a bit bewildering at first, he quickly understood their nuances. "It all boiled down to tradition," Alvin says, his long fingers sweeping gently before him. "I was very accustomed to that." His parents had made great efforts to assimilate, but despite the hamburgers and potato salad they fed their children, they remained very much Chinese. And underneath, they revered their Chinese heritage: Trudy, in fact, was readily accepted into Alvin's large family, not in spite of her Judaism, but *because* of it. "We are happy you will be joining the family," Alvin's mother told Trudy when she heard of the engagement, "because you come from the *other* Old World civilization. This marriage will be a success because you have strong traditions, too."

Like thousands of other Chinese, Alvin's grandparents had left their homeland for Hawaii at the turn of the century to find work in its many sugar and fruit plantations. Alvin's parents quickly integrated into American society, adapting to Christian mores when they began their own family. Alvin's father, an executive at a Honolulu newspaper, encouraged his four children to do the same. "You'll always have a strike against you because you're Oriental," he warned, urging his brood to study hard in college and to find lucrative and satisfying professions. The only way to succeed in Western society, the elder Wong maintained, was to *become* Western.

As a result, Alvin did not use chopsticks until he was eighteen years old. Instead of eating dim sum and pork dumplings, Alvin grew up on beef stew and pot roast. As youngsters, he and his siblings attended Catholic schools from kindergarten through high school — not because the Wongs were Catholics, but because they hoped their children would gain a better understanding of Western religion and thought. They celebrated Christmas and Easter, but were not churchgoers themselves.

Alvin never adhered to the faith. He respected the devotion of his classmates, but didn't feel comfortable enough to adopt it himself. So he sat in the back of the school chapel when the rest of his classmates took the sacraments.

A soft-spoken, thoughtful man, he had his first exposure to Judaism at Boston University in the late 1950s, when a Jewish roommate explained the basics: that Jews, for example, didn't see Christ as the son of God and therefore didn't celebrate Christmas or Easter. "Until that moment I hadn't actually ever thought of them as Christian holidays," says Alvin, fifty-four. "They hadn't been to us."

Oddly, since Alvin's parents wanted him to fit into mainstream America, they saw his conversion to Judaism as an advantage.

"They were really pleased," he says. "'Finally you have religion,' they told me." And Trudy's parents were equally pleased with the kind, elegant, and intelligent man engaged to their middle daughter. Accustomed to Trudy's adventures — she traveled widely and was the only member of the Schandler family to break kosher laws when she went away to college — they were delighted with Alvin's serious manner and devotion to their daughter. "My parents would have killed me if I *didn't* marry Alvin," she says.

Lee Schandler says that is only a slight exaggeration. "It took me about twenty seconds to fall in love with Al." She pauses. "Maybe ten. If I had been fortunate enough to have given birth to a son, I couldn't love him more." Friends, though, searched for hidden reservations. Surely she would be happier if Trudy were marrying someone of her own kind, they prodded. "My response was the same to everyone: I'll give you ten minutes in Al's presence, and if you don't fall in love with him by that time, there's something wrong with *you*."

Lee, seventy-eight, insists that Alvin's being Asian was of little import. "My children were never brought up to be concerned with anything but the person, whether he be black or yellow or red or green. We've been very blessed by having friends of all races who respect our way of worship, just as we respect theirs."

Life in Asheville, remote as it was, helped set the stage for such tolerant views. Even seders in the small town were mixed-faith affairs. Baptist preachers, Methodist ministers, and Episcopal priests shared the meal, and the story, with devout and secular Jews.

Occasionally, during her winters in Florida with other Jewish friends — or even at home in North Carolina — Lee hears the complaints of parents whose children have intermarried. She was raised in Brooklyn by Orthodox parents — one grandfather was a rabbi — but Lee Schandler shakes her head when she considers their laments. Her tone is kind but stern. "I ask them: Are you willing to give up your son or daughter because of this? Aren't you happy to have another member of the family? What about your grandchildren? Do you want to alienate them? Look at the person first; that's my advice."

Alvin feels affection for his in-laws, but not every encounter with the Schandlers was easy. Both Trudy and Alvin wince as they recall Alvin's first trip to North Carolina.

Nervous, Trudy met Alvin's plane and drove him to Asheville. As she pulled up to the Pickle Barrel, her father stepped outside, a big smile on his handsome face. Alvin hurried out of the car, and the two began shaking hands so hard Trudy thought their palms would crunch. The next thing she knew, they were locked in a bear hug. "And then Daddy asked Alvin what he wanted to eat — it was his way of saying, 'Welcome.' Alvin said he'd like a salami sandwich with mayo on white bread. Can you imagine? I just couldn't believe it. You should have seen the look on my father's face."

Of course Alvin, with his sensitivity to Jewish ritual, knew that mayonnaise is technically kosher, since it contains no dairy products. Nevertheless, Trudy felt her face growing red as she waited for her father's reaction.

But Aaron didn't flinch, and turned around to give the order. Alvin could tell that something was amiss. Bewildered, he asked Trudy what he did wrong. "There's no milk in mayonnaise. What did I do?" Trudy shook her head, aghast. "I know there isn't, but it just isn't done! We only eat mayonnaise with egg salad. Period."

Alvin laughs at the recollection. "I wanted to make a good impression, and look what I did."

Food presented yet another problem, this time at an elaborate party the elder Wongs put on for the newlyweds in Honolulu. Not to be outdone by the six hundred guests at Trudy and Alvin's wedding, Alvin's parents wanted to pull out all the stops for their son and daughter-in-law with a traditional Chinese wedding feast. Hundreds of friends and colleagues congregated in a hotel banquet room. The Schandlers flew to Hawaii for the occasion and took their seats at the table of honor for the nine-course Chinese meal.

But because Mr. Schandler ate only kosher food, much of the dinner was off-limits to him. He had asked that no special effort be made on his behalf; as the Wongs' guest, he didn't want to draw attention to his dietary differences. So Trudy quietly arranged that her father be served fruit.

As a first course, the waiter brought an elaborate pineapple boat, which Mr. Schandler ate with great gusto. When other guests were served their second course, a second pineapple boat appeared. And a third. And a fourth. After consuming nine pineapple boats, Trudy says, her dad was green. He never said a word, just ate them all politely.

A copper mezuzah marks the entrance of the Wong household. Framed quotes from Golda Meir, homemade tapestry with Hebrew inscriptions, Israeli pottery, and gold-painted panels adorn the walls. Sumptuous Chinese rugs cover large portions of the parquet floor. A black and red silk baby carrier Alvin's grandparents brought from their homeland rests behind a frame.

The main hallway is a study in Wong-Schandler history. Photos of Alvin's grandparents in the Old Country are juxtaposed with Latvian Schandlers. Slowly, the grainy black-and-white faces give way to glossy colored pictures of easier times, with subjects smiling, as only Americans do; the Wongs in Hawaii, the Schandlers in North Carolina. Finally, there is a portrait of the Wongs on their wedding day in 1975 — wide lapels and all — and of Ari and Shaaroni as children.

As richly and intentionally as the Wongs have blended their cultures, they have just as steadfastly maintained one religion. But in addition to the Wongs' huge seders, Hanukkah parties, and break-fast meals after Yom Kippur, they also spend Christmas Day with Alvin's brothers and sisters. They celebrate the lunar New Year by eating gao, a sweet cake made of rice flour, and watching the dragons and elaborately painted dancers parade through Honolulu's Chinatown. Trudy jokes that as a Chinese-Jewish family living in America, they have three chances to make fresh starts each year: Rosh Hashanah, January 1, and the lunar new year celebrated by Asians.

The 1970s were turbulent years for American Jews. The drama of Israel's Six Day War in 1967 and the Yom Kippur War of 1973 also had a lasting impact on many Jews. For the first time, a large number felt a connection to Israel and became passionately committed to its survival. Even some who were staunch opponents of the Vietnam War found themselves engaged in Israel's battles.

In demographics, there were stunning changes. The *American Jewish Yearbook* listed the population of Jews in 1976 as 5,870,000, up from the 4,240,000 listed in 1925.

But the Jewish community was not keeping pace with the American population as a whole, which from 1925 to 1975 grew by two-thirds. Demographers link high education, income, and professional status to low birth rates. The Jewish fertility rate had fallen so far that Jews had yet another distinction: they had the smallest families — 1.7 children — of any ethnic group in the United States. Indeed, Jewish women had vaulted to the national stage. Betty Friedan's feminist bible, *The Feminine Mystique,* appeared in 1963. In 1977, Rosalyn Yalow, a physicist, was the first American woman to receive the Nobel Prize for medicine. Even organized Judaism, rooted as it was in tradition, swayed to the tide of national change. In 1972, the first woman rabbi, Sally J. Preisand, was ordained at the Reform movement's Hebrew Union College in Cincinnati.

There were other changes, too. The large-scale admission of Jews to college campuses from Bennington to Stanford, as well as the integration of Jews in the workforce, meant that Jews were meeting and dating people outside the Jewish enclaves of the Northeast. It also meant they were marrying them. Studies showed intermarriage as an undeniable trend among American Jews. Between 1965 and 1974, 25 percent of American Jews married non-Jews. By 1984, that figure was 44 percent.[1]

Trudy and Alvin, of course, confirm these statistics. They met as adults, not teenagers or college students. While they did meet in Alvin's hometown, it was because Trudy's career had taken her there.

For Alvin and Trudy, their 1975 wedding was the high point of the decade. After that, the 1970s held little for them but sorrow. For all her sunny demeanor, Trudy has been besieged with health problems. The enduring pain of several back operations since her mid-twenties has kept her bedridden for months. In 1976, Alvin's mother died, followed by his father a few years later. Aaron Schandler died unexpectedly of a heart attack — on a cruise — three months to the day after Mr. Wong's death.

Not only that, but Trudy suffered three miscarriages, two of which occurred well into the second trimester. After the second, Alvin's mother begged Trudy never to try to conceive again. Having lost a small child herself, the elder Mrs. Wong hated to see her daughter-in-law suffer. As Mrs. Wong was dying, she told Trudy that her health and well-being were much more important than producing a grandchild. Desperate and depressed, Trudy began even to doubt her marriage.

"It was awful. I was beside myself, and wondered why this was happening to me," she says sadly. "I wasn't just miscarrying in the first trimester. I was losing healthy babies." At the first sign of problems with her third pregnancy, when she was five-and-a-half months pregnant, she called her rabbi to ask for a prayer. "I'll be right over," he told her, and hung up the phone. Grateful for the housecall, she began to cry.

"It was the only time in my life I wondered about our marriage," she says. She flashes a pained, wobbly smile, which leaves her face as quickly as it arrived. "I was looking for something, any explanation. And I asked the rabbi — I was crying — if God was punishing me. He took my hand and said, 'Oh, no, Trudy. God is not punishing you. God could only bless you.'" She swallows hard.

Finally doctors discovered a uterine defect, which was readily corrected by surgery. Ari was born in 1980; Shaaroni in 1982.

* *

Ari and Shaaroni Wong are as comfortable with their dual heritage
— and themselves — as any parents, interfaith or not, could wish
for. Graceful and articulate, with impeccable manners, they speak
delightedly of their combined family traditions. Much of this, of
course, speaks to the ease with which the Wongs have worked out
their lives. But some of it also stems from growing up in Hawaii,
where society has long embraced a myriad of interracial, interfaith
unions.

"I think if you're going to be Chinese and Jewish, or any
mixture of anything, Hawaii is the place to be," says Shaaroni. She
ticks off a list of her friends' ethnic make-up: So-and-so is Chinese
and Japanese; So-and-so is Portuguese and Hawaiian; So-and-so is
Caucasian and Japanese. "Nobody's just haole here," she says, using
the Hawaiian word for Caucasian. "It's cool to come from a mixed
family."

Ari Wong, who has a man's thick baritone and a teenage sense
of cool, sits back in a chair and checks his military boots for mud.
His childhood obsession with flying now channeled into membership in the state's civil air patrol, Ari spends Sundays with an ROTC
prep program and dreams of attending the Air Force Academy
someday.

Ari says he loves being Jewish and Chinese. His own bar mitzvah, much like his sister's ceremony, was a mixture of two cultures.
The welcoming dinner for out-of-town guests was held at an elegant Chinese restaurant, with gilded lions and giant goldfish shim-
mering beneath the surface of indoor lily ponds. At the ceremony
itself, a basket of red satin yarmulkes greeted male guests at the
door to the synagogue, and brilliant crimson torch ginger arrangements adorned the bimah.

The buffet table at the luncheon afterward was designed for
the Wongs' cross-cultural guests: Trudy had affixed small red stick-
ers on trays containing shellfish or meat mixed with milk, and
green ones on trays with kosher food.

Even the invitation to the bar mitzvah revealed the deliberate
intertwining of his roots: the envelope was bright red, the Chinese
color for good luck. Bold black English words, written in an Asian-

looking script, emblazoned the first page. The middle page was inscribed in Hebrew, and the bottom page was marked with the Wong family character. Ari proudly points to these details. "My mom helped a lot, but I picked the stuff out," he says.

He, too, holds a name reflecting both heritages: Ari Kol Ah Kuo. Both Shaaroni and Ari are named for prominent Jewish dead, as well as Alvin's parents, who had died by the time Shaaroni was born. In Cantonese, Ah Kuo means "Mr. Fruit tree," and Sun Lin means "Lotus blossom."

It has not always been easy, though, to be of both cultures. When Ari was small, Trudy and Alvin fed him only kosher baby food, sent by her parents from Asheville. This presented a problem: Alvin's father, still alive when Ari was a baby, loved to cook. And he frequently invited his son and daughter-in-law to dinner. Once Ari was old enough to sit in a high chair, Ah Kuo Wong served him bits of roast beef and chunks of cheese. Trudy was aghast but didn't know what to say; she didn't want to offend her father-in-law.

In a conversation with her father, she broached the subject delicately. She didn't want to disappoint him, as she had done herself in college, by breaking kosher rules. "What should I do, Daddy?" she asked. "How can I keep Ari kosher without being rude?" Aaron set her at ease. "Let him eat what he is served," he told her. "You can't be impolite to those who love you and have welcomed us so warmly. You have my blessing."

And so it is that Ari Wong feels "a hundred percent Jewish." "It's totally cool," he says. At sixteen, he loves his name and its reflection of both family histories. But it wasn't always so. He was deeply insecure about it before his first trip to a Jewish summer camp at the age of eight. "Before I went, I wanted my name to be changed to Schandler," he says guardedly, eyes darting toward his father. Alvin's face remains expressionless as he sits listening to his son, one long leg crossed over the other.

"But once I got there, everything was okay." Ari runs his hands through his thick chestnut hair, cropped short for his military duty. "People didn't say anything about Wong. What they said was, 'Wow, you're from Hawaii! Cool!' And they asked questions about that instead." During the following years, his attendance at the camp became something of a novelty. One year he won a contest for his name, and has been known during other summers as "the flying Hawaiian" and "the Chinese dude."

Shaaroni, on the other hand, has been troubled by her mainland campmates. Once, a boy told her that he wasn't going to tease her about being Chinese because he liked Chinese food. She rolls her eyes, shakes her chin-length pageboy and tucks her slim legs beneath her. With her teeth, newly liberated from braces, she tugs at a Chinese snack: a square of dried plumseed and lemon peel. "But the worst was some kid who told me Chinese people only run laundromats. He said, 'Hey, will you do my laundry?'" Her face is indignant.

Ari's only reservation about his Judaism, it seems, comes at Passover. The Wongs keep kosher and dispose of all chametz — food forbidden during Passover — for the holiday. Among the list of taboos is rice, a staple of Ari's favorite meals, which are mostly Chinese. Abstaining from rice for the holiday, he says, is his biggest hardship as a Jew. He doesn't say he wishes not to be Jewish for those eight days; he only wishes he were Sephardic. (By tradition, Jews of the Middle East and North Africa do not exclude rice from their Passover meals.)

Trudy is well known among her peers, both within the Jewish community and out. "She's a real macher," Alvin says. An active volunteer, she has also worked for United Airlines for thirty years. "Living in Hawaii, it's a good thing, too," she says, arms stretched wide as if in distance from the mainland. Some years back a *Jerusalem Post* reporter who was visiting Hawaii was so taken by her generosity that he wrote an article about the family, unbeknownst to Trudy. He included some of her kosher recipes for Chinese food, and within days, calls and letters from Israel began pouring in with requests for more. She sighs in mock exasperation, then tells this: A rabbi and a Chinese sage are discussing their lengthy histories. The rabbi points out that written Jewish history predates the first known Chinese documents by a thousand years. The sage shakes his head. "Impossible," he says. "Why?" asks the rabbi. The sage looks up solemnly. "The Jews couldn't have lived a thousand years without Chinese food!"

Jokes aside, the Wongs have found the likenesses between their two cultures striking. Both emphasize education and share a respect for elders, regardless of whether they are relatives. But for all the similarities between Chinese and Jews, the differences, too, are great. In Trudy's family, when you are upset, you yell. And yell. The only reason you wouldn't yell at someone when you are mad is if you're so angry you absolutely cannot speak. In Alvin's family, anger is something to be concealed, expressed only by not expressing. Displeasure is manifest in silence.

When Alvin as a teenager came home late, he would hear his mother's voice whispering in the darkness. "I'm here," she would say as Alvin tried to tiptoe toward his bedroom. "I'm here and I've been waiting. You said you would be home earlier." With that, she would steal off silently into her room, never waiting for a reply. "The guilt was terrible," Alvin recalls. "But that's the Chinese way."

A similar transgression in Trudy's family would have been handled quite differently. Lee and Aaron Schandler would have been furious, meeting her at the door with explosive admonitions. "Where have you been? I've been worried sick! I was about to call the police and the hospital! Don't you ever do that to me again!" Alvin and Trudy laugh at these two approaches; as parents they are anchored to them still.

But during the first year of their marriage, they were not so likely to laugh. Their first anniversary came, and a radiant Trudy fairly bubbled with joy. "Everybody says it's so hard, and it was so easy!" she exclaimed, planting a big kiss on Alvin's cheek.

"Easy?" he asked. "You think this was easy? It was the hardest year of my life." He proceeded to list his grievances, which centered mainly on his transformation as a thirty-five-year-old bachelor to a married man with a doting wife.

"I had no idea," Trudy says. "He just didn't communicate these things to me." In fact, it was a strain for Alvin to share the apartment where he had lived alone for almost a decade, and to remember to call Trudy if he worked late. He was accustomed to answering only to himself.

Fiercely protective of his privacy — another Wong family trait he says many Chinese share — Alvin says he and Trudy encountered one of their biggest differences when his mother, Sun Lin, died. It was Trudy's first introduction to the fact that her husband did not openly reveal his emotions, a concept she could not fathom. "He grieved in a way I just couldn't understand," Trudy says. "He wouldn't come home from work for hours and I didn't know why. Turns out he was going to sit at her grave. He didn't shake his fist at God and ask 'Why?' the way I would; he just accepted it and mourned quietly. I'm not used to that at all. I'm used to public grief, with lots of tears."

Alvin says the incident exemplifies his Chinese roots. "I internalize everything," he says. "That is the Oriental way. I keep it in. The grieving process is done, but it is done inside. Trudy could help me only so much. The thing that helped me the most was to be alone at the grave and to think."

Little wonder Trudy and Alvin had a misunderstanding about his feelings when his mother died: death rituals in the two cultures differ dramatically. Jews are not embalmed, and are buried as quickly as possible. The Chinese may take many days, even weeks, before interring the dead. That allows ample time for faraway relatives to pay their respect by viewing the body. Jews, on the other hand, are opposed to public viewing of the dead, on the grounds that it is disrespectful to the soul of the deceased.

And Jews are buried in simple shrouds without pockets, since according to tradition no material possessions can be taken with a person after death. Jews should also be buried without caskets or in simple ones, preferably of pine or other soft wood, which decomposes more quickly. This is in accordance with the commandment "Unto dust you shall return" (Genesis 3:19). Chinese men and women, however, are buried in finery, and morticians traditionally place a silver coin in the mouth of a man, a pearl in the mouth of a woman, to light the way into the next life.

"Our ways of grieving and communicating are totally opposite," Trudy says. Socially, too, the two are diametrically opposed.
In a restaurant, for example, if Trudy is displeased with the waiter's
demeanor, the food, or even the silverware, she makes no secret of
it. Growing up, she helped tend her father's store, and in her own
work she is accustomed to the most demanding of customers.

If Trudy has something to say, she'll say it: to the waiter, the
manager, or, better yet, the owner. Alvin shudders at the recollection of their early days. "This is just not the Oriental way," he
explains. "If you don't like something at the restaurant, you don't
go back. It's not worth the energy to complain, because they are
going to be defensive, explaining why what you don't like isn't so,
and you are going to be defensive, too. It is a matter of pride. It isn't
worth arguing about."

But Trudy can't help herself. "I can't just sit there if there's a
dirty fork or insolent service," she says. Alvin excuses himself — if
not physically, then mentally. "I don't pay attention," he says.

Early one Sunday evening the Wongs go to their favorite Chinese
restaurant. The owner, a Chinese man, darts from the kitchen to
the foyer, welcoming guests with a handshake. When Trudy and
Alvin walk in, he beams and ushers them to a round table with a
lazy Susan.

He passes out menus, which Trudy and Alvin do not open.
Instead, they rattle off a list of their favorite dishes. The owner
nods, not writing anything down. Moments later, plates arrive
heaped with delicacies: egg and tofu soup, Hawaiian fish with long
names, and vegetables steamed in ginger.

Shaaroni, who has brought a friend, picks at her food. Her
thirteen-year-old friend does the same. They look bored.

"Eat something," Trudy says. "I did," Shaaroni responds. "No,
you didn't," Trudy replies. The girls, in unison: "We're not hungry."

Trudy rolls her eyes. "It's because you were noshing all afternoon on crackers."

"We're not hungry. Can we go walk around?"

Trudy nods, then sighs, deftly poking her chopsticks into her string beans. To no one in particular, she says: "Even Jewish mothers have to give up sometimes."

In the strange synergy between mothers and daughters — mothers wanting their daughters to be independent, yet like them; daughters wanting to be independent, yet wanting their mother's approval — Shaaroni glances over her shoulder to see if her mother is watching as she saunters off into the warm evening. Trudy does, but neither acknowledges it to the other.

Perhaps Trudy said it best at her daughter's bat mitzvah when she quoted the Chinese-American novelist Amy Tan. "My daughter and I have shared the same body and the same blood. On the day she was born, she sprang from me like a slippery fish, and has been swimming away ever since."

FIVE

Two Lives

§

R EBECCA GRODIN'S parents never stopped teaching her
the lessons of the Holocaust. When she was accepted by
Brown University, they demanded she enroll closer to home — the
separation was unthinkable. Who knew what might happen? So
she chose a college in her hometown, Chicago. Her father, Sam
Grodin, a French Jew, counted Jews and Gentiles among his many
friends. But when it came to his daughter's social circle, he was
much less open-minded — especially when it came to dating. Only
Jews, he said. Only Jews. But Rebecca defied his wishes again and
again. Even today, she's not exactly sure why. Perhaps she wanted to
escape from a family over which history cast such a pall. Perhaps
she wanted to fit in, to shield her children behind the protective
coloration of an unmistakably non-Jewish name.

Rebecca Grodin is the first to say, though, that it was no coincidence that she ended up married to Rick O'Neill, a burly Arizonan
with Irish and Sicilian grandparents. "I always knew that I should
bring home a Jew," Rebecca says. "It was explicitly stated, a fact.
There was no room for negotiation. But I didn't care. I liked Aryan-
looking guys; I also dated guys who were Arab."

Intermarriage involving Jews with direct links to the Holocaust are particularly fraught with tension and guilt. One of the
slurs applied to Jews who marry outside the faith is that they are
contributing to a "silent Holocaust." That remark is painful for any
Jew, but it resonates much more deeply for people like Rebecca
Grodin, who was reminded every day that her birth was nothing

less than a miracle. When Rick O'Neill met Rebecca, he was a happy-go-lucky college student who knew little of the events that had shaped Rebecca's life even before she was born. "The Holocaust? Never heard of it. World War Two? Yeah, it happened. But it didn't make big ripples for me." Rick was ill equipped to understand Rebecca's quirky behavior — her need, for example, to keep jewels and ready cash on hand at all times. It took him years to understand how her life in modern America could be shaped by tragedies that had unfolded decades earlier. He also came with some baggage of his own: a mother who made no effort to hide her dislike of Jews and her contempt for Rebecca.

To understand the story of how Rebecca met Rick, you must begin with the tale of another Rebecca. The one who didn't survive the Holocaust. The woman for whom Rebecca Grodin was named. The Rebecca for whose sake she was implicitly expected to carry forward the traditions of Judaism and the hopes of a family. Her aunt, Rebecca Schubert.

Rebecca Schubert was a pretty girl with a doleful smile, and seemed to carry burdens far beyond her teenage years. Thick lashes fringed her dark eyes, and tendrils of black hair framed her face. She was born in 1923 in the Belarusian town of Pinsk to a simple existence: she loved to read, and delighted in helping her mother in the kitchen.

But life for Jews in the Soviet Union of the 1930s was difficult. Under constant oppression, the Schuberts — Rebecca, her older sister Sarah, and their parents — decided to head west, to Germany. Almost everything, they had heard, was easier there. Except, that is, for Jews. The Schuberts were either unaware of, or undaunted by, the rising tide of Nazism. Perhaps they assumed it couldn't be any worse than the anti-Semitism they endured in Pinsk. So in 1939 the Schuberts prepared to leave for Munich. They packed up their belongings and bade good-bye to family and friends in their close-knit neighborhood.

With a mixture of melancholy and excitement, the Schuberts hoisted their modest trunks into the southbound coach. Watching as Pinsk faded slowly into the horizon, the sisters clutched each other's hands. Rebecca laid her head on Sarah's shoulder and drifted off to sleep. When she awoke hours later, Rebecca complained of a dull headache. It persisted for days, steadily worsening. When the Schuberts crossed over the Carpathian Mountains, Rebecca slipped into delirium. Her skin burned, and her lively eyes became cloudy; surely she was unaware of her mother's frantic face, her sister's crying, and the voice of her father, the son of a rabbi, praying over her limp body. A local doctor shook his head, prescribing only cold compresses. Encephalitis, he guessed. There was nothing he could do.

Lying in her mother's arms, Rebecca lapsed into a coma. Her laugh silenced, her eyes unseeing, Rebecca drew her last breath. She was sixteen years old.

Stranded, the Schuberts, devout Jews, had little choice but to bury their daughter and forge ahead with their plans. The family wept as they recited the kaddish, each tossing a handful of foreign soil on the pine coffin that held Rebecca's remains.

The grief the Schuberts felt lingered a lifetime, but once they got to Germany, their concerns turned to the essential: survival. Their arrival coincided with the beginning of World War II. Those Jews who could afford to leave set out for more hospitable destinations.

The Schuberts, destitute, scrambled to get their bearings. Their youngest child was dead, buried hundreds of miles away in an unmarked grave. In the confusing weeks after their arrival, they managed to arrange a hiding place for their oldest daughter, Sarah: a Munich medical school. Her golden hair, clear blue eyes, and German last name helped conceal her Jewish origins. Her parents fled south, to a mountain town in Austria.

Despite the private hell she must have endured daily as a secret Jew in Nazi Germany, Sarah thrived, speaking German like a native and matriculating at the top of her class. At the war's end, she was a physician, and had even treated Nazis. But she was all alone, unsure whether her parents had escaped the war unscathed; she had no way to reach them or anyone who could inform her of their well-being.

But the Schuberts were among the lucky Jews who did survive the war. Hoping their daughter had succeeded with her imposture, they got in touch with her as soon as the Allies declared victory and were soon reunited.

After the war, the Schuberts made their way to Chicago; relatives lived there, so it seemed a logical place to settle. Sarah soon began practicing as an internist. Some years later, she met Sam Grodin, a suave and charming businessman whose many schemes had yielded him a fortune. Like Sarah, he had European sensibilities, but his bold, daring manner was a striking contrast to Sarah's gentle shyness.

Born in Germany, Sam's parents had taken seriously the growing restrictions against Jews in the early 1930s, and left for France in 1934. They settled in Marseilles, home to a thriving Jewish community. Rakishly handsome, with a shock of wavy black hair he parted carefully to one side, Sam attracted almost everyone with his debonair good looks and devil-may-care attitude. When the Nazis invaded France in 1940, Sam, nineteen, and his father joined the French Resistance. Later, he would cavalierly declare that patriotism had nothing to do with his decision. It was, he would insist in his perfectly idiomatic but accented English, the "cool" thing to do.

Perhaps it was his confidence, or, more likely, his teenager's sense of immortality that kept Sam alive. This is the story he told his family: In 1942, he and his father were captured by the Nazis and held as prisoners. Because the Nazis were aware that the Grodins were Jewish, Sam knew that he and his father had to escape. Years later, Rebecca would repeatedly ask to hear the end of his heroic tale. "What happened, Daddy?" she asked. But he would never say. Today, Rebecca says, "My hunch is, he killed a guy. Or two."

Soon after their escape, Sam, his father, mother, and younger brother wangled passage on a ship to the United States. Cousins lived in New York, and while other European Jews sought refuge any place that would accept them, the Grodins, armed with immigrant visas, arrived at Ellis Island. Soon after they landed, Sam's younger brother killed himself. "He had pretty much cracked from the pressures of the war," Rebecca says.

The young Sam Grodin vowed to continue his fight against the enemy, and enlisted in the army almost as soon as he arrived in the United States. Although he never got farther than Biloxi, Mississippi, he proudly displayed his stripes: sure signs that he was a true American. When the war ended, he headed for Chicago.

Soon after they met, Sam Grodin and Sarah Schubert fell in love and were married in a small ceremony. Since each was the sole remaining offspring of their parents, the wedding was a bittersweet occasion. Two years later, twenty years after Rebecca Schubert was buried in a makeshift grave in the Ukraine, Sarah gave birth to her only child, a girl. She named her for her dead sister.

Today, Rebecca Grodin is a pediatrician in her late thirties. On a dreary Sunday in November, she takes a sip of milky coffee and gazes outside. Her two sons are at Hebrew school, and her four-year-old daughter, Samantha, watches a video in the family room.

Both of Rebecca's parents died a decade ago, and as she tells the story of their unlikely pairing, she stops frequently to wipe away tears. As a child of survivors, she feels the obligation to carry on traditions so nearly lost. But hers is a more specific burden, the burden of a family's memory. Though her mother and grandmother rarely spoke of the aunt for whom she was named, the expectations were clear.

Rebecca has but one picture of her namesake, standing stiffly in a studio, her lips in a faint smile. Her dark eyes stare out hauntingly from the black-and-white photograph, yellowed with age. Mounted on a piece of white marble, it rests, mute and distant. "It's a tremendous responsibility to carry the hopes and wishes that I turn into everything she could have been," Rebecca says. She sighs, looks outside. "It's the responsibility of two lives."

The story of Rebecca's life, of the woman she became, is indeed a complex one. From early on, she carried the grief of the Holocaust with her, a torment that swayed even minute decisions. Sarah and Sam Grodin almost never mentioned their experiences. But they transmitted the importance of their past to their daughter almost as much in what they did not say.

Rebecca was born in Chicago, but her world was far from the American heartland. Her parents' friends were European, as was their household help; Sarah hired only German nannies and Polish maids. "It was basically to keep the Germans in a subservient position," Rebecca says. "We had Polish help for the same reason: 'You screwed us; now we're going to teach you a lesson.'" German, English, and French were household languages; Rebecca was trilingual by the time she was in kindergarten. She also heard Yiddish; it was the language in which her mother and grandmother conversed when they didn't want Rebecca to understand. "So what does a child do?" Rebecca asks. "Learn Yiddish, of course."

Indeed, she was surrounded by the culture of Judaism. And although her four grandparents were living, kept kosher, observed the Sabbath, and attended synagogue weekly, Sarah and Sam gave Rebecca a more complicated view of the Jewish faith.

The nuclear Grodin household was far from observant. Sarah attended synagogue occasionally but, unlike her mother, never lit a Shabbos candle. She frequently indulged her penchant for lobster and crab. For his part, Sam consumed mounds of ham and cheese sandwiches. "Anything treyf, my father ate it: ribs, bacon, bacon cheeseburgers. Even if he didn't like it, he ate it. And especially in front of my grandparents," Rebecca says. "Basically my father had a great deal of animosity toward organized religion."

And Sam showed it in myriad ways. Though Sarah always fasted on Yom Kippur, Sam never did. For the Kol Nidre service every year, however, he accompanied his wife and daughter to synagogue. He always made sure he and Rebecca sat closest to the aisle, filing into services at the last possible moment. Once the cantor had led the congregation in its third chanting of Kol Nidre

— the ancient prayer nullifying vows made to God during the previous year, innocently or under duress — Sam would quickly lead his daughter to the exit.

With Sarah and the elder Schuberts and Grodins praying inside, Sam would clutch his daughter's hand as he led to her to the car. They would get in and drive off quietly to the lights of Chicago's Rush Street. Then, as Jews everywhere were beginning to fast and atone for their sins, Sam would slide behind the counter of an elegant patisserie and order his favorite dessert: a plump napoleon, full of whipped cream and topped with chocolate icing. Year after year, Rebecca ordered a strawberry tart. When they had finished, Sam and Rebecca went home and watched movies on television. "This was my father's ritual, and I was his accomplice," Rebecca says. "It was supposed to be a secret. My mother suspected we were up to no good, I'm sure, but she never really knew what it was. She never asked."

Despite her father's lack of interest in Jewish traditions, Rebecca became a bat mitzvah. "Judaism was definitely in our home. We did not practice. We did not go to synagogue. But culturally, we were very Jewish. I always knew Jewishness was a part of me." Indeed, the Grodins attended first- and second-night seders on Passover, Rosh Hashanah dinners at relatives' homes, and breakfast parties after Yom Kippur.

As Jewish as her environment was, Rebecca had more than just an outsider's inevitable exposure to Christianity and its rituals. Her father's best friend was Lebanese, and her mother was godmother to a half-dozen of her Catholic patients' children. In elementary school, Rebecca once portrayed the Virgin Mary in the school Christmas play. Grandfather Schubert — the son of a rabbi — was particularly touched by his granddaughter's role. "No one was threatened by it; it wasn't as if I was going to 'turn' just because I was playing Mary," she says.

At a private Chicago high school, Rebecca was among only a dozen Jews. She was popular with her fellow students, she says, though she notes bitterly that it was not because people found her personality beguiling. Tall and curvy, with long blond hair, deep blue eyes, and the chiseled cheekbones of a Slavic model, she was invited to the society parties and formal balls that consumed the free hours of her Christian classmates. "I was invited to all of them because I was the token Jew, the Jew who didn't look Jewish," she says. Still, her closest friends were Jewish.

Her adolescence was tumultuous. There were fights over where she would go to college. Once that was settled, there were fights over what she would study. Again and again, Sam and Sarah insisted they knew best for their headstrong daughter. When she mentioned that she wanted to study law, her parents ruled it out. Out of the question, they said. So Rebecca toiled over physics problem sets and chemistry lab, all the while longing to read Shakespeare. "Basically I was raised with the belief that you can't take law wherever you go, but when the next Holocaust comes you can always be a doctor, because the human body is the same everywhere. You don't need the language, you don't need the laws. You can take your knowledge with you."

Rebecca did resist her parents' domination in one enormous aspect: her social life. In high school and college, she dated both Jews and non-Jews, but they almost always looked the same: tall, slender, blond, and blue-eyed. When her dates weren't Jewish, Sam and Sarah's reaction was not surprising. "It was not positive, that's for sure," she says.

They certainly made no secret of their unhappiness when Rebecca began dating Rick O'Neill, a burly, black-haired, olive-skinned student from Arizona. Despite his dark looks — as well as other detractions — Rick had got Rebecca's attention straightaway.

Looking back, though, they both wonder how. They laugh over the details of their first meeting and of their stark contrasts. Rick grew up far from the polyglot kaffeeklatches that marked Rebecca's upbringing, in a quiet Phoenix neighborhood. The son of Tom, a veterinarian with Irish roots, and Rose, a temperamental Sicilian American, Rick typifies the breezy self-confidence of American manhood. A good athlete and student, Rick is the kind of guy everyone remembers from their freshman dorm: irreverent, funny, a little on the boisterous side, the ringmaster of underage beer-buying schemes.

The O'Neills attended a Methodist church near their home but weren't much for religious ceremony. And as soon as he began to take his schoolwork seriously, Rick felt doubts about his faith. An anesthesiologist today, he showed his talents in the sciences early on. His favorite subjects at school — biology and chemistry — began to contradict what he was learning at Sunday school. "I got sort of a scientist's view of things by middle school," he says. "The biblical tale of creation just didn't make sense." None of this could have mattered less to his parents. Holidays were big affairs, mostly because they were excuses for festive meals. "Family, eating, and gifts, in that order," he says. "Christmas was a family day, not a religious holiday. Easter was brunch, not the resurrection of Christ. You had to get dressed up, but it was basically a brunch."

As remote as his own religion was to him, Judaism was even farther away. "Jews didn't mean boo to me," he says. He recalls his parents using the expression "I jewed him down" when they were able to negotiate a lower price for something. He insists the comment was only part of the vernacular, not meant with rancor.

Rebecca rolls her eyes at this. "Yeah, right," she says. He shakes his head and rolls his eyes in return.

"It was used in this case with no appreciation of what that might do to a Jewish person in their presence, but not with any pejorative content. There was no appreciation for the culture, history, background — anything Jewish whatsoever. It's not as if I grew up learning that the Jews killed Christ or something."

In fact, Rick didn't much concentrate on history of any sort. Focused on becoming a doctor, he paid little attention to the social sciences. He was particularly uninterested in history: of the Civil War, of World War I, of World War II. "It was no big deal to me," he says. "I never thought I'd have to know about it."

Rick flourished in college in the Midwest, far from his family. On campus, he was gregarious and fun-loving, popular among his classmates despite his grueling schedule. One reason for his notoriety was his vast T-shirt collection, the prize of which bore the inscription TO ALL YOU VIRGINS, THANKS FOR NOTHING. He wore it often, Rebecca says.

Rick, who is about to take a bite of coffee cake, suspends his fork in midair. "I did *not* wear that," he says. "I owned it, but I didn't wear it around campus."

"Yes, you did," Rebecca says. She turns from him defiantly; even if he didn't wear it, it's a good story.

"I didn't even know anybody *lived* between California and Texas," she says, stretching her arms wide, as if they framed a map of the United States. She thought Rick was a "cowboy." And Rick wondered of Rebecca: "Who is this person? And why is she on such a high horse?"

He did, at least, have one advantage when it came time to ask Rebecca for a date: he wasn't Jewish. Rick and Rebecca were surprised to discover that they actually had fun together, first impressions aside. After their second date, Rebecca's roommate told her, "You're going to marry that guy." "Sure," Rebecca remembers saying. But the second date led to a third and a fourth. Soon, she realized she was in love.

It seemed that her relationship with Rick O'Neill was coincidence: two smart premed students meet, hit it off, fall in love. Rebecca often looked back, at her parents' fears, and forward, to her own life as a mother. Her pairing with Rick was deliberate, shaped, ironically, by her parents' fears of loss. "Of course part of it was the survival thing I grew up with. But I will tell you that to this day the fact that my children's last name is O'Neill is comforting to me." She taps the table with her fingernails. "They will not be among those automatically targeted. It's just a fact."

Nevertheless, Rick, a convert to Judaism, and Rebecca identify themselves very much as Jews. But the legacy of fear lingers. Even in wholly Jewish surroundings, their synagogue, she likes the mystery of her family's obviously Christian origins. "Even some Jews wonder, 'Are they, or aren't they?'" she says. Although

Rebecca has kept her maiden name, there was never any question about their kids' surname. The Jewish O'Neills? It sounded just fine to her.

Rick has become accustomed to the fears that, born of her parents' wartime experiences, often propel Rebecca. But it was not always so. When they were first dating, Rick was totally oblivious of the passions behind the Grodins' reluctance to accept him. Her parents were obviously displeased that he was not Jewish, but he was baffled as to why.

Rick represented a rejection of the past and the losses the Grodins themselves had suffered during the war, a slap in the face to the Jewish people. Although he was not a religious man, Sam Grodin felt his culture — and its continuation — to be of utmost importance. In his actions he had shown disrespect for Jewish ritual: sneaking out of synagogue for dessert while other Jews fasted, eating bacon cheeseburgers with the gusto of a teenage football player. But when it came to the Jewish people, his feelings were clear.

"My father didn't believe in God. He basically shook his fist at the whole idea of religion," Rebecca says. "But when it came to Jews, nothing mattered more."

And so Sam Grodin made fierce attempts to keep Rick and Rebecca separated. Because Rick and Rebecca went to college in Chicago, they saw the Grodins frequently. The encounters were uneasy, to say the least. Sam called Rick "what's-his-name" whenever he referred to him privately and never uttered his name when speaking to him directly.

"They didn't welcome him at all," Rebecca recalls. "It disturbed me a lot, because I was very close to them. We fought about it. My father did not approve; he would not approve of Rick. And soon it became clear that any relationship my father and I had was not to include Rick. So we just pretended he didn't exist, but my father knew that when push came to shove I would choose Rick over him."

By the time of their graduation, Rick and Rebecca had been

living together for several months. Rick's plans to become a doctor were on track. He had qualified for generous grants to medical school in Arizona, an opportunity he could not afford to pass up. Rebecca, meanwhile, had applied to medical schools throughout the Southwest with the hope that she and Rick could carry on as before.

But that was not to be. "My father's goal was to keep us apart," Rebecca says. Sam, Rebecca says, "pulled strings" for her to go to medical school in Chicago, which she began that year. Rigorous coursework and a thousand miles of separation would undoubtedly weaken the relationship, Sam believed, but he added a little incentive of his own. He introduced her to as many eligible young men as possible. He and Sarah arranged meetings with their friends' sons, insisting that Rebecca go along, as much for herself as for them. "So I went on a lot of first dates," she says. "Never second ones." Rebecca was undeterred. Her father had succeeded in keeping her in Chicago, but he was not going to win the battle of her heart. She continued to see Rick as often as possible, and they spoke on the phone almost nightly, racking up bills of four hundred dollars a month.

Back in Arizona for his first year of medical school, Rick ate dinner with his parents a few times a week. For all their frequent meals, however, he assiduously avoided discussing his personal life. Though he and Rebecca had been together for two years by this time, he had not yet mentioned her to his parents. "It just hadn't come up in conversation," Rebecca says.

Rick puts his hand up as if to stop her words. His reluctance to mention the topic to his mother was quite deliberate. His mother became enraged when she discovered that Rick and his high school girlfriend had slept together. Rose called the girl's parents to tell them; she was furious with the girlfriend, not with Rick. "It was a massive issue with her," he recalls. "Basically no girl was going to come between her and her son. To her, my girlfriend was a slut, a tramp, whatever. So in my family we learned that the best way to deal with issues was avoid them," he says. He pauses. "Jews do not have a monopoly on guilt. My mom lays major guilt trips. I wanted to avoid confrontation, so I avoided discussing Rebecca."

And so for Thanksgiving his first year home, when Rebecca was scheduled to visit Arizona, Rick arranged for Rebecca to stay with his parents rather than in his apartment. He would pass her off as a "friend" until he could explain the whole story. Rebecca went along grudgingly; she, after all, had endured her father's fury over Rick for years.

"When I told my mom, her reaction was thermonuclear," Rick says, wiping his brow in mock exasperation. He starts to say something, but Rebecca interrupts.

"She sent me a letter calling me a Jewish slut," Rebecca says. "Calling me a Jewish slut. Letting me know it was my Jewishness that contributed to our relationship."

"It wouldn't have mattered what you were," Rick says. "For her, it was betrayal. She didn't approve of people living together. And my father didn't like being kept in the dark. But the fact that Rebecca was Jewish was also an issue."

Rebecca turns to speak, almost as if Rick is not there. "Rick grew up in a home where there was anti-Semitism, whether he realized it or not. I get along with my mother-in-law very well now, partly because I stopped dealing with her the way his family deals with her. I treat her the way I treat anyone else."

"She's the first living person to ever confront my mother and survive," Rick says. Rose, for her part, held nothing back. "You're out," she told Rick. "You're cut off." The message was clear, he says: "'Be sensible. Forget this whimsy.' I expected my dad to come through for me — he's a pretty pragmatic guy. I went to him and said, 'You know, Dad, can't you referee this?' And he couldn't. My mom had the idea that if she pulled the apron strings tight enough, I'd come back to Mama. Well, it didn't happen that way."

Although Rebecca seethed over that first letter, she never mentioned it to her future mother-in-law. "I didn't really know what to tell her, because I had never had anti-Semitism thrown in my face quite as clearly or directed specifically at me. Before, it had been directed at all Jews — I was a part of a bigger thing. But this was directed at Rebecca the Jew."

"I think it was directed at Rebecca the son-stealer who happened to be Jewish," Rick says quietly.

Family members on both sides counseled Rick and Rebecca to pay no attention to their parents' antics. Rick's brother, accustomed to his mother's rages, shrugged it off. "Let them chill," he advised. They heard a similar suggestion from Rebecca's Orthodox grandmother. "This will sort itself out," she said. "You're in love." And they were. But what both Rick and Rebecca came to realize years later was that at least part of that love was fueled by rebellion: Rebecca's against her father, Rick's against his mother.

Throughout medical school, Rick and Rebecca shuttled regularly between Phoenix and Chicago. The Grodins began to realize, Rebecca says, that Rick was in the picture to stay. Sarah Grodin, in fact, became quite fond of him. When the topic of Judaism came up, Sarah was frank. "Look," she told Rick, "this is an issue for us. It's important. She's an only child, and she has no cousins. So this is it: the whole family boils down to this one child. And it's very important to us what goes on from here. It's not the name so much; it's the essence of things."

Even Sam started coming around. "Once her father started accepting me as a decent person, it became clear that the Jewish issue was a big part of it, but there was more. I had come from a relatively sheltered life in the Southwest. Here, I was exposed to all different kinds of people." He splays his fingers and thrusts his hands in opposite directions. "And I started appreciating a variety of 'isms' that I hadn't fully understood before: racism, sexism, anti-Semitism. I started to appreciate that I was guilty of some of these things, both passively and aggressively. Once I realized they could accept me as me, I was willing to work with this Jewish issue."

So Rick began attending an introductory course on Judaism at a Reform congregation in Phoenix. Rebecca, though pleased, had never asked Rick to take this step. But she was hopeful that, at the very least, the class would enlighten Rick about the Grodins' emotional reaction to their relationship.

She also realized that marrying a Jew was important to her. "At first it was no big deal that Rick wasn't Jewish," she says, "because, I thought, 'What difference did it make?' The more serious it got between us, the more I realized he could be a partner. And then I realized that this was potentially a big problem. Because it was very clear my kids were going to be Jews."

"It was clear that conversion was going to have to precede our marriage," Rick says. "We didn't want to go on unmarried forever. We'd already made the commitment personally, and we wanted to move on."

In his Judaism course, Rick instantly liked what he was learning. He had never much believed in heaven's salvation or hell's damnation, but he immediately fastened onto Rosh Hashanah and the Days of Awe. He especially liked the Jewish notion of man's responsibility to atone for his wrongdoings to his fellow man, rather than praying to God for forgiveness. He was impressed that Jews see rabbis as learned peers, not as intermediaries to God. He was also drawn to the communal way Jews mark life's milestones, from a bris to a bat mitzvah to sitting shiva. And so, a year after he began his studies, Rick converted to Judaism. It was December 24. He asked Rebecca to marry him the next day. It all seemed a pointed attempt to vex his mother: choosing Christmas Eve as the date of his conversion, and Christmas Day, the first day of his life as a Jew, to get engaged to a Jewish woman.

Rick gets up, makes a fresh pot of coffee, sits back down, and dismisses that suggestion — or at least part of it — as coincidence; it was more about where Shabbat fell and the rabbi's schedule. "But it was also this: 'This is where I am. You can support me and enjoy it, or if not, I didn't do it to spite you. Or *despite* you. It wasn't a fuck-you either way.'"

The Holocaust shadowed even the date Rebecca and Rick chose for their wedding. Meticulously organized, Rebecca had planned since childhood to have a spring wedding. She chose the site, and the day in late April, almost a year in advance. Months later, she learned that the date she had picked was to be the first Yom Hashoah, Holocaust Remembrance Day. Everyone — her parents, her friends, her family rabbi — told her to revise her schedule. "We looked at each other and said, 'Bad things happen to Jews every day of the year,'" she says. "'Why not make something good happen, on this day especially?'" The date remained as it was.

But soon afterward, Rebecca began to have doubts: niggling at first, then overwhelming. Rick's conversion, far from making her task easier, seemed only to complicate things. "I had not asked him to convert," she says. "I made that very clear. I was somewhat frightened that if he converted, I was trapped into a marriage. I didn't want him to convert and then think, 'But what if I don't want to marry him? Would I have to?' My initial reaction to his conversion was: 'Don't do this.' He insisted after the first Judaism class he took that he would've continued down the Jewish path regardless. I don't know about that. Because when push came to shove, Rick was much more ready to marry me than I was to marry him."

Rebecca attributes her reluctance, in part, to the bald contempt in which Rose O'Neill held her and her family. The Grodins, who had become very prosperous, lavished gifts on Rick and their only child. "My parents saw it as though Rebecca's parents were buying their son," Rick says. "My mother saw it as, 'Oh, he's with them now.' It was really unpleasant." Rose was overtly rude to Rebecca and disparaged her to family members.

Three months before they were to be married, Rebecca decided to call it off. After a heated argument in the parking lot of a Phoenix hotel, she wrested her diamond engagement ring off her finger and thrust it into Rick's hand.

"It was clear to me where we were going," she says. "There would have to be a choice, because I never wanted to see this woman again in my life. Why should I put up with this crap? What had I done? Nothing, besides be Jewish."

"I tried to convince my parents that there didn't have to be a choice," Rick says, "but until they could appreciate that, there was going to be one. They could see it as me slamming the door — it's her or us — but it didn't have to be that way. My actions, my language, the look on my face — all of it was enough to make her realize that this wasn't just a passing —"

"Fancy," Rebecca inserts.

"This wasn't just rebellion for rebellion's sake; this was the real thing. And they'd better make a decision."

Rick and Rebecca soon resolved their parking lot quarrel, and on the eve of her son's wedding Rose wrote Rebecca a letter. In it she apologized for the first damning letter, which had been written four years earlier. Neither had ever mentioned it to the other. In the second letter, Rose said she realized she had been wrong, and wanted Rebecca to accept her not just as Rick's mother, but as her own mother, too.

"In my actions," Rebecca says, "I have accepted her. But in my heart, I never can."

The wedding, a grand affair, was held in one of Chicago's most distinguished old hotels. Everyone was on best behavior. The O'Neills, much to Rick's surprise, even walked him down the aisle in accordance with Jewish tradition. Rick's father wore a yarmulke, fixed to his head with Rose's bobby pins.

Not long after the wedding, Sam Grodin died unexpectedly. Sarah, ill with diabetes, passed away a year later. The loss Rick and Rebecca feel for her parents is palpable. She speaks of them wistfully. Even Rick, who rarely lets his emotions take hold, weeps freely at the graves of his in-laws. Rebecca's grief was in some ways compounded by the struggles she and Rick continued to have with the O'Neills. Although the initial outbursts had been smoothed over, they left scars. The disappointment they would come to feel began even as Rebecca was pregnant with their first child. When Rose heard what names her son and daughter-in-law were thinking of, she expressed her dissatisfaction out loud.

"'Benjamin? Sam? Joshua? Those sound awfully Jewish, don't they?'" Rebecca recalls. "It was a reaction to Jewishness. Then she'd come up with Christopher or Brian or John. Those are perfectly nice names, but not for a Jewish child."

Rick wishes his parents could have a closer relationship with his children, but he doubts that one will ever develop. Clearly, it differs from the one he and Rebecca believe the Grodins would have enjoyed.

"Considering what Rebecca's parents suffered through, it's too bad they didn't get to see the results," Rick says. "They got a converted Jewish son-in-law. But they missed out on our kids. And I think that's a tremendous tragedy."

Despite the prosperity she enjoyed in the United States, Rebecca says, her mother never escaped her "shtetl mentality."

Rick, who has been listening to his wife hold forth as he chops onions and jalapeño peppers for an omelette, interrupts. "Your mother? What about *you?*" he asks, gesturing toward heaps of food on the counter and table. He opens the refrigerator door to reveal still more copious supplies. "Look at this place!"

To be fair, four guests are expected later that morning for brunch, and with three children, grocery bills are undoubtedly high. But it does seem like a lot of food.

"I grew up as a survivor," Rebecca says. "I very much grew up as the child of survivors. That's my mentality. I believe it could happen again. I have lots of jewelry because I grew up with the idea that if you have to take it, it's portable. I grew up with the idea that if I had to lock my doors and walk away, I would. I have cash in this house. That's something that puts me in a very different place from my peers."

She sighs. "My Jewish friends with American parents don't feel the same way I do," she says. "But loss is in my psyche every day. It doesn't stop me from doing anything, but it really is a part of my life. Yesterday Rick got a phone call from work, and it wasn't someone who usually calls. My immediate response was: 'There's been some horrible disaster and they're calling in every doctor in the city.' If he's late coming home from work, my instinctive fear is that there's been a horrible car accident, he's been killed, and I'm a single mother."

That his wife thinks the worst is nothing new, Rick says. "That's always her response. She's always waiting for the next Holocaust. She keeps a variety of stuff that would get us across the border — our passports are always current — and we'd just go. Rebecca's attitude is what the European Jews — those who were lucky — had. And that is, just to go, blend in somewhere else. If it were up to me, we'd get a couple of semi-automatic rifles and train the kids. I realize that it's totally un-Jewish. We don't even own a gun; Rebecca won't let me. I say, if you want to be protected, you protect yourself. That would be my initial response. Even that's changing, though. At twenty-five you think of bad things as a total impossibility. You're immortal. Nothing bad ever crosses your mind — or at least for me it didn't. Then when you're thirty-five and you have kids and a family to protect, there are more threats. Sometimes they creep into your mind. But never like they do for her. That's because of who she is, what she comes from, what happened to her family. My reaction is totally non-Jewish. Some things you can't change."

He may be a full-fledged Jew, as is any "Jew-by-choice" under Jewish law, but Rick occasionally finds himself at odds with tradition. The first year he converted, he and Rebecca brought home a huge pine tree at Christmastime. "I'm not giving up my tree, you know," he declared. Rebecca was thrilled: she could get the tree she had always wanted, yet not take responsibility for it being "hers." Rose and Tom were in town from Phoenix, and had brought as a gift a wreath of red chili peppers; Rick hung it on the door. One evening, Sam and Sarah came to visit. As they left to go, Sam took Rebecca aside. "I couldn't care less about the tree," he told her. "I'm not pleased that you have one, but the wreath really bugs me."

"It bothered him because it signifies the crown of thorns around Christ's head when he was crucified," Rebecca says. "He could tolerate everything else, but not the wreath. I heard that." She taps her chest with her fist. "And I think somewhere deep inside me, it made me realize that, as nice as this tree was, it wasn't for me."

After that, there were plenty of excuses not to get one. The following year, Sam Grodin died. The December after that, Rick and Rebecca got a pair of new puppies, and were sure the tree would overexcite them. The next year, Ben was born. Finally, some years later, Rebecca asked Rick, "What's the story? Are we ever going to have another tree? I have all these Christmas decorations. Are we ever going to use them again?" Rick replied, "You know, Rebecca, we're Jews. And we're not going to get another tree."

Rick and Rebecca resolved the dilemma of a Christmas tree easily, with no hurt feelings, no loud fights, no sullen misunderstandings. He doesn't miss it, he says. A few years after he had converted, he came to realize that there were tangible things he would do, or not do, in his life as Jew. That was the easy part. It is the intangible that trips him up every now and again.

Perhaps because Rick's childhood experiences were so wholly American — free from the anguish the Grodins endured — he doubts that he will ever fully emotionally experience what it is to be a Jew. It is not for lack of effort. He attends synagogue with his family regularly — unlike Rebecca, he wishes they would go more frequently so that he could learn more prayers — and is active in his children's religious education. Rick is as enthusiastic about the celebration of Jewish holidays in his home as are his wife and children. He fasts on Yom Kippur, abstains from grain products at Passover, and grates potatoes for Hanukkah latkes he makes with his kids. At their local Jewish community center, he is outspoken about the need to welcome the Gentile spouses of Jews into Jewish life.

But like many converts, he feels that his efforts cannot replace the childhood memories of most of his Jewish peers, their family stories, traditional recipes. Songs and smells that evoke powerful feelings for Rebecca often mean little to him. On Yom

Kippur, Rebecca's eyes brim with tears at the melody of Kol Nidre. "I appreciate the significance and the beauty of it," he says, "but I don't think I'll ever be able to feel about it what Rebecca does."

Rick and Rebecca both say Rick knows more about Judaism than Rebecca does — after all, he studied it as an adult, rather than learning what was expected for bar mitzvah preparation. When the kids come to her with a religious question, Rebecca points them to their dad for the answer. But for all that, he still feels removed from the fold, like a naturalized citizen who is reminded on the day he takes his oath that he was born elsewhere. At their community center, Rick took Sunday morning toddler-father activity courses with each of his children when he or she was three. "It was a sort of religious Gymboree for dads who felt guilty that they didn't spend enough time with their kids," Rick says. But he went good-naturedly, cutting and pasting construction paper dreidels and burning bushes.

One morning in early February Rick sat in the class with Joshua, his second son. The teacher called out brightly, "Now, boys and girls, does anybody know what we're going to make today?" In a stage whisper, Rick leaned over to Josh: "Valentines," he said. The teacher's head snapped in his direction. Her eyes flashing, her tone indignant, she said, "We would *never* make Valentines in this class. That is a *saint's* day. That is not Jewish!"

"She came down on me like a ton of bricks," Rick says. "It was as if I had identified the Father, Son, and Holy Ghost. I was like, 'It's Valentine's Day, lady, relax. I guess that rules out Halloween and Saint Patrick's Day, too.' She was so humorless, she said, 'That's right.' I felt like it was 'Spot the Goy'!"

He laughs. "I'm not sure I'm ever going to totally peg the Jewish meter. I may never get to the top of the little indicator, but I'm not worried about second thoughts or anything like that. Now that I'm converted and acknowledge myself as Jewish — converted Jewish, but Jewish — I don't necessarily have the same feelings as, say, Rebecca did when we went to Israel. And I've got to be honest:

I'm pretty sure I may never totally get there. I don't think that means it's a failure. It's not as if I stood there in the Church of the Holy Sepulchre, thinking, 'Gee, maybe I should've hung on to Christ.'"

Christian shrines aside, Rick never imagined how he would feel, as a Jew, on his first trip to Israel; he had paid scant attention to it. Occasionally he would argue with Rebecca about the need for a peace process. Rebecca passionately disagreed; her allegiance to Israel is unwavering. She even says she can envision moving there someday, although Rick points out that she says the same thing when they go skiing in Colorado.

Some of Rebecca's family settled in Israel after the war, and a cousin died years ago in the Israeli army. She fondly recalls a trip there as a child, when she made a pilgrimage to Grandfather Schubert's grave on the Mount of Olives. So when a bar mitzvah invitation arrived from an Israeli relative, Rebecca decided that the entire family would attend.

Once she arrived, Rebecca says, "I felt I was home. I felt I was with 'my people,' for lack of a better word. I was in a Jewish land. I was in a land where the numbers, the proportion of Jews to non-Jews, was greater. Here, I'm part of a minority no matter what. It was a great feeling to know that I was one of many."

Rick and Rebecca pulled out all stops for their children: they stayed at the five-star King David Hotel in Jerusalem, and got rooms that looked out on the marvels of the old city. They hired an American-born guide to help them navigate through the country's many special sites, from the Dead Sea Scrolls to Christendom's holiest places. They even visited a kosher vineyard, where the children stomped on grapes, along with the regular workers.

Much as they enjoyed riding on camels and eating falafel, the O'Neills liked their guide better than anything else on the trip. They especially liked his tour of Masada, the ancient fortress atop a mountain where besieged Jews committed suicide to avoid the invading Romans. "Our guide was phenomenal. He made every rock breathe and the baths drip water," Rebecca says.

"In a three-and-a-half-hour tour, he gave us a million facts of what had happened there. But he also mentioned that the only time a Jew is permitted to commit suicide is when he or she is asked to give up Judaism," Rebecca says. "Which is what these zealots were doing: they would rather die than give up their faith."

Days later, near the end of their trip, the family visited the Museum of the Diaspora in Tel Aviv. At an interactive exhibit, museum-goers are given brief scenarios about Jewish history, then asked to make one of two choices to determine the outcome. Ben, the eldest, read his circumstances out loud. His slip of paper said: "You live in Vienna in the 1860s and you have a choice. You can remain in Vienna but not practice your Judaism, or you can move to Israel."

Ben said, "Well, I have to move to Israel." Rebecca asked him why. He replied, "If I stayed in Vienna I would have to commit suicide, because the only time Jews can kill themselves is when they are asked to give up their faith." Their guide, who was still with them, leaned against a wall, looked at Rebecca, and said, "Oh, my God." Rebecca was astonished: her eight-year-old son had absorbed more than she had ever envisioned. "He had given the comment on suicide no more import than 'And here's where the baths were.'"

The last night of vacation, the O'Neills had time to waste before they boarded their plane. It was a hot July evening, and after dinner they strolled along the promenade in Tel Aviv. The scene was beautiful, Rebecca recalls. The sun was a red globe sinking into the sea, and fishermen were returning home with the day's catch.

Then she snaps. Her eyes narrow and her posture becomes rigid. "It was just gorgeous, except for our kids. We were yelling at them, because they were hocking up to us about why we weren't buying them this *crap*. And we yelled back: 'Don't you understand you're watching the sun set over the Mediterranean? Don't you understand that some people never get to see this in their lifetimes?' We were furious. We said: 'Look, what did you get from this trip? We have spent a *fortune* bringing you here. Would you like to tell us what you got from it?'"

Ben spoke first. "I really got a sense of family," he said. Rebecca's words come out in whispers. "He didn't mean *our* family; he meant Israel. He meant the greater family. He meant the Jews." Josh, their seven-year-old, said: "'I just liked everything. I liked the food, I liked the atmosphere, I liked the people, I liked everything.' And it was true. He is my most difficult child, and he was absolutely at home. He ate everything. He didn't need us to help with anything. The fact that there were soldiers around with guns didn't faze him. He just felt at home." Samantha, only four at the time, looked solemnly at her parents and said, "I just like knowing what it feels like to be a real Jew."

Rebecca wipes her eyes. "This is nothing they get here. This is what Israel did for us. It's nothing I teach them here. But that's what it was. Whether it's on a gene or not I can't say, but I've never even talked to them about what Israel means to me. And it's certainly nothing they get from Rick; his attitude is, yeah, well, Israel's important, but there should be a peace process. At the end of our trip, though, even he had a different feeling. His comment was 'This is the motherland; this is Jews' land. Let the Palestinians find someplace else.' It wasn't as emotional as mine. But my kids reacted the way I did: in the core. This is what happened."

She pauses, stepping outside the narrative of her Israeli trip. "There's a part of me that keeps going deeper to my roots. I would never become ultra-Orthodox. We don't go to services very often. I can imagine keeping kosher someday. More often than not, I would say, we light candles on Friday night. And we have Shabbat dinner. It may be Chinese food, but yes, we have this dinner together and we signify Shabbat. I do the Jewish holidays here. Many of the traditions are the traditions I grew up with. I don't even know how I let the kids know, but they know.

"We are part of a larger family. This home or whatever home we're in as a family is why Judaism survived 5755 years. It's because it's centered on family and centered on people helping people and a community. If I had to leave tomorrow with just my family, I could do it, because it's really all I care about."

Rick leans back in his chair. "For me, it's the fact that, to a certain extent, I don't die when I die. I'll go on living through my kids. You live through your kids. And hopefully through the next generation, as yet unborn, that's where you make your contribution."

SIX

Keeping the Faith

§

MAX AND JONATHAN Lehmann stand straight and tall.
They laugh the deep, throaty laughs of those who appreciate good jokes and know how to tell them. Five years apart, the
brothers bear a striking resemblance, with brown eyes, broad
shoulders, and smiles that could melt snow. Dark curls fringe their
faces, though Max notes with chagrin that he has fewer than he
used to. Max, thirty, and Jonathan, twenty-five, were born and
raised in an affluent San Diego suburb. The blessings of their
abundant state were heaped upon the brothers: gifted both as
students and athletes, they excelled in nearly everything that came
their way. The sons of Michael Lehmann, a Jew with Czech roots,
and Megan Summers, a fourth-generation California Protestant,
they were raised as Jews. When they reflect on what that meant,
Max and Jonathan recall warm evenings of Hanukkah gifts and
latkes, as well as elaborate Passover seders. And they fondly recall
summers spent at their predominantly Jewish camp, where they
met Jews of all stripes: rugged Israelis, chess-playing Russians. Both
became bar mitzvahs, an achievement they note with great pride.

So much of Max and Jonathan seems set along the same path:
they attended the same university and took many of the same
courses. In the flesh and on paper, the two men are indisputably of
the same family and certainly of the same tribe. But when it comes
to the ideas the brothers have about Jews, Judaism, and who they
are themselves, you would hardly believe they grew up in the same
house. Max is quick to point out that he is only "half-Jewish," and

harbors little affinity for Jews in general. Although having children seems a far-off notion, he can't imagine he would raise his in the Jewish faith — or any faith, for that matter. "I'm an agnostic." Max says this dismissively. He counts no Jews among his closest friends — not by design, he says, but not necessarily by coincidence, either. He finds Jews insular, and says he objects to clannishness, whether practiced by Jews, Cubans, or Koreans. "This is America; this is California," he says, his arms gesturing wide. "That kind of thinking — it's a sick way to live."

Jonathan, on the other hand, has a vast array of Jewish friends and is an avid student of Jewish history, both ancient and modern. Much to his left-of-center surprise, he finds himself defending Israeli politics in the oddest of circumstances. An agnostic, like his parents and brother, Jonathan can't imagine bringing up children with any organized religion. "But I'd like to work out a way to pass Jewish culture on," he says. "I'm pretty clear on that."

Max's ideas on the subject are far more complex and serve as an example of how corrosive knee-jerk negativism toward intermarriage can be, even generations later. But their dichotomous views were surprising. How could two brothers forge such different views of their identity? Was it personality, birth order, experiences outside the home? Or was their something about their family life? Siblings in wholly Jewish or wholly Christian families often come to hold different notions about their ethnicity or their relationship to God. But with an interfaith family, the question that inevitably arises is whether it stemmed from the blending of cultures or of religions.

Michael Lehmann and Megan Summers Lehmann are great contrasts, to be sure. He is an olive-skinned man with black hair, a warm, affable manner, and a strong, firm handshake. She is a willowy blonde with California good looks and a tentative laugh. Their modern house at the top of a treacherous driveway, with spectacular views of the Pacific, sprawls gracefully from a hillside. Set into the Lehmanns' deck is a bright turquoise pool, the kind that, from the air, makes Southern California look as though it is studded with dime-store bijoux.

Megan Lehmann seems guarded at first, revealing little of her background except the essentials. As she sits in a chair, the sun at her back, Megan crisply conveys her past. Her mother died when she was four years old, leaving her and an older brother. Her father, overwhelmed with grief and the care of two small children, sent Meg and her brother to boarding school. A grandmother, who was as devoted to Meg as Meg to her, died when Meg was thirteen.

Religion played only a small role in her life. Her parents were of different Protestant denominations but had never been churchgoers. At boarding school, Meg occasionally attended services with friends. But the solace her friends found eluded Meg. "It didn't work for me at all." She shrugs. Her world was solitary. Her best friend, in time, became her schoolwork; it was the only thing she could count on.

Michael's childhood was as far from Meg's emotionally as it was geographically. Growing up in Manhattan in the 1930s and 1940s, he was the object of his family's love and attention. The first-born son of a Jewish dentist from Prague, Max, and his wife, Anna, Michael was surrounded by his own kind. If his neighbors weren't Czech Jews, they were other Central European intellectuals, and had brought the genteel manner of Budapest, Munich, and Warsaw salons to the Upper West Side. Although Michael became a bar mitzvah, the Lehmann family — Max, Anna, Michael, and his younger brother, Julian — worshiped at their synagogue only occasionally. "The rules and regulations of Judaism were somewhat of a mystery to me," Michael recalls. "Our family was less than scrupulous about religious practice."

Michael Lehmann and Meg Summers met in 1956, as Michael, a young surgical resident at a Los Angeles hospital, was hurrying to make his rounds one evening. He couldn't help noticing that the admissions clerk — a woman he had befriended — was missing.

In her place sat a tall, slender young woman, a solemn beauty with short blond hair and large gray eyes.

"Where's Peg?" he demanded. The woman looked up and answered bluntly, "I don't know where Peg is, but I'm Meg." With that, the couple began a courtship that spanned three years, transcontinental cities, and the erratic hours of a medical internship and law school. But probably most challenging to the relationship was the cultural clash posed by Michael's Jewish background and Meg's lonely childhood, without faith or family.

Neither of them paid any attention to these facts at first. Michael was so smitten by Meg's quick wit, intellectual drive, and elegant good looks that he hardly noticed, he says, that she wasn't Jewish. Meg, for her part, says she scarcely knew Jewish from not Jewish in the first place. Michael was brilliant, handsome, and funny; that much was obvious. But what seemed so striking about him was his confidence, his ease with others — colleagues, superiors, family members. It was everything Meg lacked. "Part of the attraction was Michael's knowing who he was and how he fit in." Her face, chiseled and tanned, flickers with sadness for a moment. Then she declares matter-of-factly, "I really didn't know who I was. My background was a zero. So I welcomed this sense of belonging."

The relationship quickly flourished. They talked about books — the classics, contemporary literature — and their shared interests in architecture and the arts. "I wasn't all caught up in whether or not someone was a certain something. I had other priorities," Michael says. "If we weren't a perfect match, it had nothing to do with religion." He adds, "And in terms of intermarriage, I feel that it's such a mild intermarriage, I don't even consider it intermarriage."

His family saw it differently. He runs his hand over his face. He stares into the ocean, as if he is genuinely puzzled by the memory of the first time he brought Meg home to meet his mother. He was nervous, of course, but expected his mother and stepfather to be, at worst, politely distant.

For Meg, the experience was even more tense than for most young women. She was anxious to meet her future mother-in-law and was more than eager to please her. Probably more than she realized, Meg, motherless herself, wanted Anna to accept her. In Anna, Meg had envisioned a woman who could guide her through female milestones: becoming a wife, becoming a mother.

As she and Michael entered the apartment building together for the first time, Meg took a deep breath, checked her face in her compact mirror, and followed Michael into the apartment. Her heart thumping in her chest, Meg asked, "'What do you want me to call you, 'Mom' or 'Anna'? She answered, 'I had always hoped that Michael would marry someone Jewish.' And she launched into a tirade against me."

It is clearly a painful memory. "How do you think it felt?" she snaps, hurt, when asked. Megan seems startled at the notion that the addition of a non-Jew to a Jewish family, or a Jew to a Gentile one, could still stir such rancor and bitterness. "I had no idea," she says. She shakes her head. "No idea."

The couple carried on with their plans to marry. Michael was in the midst of a grueling residency, so he asked Meg, who was finishing her undergraduate degree, to reach a rabbi for the arrangements. The first rabbi she spoke to, she says, was outraged at the idea of a Jewish man marrying a non-Jew, and sent her away. Michael was perplexed by the exchange. Hoping to avoid more unpleasantness, Meg began exploring conversion. She found a Hillel rabbi on a college campus who agreed to marry them, but he suggested first that Meg study the basic tenets of Judaism with him. But the rabbi was busy, and the time they planned to spend in study soon dwindled. Meg began to think twice about exactly what it meant to become Jewish.

"I quickly realized that to convert, you had to study certain principles and doctrines and pledge to abide by them," she says. "That had nothing to do with the way Michael was Jewish. Converting to Judaism is a very small part of what it means to be Jewish. What it is to be Jewish is something that's in your blood, mind, psyche. I also got this insight: I would be signing a piece of paper that had absolutely nothing to do with Michael, so why do it?" The Hillel rabbi married them anyway, under a chuppah, in the presence of a few relatives and friends. "I bless the rabbi to this day. It made Michael's family happy, and my family didn't care."

In her marriage, Meg had few traditions she was eager to pass on. Christmas, for example, difficult for most interfaith couples, never surfaced as a problem for the Lehmanns. The holiday cheer shared by others served only as reminder of the loneliness she had endured as a child. Once she and Michael were married, a tree was out of the question. Meg didn't want one in her house.

Many interfaith couples decide as time passes what they will do with their children, but not the Lehmanns. Meg was firmly decided long before she ever became pregnant: her children would be raised as Jews. In fact, it was essential for Meg to have Jewish traditions in their home. Michael didn't seem to care either way, but Meg was determined. It was she who initiated Hanukkah and Passover celebrations. When holidays approached in the first years of their marriage, she asked Michael for a seasonal roadmap: menu ideas, whom to invite, ritual decorum. Mostly, though, he had only a vague idea of what to do. "It wasn't as if he brought to me what the holidays were. He couldn't really help me very much when it came to that," she says. "So I tried from what he told me, and guessed what I didn't know. I found out the rest from people at delicatessens." She laughs at the number of Jewish coffee table books she sees now, which spell out menus and give context even to the condiments of traditional meals.

"I wanted to please Michael. I was open to Judaism, I was excited and fascinated by it. Then there was the intellectual aspect, which I so enjoyed. The ritual and tradition were so rich — my perception was that I had no family. I did, but I didn't grow up with my brother or anyone else in my family. Now I have family. I'm close to my brother, but Michael's sense of knowing who he was and who his people were —" She pauses. Her hands flutter in the air to brush some stray hairs off her forehead; she doesn't finish the sentence. "I was delighted to do it and I wanted my boys to have it, too. I wanted them to have that sense of who they are, that sense of ritual and tradition, of belonging." Even if she would never fully immerse herself in Judaism, at least her children, Meg hoped, could be part of the community — the larger family — she had never had.

As the years went on, and the boys were born, the Lehmanns invented their own family traditions. "With Hanukkah, we kind of made it up as we went along," Meg says, "with eight presents, one each night for one year, or eight presents on the last night the next." But the Jewish ritual she had established in their home did not pass muster with the elder Lehmanns. Though Anna and her second husband, also a Czech Jew, were delighted with their grandsons, they never warmed toward Meg. Anna, a tiny woman who favored knitted shawls and dyed her white hair so black that it was almost blue, doted on Max, named for her first husband, who had died a decade before. But in the early years of Meg and Michael's marriage, the family could find little good in the stranger among them. And they made it no secret; family get-togethers were always riddled with tension.

One in particular stands out.

The sun was just dropping into the hills, and the chill that marks even Southern California evenings began to set in. Several family members — aunts, uncles, cousins, grandparents — had converged at a desert resort, and Michael, Meg, and little Max, then in preschool, drove to meet them for dinner.

Everyone was seated around a steaming brisket. Anna got up to bring to the table something she had forgotten. Meg suddenly realized she had forgotten a drink for Max. "Oh," she called to her mother-in-law in the kitchen, "would you mind bringing out a glass of milk for Max?"

No one spoke a word, but everyone turned to stare at Meg, their faces showing disbelief. Mouths were drawn tightly, and stares, she recalls, were hot. Finally someone spoke, an uncle who had been particularly belligerent about the couple's marriage. "I never thought that *Michael* would marry a woman who would ask for milk at the dinner table," he muttered.

Meg, stunned, felt her face grow red with humiliation. The family, loose about many rules of kashrut, did not mix milk with meat. Max sensed his mother's embarrassment in an instant. "It's okay, Mommy," he said, the only person daring to speak.

Unlike other family gatherings, when slights or attacks on Meg from Michael's brother, mother, or uncle were indirect, this was undeniable. For years, Meg asked herself after other get-togethers: "Did I hear that correctly? Did I misunderstand that comment?" There were always subtle, behind-the-scenes remarks that nobody else heard. She herself couldn't put her finger on some of them. She began to wonder, "What's wrong here? Am I losing my mind?"

Meg believes her husband didn't do enough to shield her from his family's wrath. He agrees, guiltily. Even his recollections of the period seem tortured, his language stiff. "How my mother and brother may have acted toward Meg was not something I fully perceived," Michael says. "I did say, in good conscience, 'Don't pay attention,' because I failed to realize the intensity of what was going on, and the way it was received. I think I underestimated it all. If I were to do something differently, it would be to approach it more forcefully. I regret that now. It wasn't with malice aforethought; I just underestimated the dynamics." He sighs. "I did the wrong thing," he says.

"I'm not sure I made it clear, because I myself didn't know what was hitting me sometimes," Meg says. "And when I would mention specific incidents, and he'd say, 'Don't pay attention,' it was very difficult. I didn't have anybody else to talk to."

"I think there are cultural differences that, had I understood, would have made my life much easier," Meg says. "The ways that people are in the world are what they bring from their backgrounds. There's a certain sarcastic manner which I took as painful in the beginning."

Michael shrugs. "My saying 'Don't pay any attention' was really my way of saying 'Meg, I'm on your side.' It may not have been very effective — I never directly talked to my mother. I mostly indicated to my mother how much I was enjoying my marriage to Meg." Which Anna, no doubt, did not welcome.

"If you imagine these people coming from the shtetl, where

togetherness was their survival in an alien world, intermarriage was absolutely inexplicable to them. Watch *Fiddler on the Roof.* It all boils down to 'our people, our faith, our traditions,' because it's all survival. My parents were only one generation from that, from the shtetl."

In the mid-1970s, Meg began to feel that Max was too isolated from other Jews, living, as they did, in a mostly Christian suburb. So she set out to find a predominantly Jewish summer camp for him, and was intrigued by one set deep in the ancient redwood forests. It revolved around sports: kayaking, tennis, and hiking.

Though only eleven, Max was already an overachiever, intent on pleasing his parents — and himself — with top grades. "I thought, 'Well, we'll give him a rest.' So we sent him off, and the first postcard we got said how awful the food was." Two weeks went by, and Meg and Michael received another miserable postcard. "I remember thinking, 'Why did I do this? Why didn't I send him to one of those normal upscale WASPY camps?' When we went to pick him up, at the bus, I was really ready to hear the worst. When he got off, he said he'd had a marvelous time. I said: 'What?' What I'd wanted to happen had happened. He came back and he wanted to be bar mitzvahed. One of his counselors was an Israeli who played baseball. He was exposed to all kinds of Jewish kids — Russian émigrés, the whole works."

Max had expressed no interest before that point in being a bar mitzvah, and Michael hadn't pushed the issue. While they celebrated Passover and Hanukkah at home, Judaism had had no formal context until then, since they did not attend synagogue.

"It was I — and Michael will agree with this — who took the initiative. 'Wait a minute,' I said; 'we want to get him bar mitzvahed.' I feel to this day, whether it's through Judaism or whatever, it's critical to know who you are in that sense of roots and belonging. So although I was pushing a direction that wasn't who I was, it didn't matter."

Meg arranged a meeting with the nearest rabbi, at a Reform temple. She entered his chambers with the same earnestness she had felt before she met her mother-in-law, eager to do the right thing. The rabbi motioned her to sit, then asked bluntly whether she had converted. Well, no, she said, but Max had been raised as a Jew. The rabbi stood up. "You haven't converted. Your son will never be Jewish."

Her long, delicate fingers rigid and splayed, she throws her hands to her face as if to protect herself from the memory. She shakes her head. The rabbi's reaction left her wondering how her plans would ever turn out. She could not know, of course, that six years after that day in 1977, the Reform movement would recognize the children of Jewish fathers and non-Jewish mothers as Jews, provided they were raised as Jews. To Meg, it was yet another painful rejection by the family she wanted her children to be part of.

The rabbi, Michael recalls, was worried about Max not having the right of return; that is, the right of Israeli citizenship granted to all those born of Jewish mothers. "I can tell you that Max's having the right of return was not my uppermost thought at the moment." He pauses. "And I said, 'Well, we'll just have our own. I'll collect ten men for a minyan. We'll go to a mountain and have a nice bar mitzvah ceremony on our own.'"

But Meg insisted that the process and the ceremony be conventional. Enough of Max's Jewish life was already in the margins, she thought. Not this, too — some funky 1970s bar mitzvah on a mountain. So once again she searched for a rabbi who was willing to bend the rules. Several weeks later, she found him at a synagogue an hour's drive from her house. The rabbi welcomed her warmly. Even though Max was several years behind his peers in preparation for the bar mitzvah ceremony, he offered to help Meg in any way he could.

The event, held on the eve of Max's fourteenth birthday rather than near his thirteenth, as with most boys, was a smashing success. "He did a beautiful job," Meg recalls. "I did it for Max, but I also felt I had given Michael's family all that I could. After Jonathan was bar mitzvahed, too, I really felt I had done something wonderful. It was I who drove the boys back and forth to Hebrew school. I put a great deal of myself into it. And for them, I think I did what was right."

She thinks about this a moment, then adds: "But they're not *all* Michael and his family. They are also who I am, whatever I am, and who my brother is, and we *are* WASPs. Religiously we are nothing, but it's not all the Jewish culture. I used to lead them to believe that's all there was, but that was sort of a reflection of our relationship. I think the boys will always have their Jewish identity. You can't get away from it — the humor, the kind of irreverence and unconventionality.

"I'm certainly not Jewish, but depending on who I'm talking to, I might say, 'I'm Jewish by marriage' or 'Jewish in spirit.' I very much enjoy my affinity and the opportunity to be a part of all this, as are my boys. But in recent years I'm also very clear that I'm not Jewish. And I am very glad that I didn't convert, because it wouldn't be who I am. I am now a blend of what my life has brought to me, and I'm much more aware of that other side than I was in the early years. I would have converted. I keep a Jewish home. I have come in my own evolution and development to realize that the boys *are* Jewish — but they are something else as well. In other words, I've come to appreciate who I am a great deal more."

It is early morning, and Max squints as he leans back into the booth of the restaurant. He orders no coffee, only ice water. A gregarious, warm man, Max has a smooth, sonorous voice and greets his friends with big grins and bear hugs. A recent business school graduate, he has three successful health clubs of his own, one of which he is busy launching. Even so, Max has an active extracurricular schedule: hiking in the California hills, skiing at Lake Tahoe, white-water rafting in the West's most challenging rivers. Trim and lean, Max orders yogurt with fruit for breakfast, a statement as much as a choice. He is very much a part of California; he is a gourmet cook, and has a kitchen equipped with state-of-the-art pots and pans. He grows fresh herbs in his garden and looks upon his native state with an almost nationalistic pride.

When the conversation veers toward intermarriage, his mood changes perceptibly. "I was always Jewish," he says, "even though I was only half-Jewish." But in the next breath, he adds, "When I was growing up, I found Jewish people unattractive." He says this last word hesitantly, as if he were searching for a less disparaging one. "Just because a lot of examples I had of Jewish people were unattractive. My relatives on my father's side, my father aside, were not physically attractive, and very few of them were emotionally attractive.

"There wasn't a lot of playfulness and there wasn't a lot of fun. They didn't fit into California the way I found my life was developing. I would run around and get dirty, and they wouldn't like that somehow. They liked me — no doubt about that. I was the star child. I was the first-born son of a first-born son, and there weren't a lot of kids on my dad's side of the family."

Max's discomfort with his Jewish identity rests on many factors. Growing up as he did in an affluent community, being "half-Jewish," Max says, "wasn't always an easy identity to have." With the picture-book surroundings of the Lehmann home — its vistas of the ocean, a table set up outdoors for doing homework, parents who commanded respect among the neighbors — growing up was far from painful. Yet Max felt he stood out. Among his peers, he didn't know a single Jew.

"So being half-Jewish was a lot of Jewish, as opposed to just half. And I was thankful that I was just half because that made me okay to the other half. As a kid I remember thinking, or I'd say, 'Well, my mother's not Jewish,' because I felt the need to fit in." Max says his friends never questioned his differences; the isolation he felt was internal, not imposed by others. "I always fit in very well with friends — it wasn't like my Achilles' heel that brought me down in the group in any way. It was a matter of wanting to feel like everyone else. As a little kid it's not abnormal to want to be exactly like everyone around you, so that you don't stick out in any way but fit in as well as you possibly can. And this was the one thing about me that stuck out."

People would make Easter plans, but the Lehmanns wouldn't.

They would spend Christmas with Meg's brother, who lived nearby, but never have a tree of their own. "I felt kind of weird about that, but I didn't really want one, either. I just knew that not having one made me different from other people."

Regardless of his perceived differences, Max excelled. A brilliant student, he vaulted to the top of his class, even skipped a grade. Tall and powerfully built, he exuded confidence, never betraying for a moment that he was as much as two years younger than some of his classmates. Indeed, Max soared through the years that trouble some kids the most. In high school, he was student body president. He was a National Merit Scholar. He was captain of the varsity basketball team. He was handsome and had a pretty girlfriend. He came from a good family. But to his girlfriend's parents, not good enough. Though Max had dated her for four years, when the girl came out as a debutante, her parents forbade Max to escort her to the ball. "Why? They were uncomfortable with me escorting her to the ball because I was Jewish." He goes on. "I had everything going for me and they knew it. But there was some serious concern about Max Lehmann escorting their daughter to a debutante ball."

He scowls. "I thought it was ridiculous, and I blamed her parents and hated her for it."

As complicated and painful as not "fitting in" among peers can be to a child, it is perhaps even more devastating not to be accepted by family members. Max was acutely aware of the differences Michael and Meg had with Michael's parents. Even though they were manifested in small, subtle ways, Max picked up on them. And even though his grandmother and his Uncle Julian lavished praise on him, he knew they were less than accepting of his mother. As a little boy, Max was devoted to Meg, as he is today; he speaks of her with reverence.

"The main stress I felt from my father's family was the stress they put on my mother," he says. "I knew she wasn't happy, and I knew my father wasn't going to do anything about it. I just didn't see any parallels between myself and my father's side of the family, even though I didn't mind their presence most of the time. I never really enjoyed my father's side of the family. I always wanted to be much more like my mother's family. They were good-looking, athletic, well-adjusted Californians." Max pauses before he says "Californians," as if he were certain that residence in a state amounted to a sort of ethnicity.

"There just wasn't a lot of joy when my father's family was around. I was — and am — a sensitive person. I guess I get that from my mom. And I felt the tension regarding my father's family very intuitively. Nothing was ever really overt, but I'd pick up on little comments like, 'How long are they going to stay?' or 'They're impossible.' As I look back on it, there was a definite feeling of tension in the air."

Indeed, he remembers his father's family with dread. It wasn't as if they spoke in loud voices or had habits that were impossible to endure. "They were boring, actually. There was a lot of sitting around and doing nothing, just getting in the way. They were unappreciative, too. They expected to be waited on hand and foot by my mother when they came to the house. Rather than lots of 'thank you's,' it was like, 'Can you get me this? Can I have a glass of water?' Essentially, it was, 'Can you do more?' And my mother was always working. She'd take off work to be with them. It wasn't as if she was a housewife."

Max frowns and says, "And you know what? They weren't role models." He pauses for a moment, looks out the window, takes a sip of water. His hands together, fingertip to fingertip, he erects a barricade, pinkies resting on the table. "There was a big Jewish wall. The real influences in my life weren't the Jews. I wasn't comfortable with these people when I was growing up. I didn't see them as being kind or having fun. I don't think it's surprising that I'm not attracted to them, because I didn't have a lot of circumstances in which I felt comfortable with them when I was younger."

He shrugs. "There was a lot of darkness there. And the darkness in my father's family was the pain they created for my mother. I didn't want to be like them. I definitely wanted to be like my mom's family. There's a lot of pain there, but by the time I knew my mother and her relatives, the living examples of them were so different from my dad's side. Almost across the board they were interesting, warm people.

"But personally I must add that life wasn't too rough. They treated me well. I was the son of Michael, and I was named for Max. In a way, it was as if Michael was so wonderful, my mother could never be enough."

He leans back and takes a deep breath. His eyes narrow. "This is a huge stereotype, but when I think of Jews, I don't think of athletes, I don't think of people who are health-conscious, I don't think of people who are connected with their feelings and people who enjoy art, and I know they do. It's just that in my growing up the Jewish part was . . ." His voice trails off.

What he says is so outlandish, he can't possibly mean it. Everybody can tick off Jewish contributors to the world: to the arts, to medicine, to psychology. Marc Chagall. Beverly Sills. Jonas Salk. Sigmund Freud. Even people who don't follow sports know who Sandy Koufax is. What Max really seems to mean is that the Jews he knew, the Jews who had formed his images of Jews when he was a small child, were doleful souls who made his mother, already wounded by her many losses, suffer even more. They lacked humor and flexibility. And as a young boy, Max couldn't see past it. His view of Jews, of his extended family, and what it means to be Jewish all took root in the bitter, strained interaction between his Gentile mother and his Jewish family. Max sees the unpleasantness in his family as a by-product of his parents' interfaith marriage. But was it? Perhaps these two families, separated by culture, language, personality, and geography, would have disliked each other just as bitterly if one were Lutheran and the other Southern Baptist. It is impossible to say.

Max concedes this much. He knows things improved between his mother and grandmother, but it's hard to forget early experiences. Yet much as Max says he is "half-Jewish" — a phrase that is perhaps even more telling than he realizes — it is important to note that many of his experiences with Jews are positive ones. It seems, however, that they came too late.

Although he had never expected to, Max ended up liking summer camp. He laughs about the worrisome dispatches he sent to
his parents — "What do you expect? I was eleven." Then came his
Hebrew lessons and occasional attendance at the temple. "It was
my first experience with Judaism in which finally it was okay who
the Lehmanns were," Max says. "It was that positive experience
that made me feel, 'Okay, I want to do this.' It happened one and a
half years before my bar mitzvah, and it really made me feel different. I'm proud of that, and I was proud to be a part of that
congregation. The rabbi is a wonderful man. He has a warm, welcoming spirit that makes you feel special to be a part of his congregation and lucky to know him."

Once ensconced in Hebrew school, Max had the sense that his
upbringing was not "authentic" when compared with that of his
classmates. "But I was glad. I didn't want to be a full-blooded Jew. I
didn't see any reason why that would make me happier."

He looked forward to his bar mitzvah, however. "I wanted to
do what it took to meet whatever criteria they had. I wanted to do
it; it was my decision. And I knew how much it would mean to my
father even though he would never say it. The temple turned me
around. It was one of the first positive experiences with Judaism
that I had." He smiles. "And my bar mitzvah: I was very proud of
my accomplishment. I thought I'd done a great thing. I felt a part
of Jewish society on that day."

Max leans over the table. "To this day I feel a bond when I'm
around Jewish people, different from the way I feel when I'm
around other people. There's an unspoken understanding that,
because we're both Jewish, we're going to be more honest, more
open, probably more trusting. That's a very Jewish experience, to
sit down with somebody else who's Jewish and know that I understand who that person is, probably much more than they know me.
They're pure-bred Jewish; I'm half-Jewish.

"Although I'm not pure bred, it's a tie to a history and a culture
from long ago. It's my perception of how I fit into the world, where
I come from. I think everyone needs to have a sense of place, and
who he is, an identity. I think it would be very confusing if you

were adopted and had no idea what your ethnic heritage was, and you just had to guess from your appearance. You'd always wonder. For me, it's different. Two thousand years ago, where were my relatives? I know. Well, I probably can't tell you exactly when they went to Czechoslovakia, but you get the point.

"It makes me proud to look at the positive contributions Jews have made to society, but I'm also very conscious of the negative associations that have gone with that positive success. The outsider's opinion —" Max shrugs. "I can step away and see that other people resent it. The exclusiveness." He pauses.

"I can understand both worlds, but I'm a member of neither. It's lonely at times, but it's not as if I think about it a lot. I know I'm very accepted by both worlds, so I don't have to feel a lot of loneliness. I know I don't have to fit perfectly into either one."

But Christian beliefs and customs are even more foreign to Max than Jewish ones. "To this day, church baffles me," he says. "In fact, the nuances of other religions baffle me. But in temple, well, I felt comfortable there. I *do* feel comfortable there, although I can't remember the last time I went.

"I liked the cantor singing, the people kissing their prayer book after they'd touched the Torah with it. In a strange way, the Jewish sense of community, which pervades the religion as well as social interactions within the temple, I found warm and accepting. And it was nice to know it was there."

Even though he was at home there, Max still felt removed from the congregation. This time, instead of his Jewish father in a non-Jewish neighborhood, it was Meg who made the family stand out. Rather than feeling out of place, Max enjoyed the fact that her angular blond looks made the family different. "I was proud of it," he says.

Max appears to be on both sides at once. Like anyone, his identity is clearly a reaction to things in his family — from where he grew up, to the messages he received from the prevailing culture, to the animosity Michael's family unleashed against Meg. He was acutely aware of all of it.

"Something that my parents did very well was to raise their

children in an environment where we knew they would accept whoever we married, as long as they felt that the person loved us and we loved that person, whether she was black or Asian or Latino. That comes from their own painful experience. But I'm proud of that, proud of how they see things. We have a black member of the family on my mother's side, and a Cuban — all of it's okay. I take a lot of pride in my family's openness to people of different races and religions."

His long-time girlfriend is Chinese American. They have tentative plans to marry, but children, Max believes, aren't likely to come any time soon. He is not sure how he would raise them; he can't envision them as Christians, yet he can't imagine them as practicing Jews, either.

But he leaves room for maneuver on that one. About synagogue, he says, "Maybe it would become more important if I went now. I haven't been in so long; if I went maybe I'd realize I should go more often." He laughs. "I'm more proud of my heritage now than I was as a child. I've found more people like me, and have a broader perspective. I understand where I fit in better, and I like it."

Max's brother, Jonathan, sits in an organic coffee shop-cum-bakery, relaxed despite the flurry of activity around him. He has just got off work — as a health policy adviser in a Democratic congressman's office — and he picks at a muffin. The café is filled with the unmistakable smell of burned sugar. The din of the server shouting latte and espresso orders seems to grow louder by the moment.

Jonathan has the appearance of someone who, as the French expression goes, feels good inside his skin. He grins easily, and carries himself with a casual elegance that seems, well, Californian. Jonathan's memories of growing up are radically different from his brother's, strikingly so. "I actually never felt a lot of conflict," he says. "A whole lot of things came together to make my situation pretty easy. By the time I was aware of the situation, my parents had obviously had to make some choices — how they were going to celebrate holidays, what kind of exposure we were going to have to both religions and cultures — and I had the benefit of those decisions having already been made."

The more he talks, the more it seems as though he is talking about an entirely different childhood from the one his brother recounted. Where Max saw an overwhelmingly non-Jewish environment, Jonathan remembers being surrounded by Jews. There were, in fact, a few Jewish families in the town. But numerical facts and emotional experience are two very different things.

He shakes his head. "I actually had quite a number of Jewish friends, both in grammar school and high school. Whether it's a statistical anomaly or whether the population changed a lot in our town within five years, I don't know, but that's how it was.

"If someone asked me, when I was growing up, I always identified myself as Jewish." He shrugs. "I mean, I'm Jewish." He points his hands, palms turned inward, at himself. "I'm not religious — I'm agnostic — and I don't have a lot of faith in any kind of organized religion. But as far as cultural ties and cultural identity go, I'm Jewish."

Looking back, Jonathan has none of the bitter memories Max has about his father's family and their unkindness toward Meg. By the time Jonathan was old enough to remember, Grandmother Anna had developed rheumatoid arthritis and lived in a nursing home. Meg readily admits that, to her surprise, Anna's illness brought out a gentle side in her that Meg had never witnessed. And that is what Jonathan recalls: his grandmother as a sweet old lady, frail and foreign. She would struggle to her feet when her grandchildren entered her room in the nursing home. "I mainly remember her giving me these old-woman kind of kisses," he says.

Of course, Jonathan knew that there had been tension between his mother and grandmother. But by the time he was old enough to be aware, the women had ironed out some of their differences. "I guess I knew that things between them were not always great, but they always came across as good enough. And frankly, at that age, I had no idea of what other people's relationships were. I had nothing to compare them to."

He pauses. "I suppose being the child of an interfaith couple could be a problem for some people, but it's never been one for me. It's probably a product of having some Jewish friends in a predominantly Christian environment. I've always had enough Jewish friends that I've never felt alienated." Even growing up in a community that seemed to prize blond good looks, Jonathan was happy he was different. The lack of a Christmas tree barely fazed him, he says. He helped decorate the neighbors' tree and had eight nights of Hanukkah at his house. "When you're little, all you care about is presents. So eight nights — it was a pretty good deal."

"I don't know to what extent that was a product of conscious choices by my parents or what, but I don't identify with Christianity at all. I didn't feel I was missing anything, not having Christmas."

Given the importance of California in Max's life, it seems that Jonathan would give it equal rank. Instead, he says, "I'm Jewish first, Californian second, American third. I don't know quite what forces have produced all this. It's never been a problem, my Jewishness. I've never been exposed in any direct way to anti-Semitism. No one's ever confronted me in any overt way with an anti-Semitic remark. Obviously I've read and heard about it, but I've never been exposed to it." He brushes crumbs off the table. "I take pride in being a little different. Our society is dominated by white Christian males, and I'm proud of the fact that I'm Jewish. Or at least that I identify myself as Jewish. Obviously the only organization that considers me truly Jewish is American Reform Judaism. But I identify myself as Jewish." He points to himself.

"I enjoy being different. It's unique. I'm a little outside American culture. I'm slightly to the left of center politically, and I enjoy taking less-than-orthodox stands intellectually. Part of it is that I enjoy looking in from the outside — finding Christmas so commercial, stuff like that. And maybe because the difference has never caused problems for me, because I've never been persecuted for it, I can take pride in being Jewish. There are a lot of things to take pride in about Judaism; I think it's neat that Jews have sort of swept science's Nobel Prizes. And their contributions in the arts. It goes on and on."

As for his own intellectual achievements — which number many — Jonathan's formal induction into Judaism was among the greatest. Like Max, Jonathan became a bar mitzvah in the Reform temple the family attended for the High Holy Days.

"I looked forward to it; I really did," he says. "And my pride in it went well beyond the fact that I was going to get cool cameras and Swiss Army knives. My feelings about my bar mitzvah were wrapped up in the fact that educationally I had achieved a real feat — as a young boy I had severe dyslexia, but by eleven or twelve I was overcoming that. My bar mitzvah, my reading of Hebrew — it was all a big success in many ways, but mostly because it boosted my self-esteem in accomplishing intellectual projects. I mastered the Hebrew. I really took pride in that."

Like many Jewish thirteen-year-olds, Jonathan dropped out of Hebrew school immediately after his bar mitzvah. "My parents gave me the choice of having the ceremony or not. I said 'Yeah,' but it was never like, 'Oh, great, I get to go to Hebrew lessons now.' After my bar mitzvah I dropped out; the reward of a trip to Israel if we continued our education wasn't enough to compel me."

Much like the other members of his family, he found that formal identification with Judaism mattered little. "But I do identify with Jewish culture, although it's never been a great passion. I think I got more involved when I became a history student." Deeply thoughtful, articulate, and well read, like the other members of his family, Jonathan seems much older than his twenty-five years. Active in Democratic politics, Jonathan has, since he was a teenager, volunteered for a wide range of causes: environmental, human rights, and health-care reform organizations.

"All these things are important to me, and I've acted on them. My desire for higher education, my concern for social justice — I don't know if that's a result of my parents' design, or if it came from my dad's upbringing, or what, but that's how I turned out."

Once in college, he settled on history as a major and began to study the history of the Jews. As a graduate student, Jonathan took a special interest in Jewish history, first in Europe, then in the

Middle East. It wasn't, however, something he had intended. As an undergraduate, Jonathan spent a semester in Cracow, Poland, where he found himself haunted by the remnants of Jews who once thrived there.

"I kind of knew what to expect from all that I had studied, but seeing some of these things and being confronted with Auschwitz and Dachau and Germany — it certainly does bring it to life."

Once, he attended a seder at the city's Jewish community center, held in a decrepit building in the once-grand Jewish quarter, Kazimierz. Still home to a handful of Cracow's elderly Jews, Kazimierz now draws tourists, who wander through its crowded cemetery and tattered eighteenth-century synagogues.

"Here we were, these young Jews; and these old people — Holocaust survivors, hobbling around — were so happy to have us. The odd thing is, the only language I had in common with them was German. So I was sitting next to this old guy, both of us eating matzoh, and we're talking in German. I felt really weird about that, speaking to this guy in German. But what could I do? I didn't know Polish well enough to carry on a conversation. It didn't seem to matter to him. That I was young and Jewish was enough."

Unlike Max, Jonathan cemented his Jewish ties as he grew older, although he says it was not a conscious choice. "There was never a time when I was indifferent and then wasn't. There was never something that kind of clicked. I just think my interest in Jewish things in general has gradually progressed with my knowledge of Jewish history. There was never a certain moment I suddenly discovered myself as a Jew. Organized religion is not for me."

Like many Jews, regardless of their religious devotion, Jonathan finds himself concerned about Israel, particularly after his visit there some years ago. "If someone is bashing Israel, I'll be the first to defend it. That's my first instinct, to stand up for Israel. If there were suddenly an Arab-Israeli war, I'd be cheering for Israel." He waves his fist. "And I'd implore the United States to sell Israel whatever war toy it wanted. At the same time — this is my instinct — when I'm around people who are sort of gung-ho Israel supporters, I'll be deeply critical of Israel, of its policies toward the occupied territories and Jewish extremists.

"Going to Israel didn't make me feel more deeply Jewish. I didn't think, 'Oh, thank God, I've finally made my way back.' But I will say this: I found it fascinating. There were all these different people: blond Russians, dark Ethiopians, Mediterranean-looking Sephardim. It was really great. It was very stimulating, more so intellectually than emotionally. Emotionally it was interesting to be in a place full of Jews, since I'm so used to the opposite, and it was stimulating to be in a country where Jews were interacting with Jews on every level."

He looks down at the remains of the multigrain concoction he has just eaten, and shrugs. "The food in Israel was fantastic. I expected matzoh ball soup and gefilte fish — your standard Ashkenazic fare. Instead, there was all this great Middle Eastern stuff — hummus and falafel. I liked it. I like all Jewish food. Bagels to me are the ultimate — they are the one thing I never get sick of. I could eat them nonstop. And here's a kind of trivial way I think I take pride in Jewish things: when I see some of my goy friends eating some blueberry–chocolate chip–bran bagel, I love just mocking them."

His face full of scorn, Jonathan waves his hands. "And I go, you know, 'What is this, a blueberry bagel? What a goy thing to do! You should eat an onion or a poppyseed bagel or none at all! Do you have any idea how many Jewish grandmothers are spinning in their graves right now while you eat that blueberry bran bagel? I mean, it's *purple!*' It's little things like that, I guess. I sort of think of them as my own, whether it's matzoh ball soup or authentic bagels." He laughs.

"That's something that's always been interesting to me, that Jews hold this unique place in world culture. Judaism is a religion, but it's also a culture. It's a weird hybrid, and I can't think of another example. It's hard to see the threads that tie Jews together around the world, but they're there."

Marriage and children seem prospects for the distant future.

There are no serious girlfriends in the picture, and if there were, Jonathan, like his father, does not consider Jewishness a prerequisite. "If I were attracted to a Jewish woman, her being Jewish would be low on the list. I'd have to be attracted to her physically and intellectually first. Our personalities would have to match. But maybe if she were Jewish, we'd have a greater synergy. I just don't know." He takes a sip of his drink.

"I wouldn't have a problem marrying a non-Jew. And as far as raising kids, I'd like to do a bit of what my parents did. I'd want my kids reared with an understanding of their Jewish background and culture. We'd have Passover seders and Hanukkah candles, but at the same time I wouldn't mind having a Christmas tree." He pauses. "I'd hate to see Jewish culture in America lost, swallowed up by some white-bread mainstream. What appeals to me about Judaism is its distinctiveness."

Just as quickly, he adds, "But I find it distasteful to discourage marriages of Jews and non-Jews or whites and people of color. Yet I'm sympathetic to the idea of losing Jewish culture.

"I'd like my children to grow up with an understanding and an affinity to Jewish culture, to the whole concept." He pauses again, as though this is a topic to bring up several years from now. "I'd be very surprised if I ever became superreligious. But one thing's for sure: if I ever married a non-Jew, I'd never want a priest there. I just couldn't do that. Part of my Jewishness comes from my total lack of connection with Christianity, particularly Catholicism. I find the trappings of the Trinity just give me the heebie-jeebies. All of that — the angels, the cherubs, the Holy Ghost, and all of that mumbo-jumbo — it's not for me.

"While I may not be the most Jewish of Jews, the fact is that I'm not a Christian. And if I were to pursue anything in the future, it would be Judaism.

"I don't think there should be a fear of Jews slipping into Christianity. That's illogical. There will always be Jews. Maybe not active, religious Jews, but there will always be Jews like me: agnostic but Jewish. That's pretty much where I end up."

SEVEN

Equal Time

§

O NE STIFLING MORNING in August 1985, Linda Lowenstein woke early. She opened her eyes, looked at the clock,
and sleepily remembered that this was no ordinary Sunday. She
tapped her husband, Doug, on the shoulder and padded down the
hall to get their infant daughter, Camille, from her crib. Usually,
the Lowensteins rose in a leisurely fashion on weekend mornings.
But today, Linda hurried downstairs to scramble some eggs. She
strapped Camille into her high chair and flipped on the radio. She
listened to the news without hearing it; her mind was on the events
of this day, not yesterday's. In a brick Maryland parish at eleven
o'clock, Camille would be baptized.

It wasn't Linda's idea, this whole thing. Not at all. She was
doing it to please her mother, Maria, a devout Roman Catholic.
When Linda and Doug adopted Camille in Korea, it was Maria
who insisted that the baby — Maria's first grandchild — be baptized. Linda knew her Jewish husband was uncomfortable with the
idea. But it wasn't as if he were religious. Doug was hardly even a
cultural Jew, to tell the truth. He had become a bar mitzvah in
Detroit, but that was it as far as his Jewishness was concerned. He
professed to know next to nothing about his faith, his people.
Whereas Linda, the only child of Filipino immigrants, had had an
upbringing steeped in Catholic tradition. In her Chicago neighborhood, she was the only Asian child, but it hardly mattered in the
uniformity of a parochial school. She may have had dark skin,
but she dressed just like her blond Polish and Irish classmates:

starched white shirt, blue and gray plaid skirt, white bobby socks, polished loafers. The nuns were there to rap your knuckles if you got out of line.

All of this hardly mattered between Doug and Linda. Her background, his background — both were really ancient history to the Lowensteins. They had come of age in San Francisco in the early 1970s, when religion was more spiritual experimentation than dogma.

Camille's baptism was going to be just one little thing, Linda assured Doug. It doesn't mean we'll be going to church. It doesn't mean I'm going back to my roots. It doesn't mean anything other than it will get my mom off my back. Maria had taken charge of the christening, and Linda hadn't argued. Funny; usually she stood up to her mother. But this seemed important to Maria, and Linda didn't want to disappoint her. And what was baptism, after all? Maria reminded her, although it was hardly as if Linda had forgotten, that it was the first of the sacraments, a public commitment to raise a child within the church. The holy water — a sign of new life — would also purify the child of sin. These things were not only important, Maria said, they were essential. So she presented Linda with a choice: the baptism could be a special service, just for them, or be incorporated into Sunday mass. Linda opted for the Sunday mass. "I thought it would be less obtrusive," she says.

Doug, a doctor, thinks often in medical metaphors. He remembers it this way: Camille's christening would be like a shot, a vaccination. It would last for one painful instant, but he wouldn't have to deal with the issue again. "I guess once I rationalized it that way, it wasn't so bad," he says.

But Doug harbored deep reservations, about the baptism — and about Catholicism. Years before, he had gone to midnight mass every Christmas with Linda in a liberal Berkeley, California, parish. "I think I've spent more time in church than I ever did in shul," he says. "In synagogue I feel much more alien than in church. I'm not familiar with the rituals in synagogue. I don't know what's going on there. I didn't always feel comfortable in church, either — I'd sit and make jokes about the cross to Linda when we went. And she'd take it! But then I'd look at the ceremony where they're eating the host and drinking the wine. Basically this is supposed to be the body and blood of Christ. And I'd think, 'These people are really primitive.' It was like devil worship, only with Christ substituted for the devil." He laughs uncomfortably, then adds, "Judaism's primitive, too. All religions are, I guess. But some of this Catholic stuff . . ." He doesn't finish the sentence.

So Doug was hardly pleased when the priest summoned the Lowensteins to the altar for Camille's baptism. Linda, Doug, the baby's godmother, and Linda's father, Ernesto, who stood in as a proxy for the godfather, made their way up the aisle. Linda held Camille, who wore the same elaborate christening gown she herself had worn in the Philippines. As soon as they assembled before the priest, the baby began to fuss — she was hungry. But the baptism was under way, all eyes on the Lowensteins. "Do you denounce Satan in all his forms?" the priest intoned, looking at Linda. Her face flushed. Camille screamed. She shrieked. She squawked. The priest dabbed the baby's head with holy water and murmured soothing words, but Camille was not to be calmed. Linda was embarrassed. "I knew I'd made the wrong choice — we should at least have been there on a day without all those people," she says. "I felt so bad for my husband. It was really nice of him to go to church when I wanted him to go."

Doug never hinted at his displeasure. But beneath his calm demeanor he made a hardened vow: their next child would be raised a Jew. Linda concurred. "After Camille's I knew we could never do another baptism. We never discussed it. I mean, it's not fair. My husband's Jewish. I just assumed our second child would be, too." And so, when Linda and Doug adopted a newborn boy three years later, they gave him a Hebrew name, David. They felt a bris was unnecessary, since he had been circumcised shortly after birth. Their minds were made up, anyway: David would be Jewish, no question.

Linda and Doug say their decision — to raise one child as a Catholic, one as a Jew — raises eyebrows among friends and acquaintances. But to them, it does not seem strange. At an interfaith class at a local Jewish community center, Doug and Linda have met young Catholic-Jewish couples, just starting out, who ask them dozens of questions. They shrug most of them off; in their twenty-five years together, they say, religion has never surfaced as a problem. They attend this class because David, now seven, has started going to Hebrew school in preparation for his bar mitzvah, and they thought they could learn something about bringing him up as a Jew. Besides, they were curious about how other interfaith couples reared their children. "When people talk about how they're going to raise their kids and what kind of a home they're going to have, I realize we approached it in a half-assed manner," Linda says. "We didn't think about it at all. People there think it's the most unusual thing they've ever seen. We didn't decide to do this before the children were born; it just sort of happened. I think I still might have done an equal-time thing if David had been a girl. I don't feel guilty about what happened with Camille. What's done is done."

Ernesto Cruz, Linda's father, was born to a Catholic father and a mother who was a member of the Philippines' Protestant minority. His mother died when he was young, and his father's mother saw to it that he was reared with a proper Catholic foundation. As a teenager, he left his country for San Francisco, where older brothers lived. In America, religion lost its importance. Ernesto went to college and became an accountant; when World War II erupted, he served in the U.S. Army in the Philippines. When he met Maria de la Rosa in Manila, church suddenly re-entered his life.

For Maria, faith was a sustaining force. More than anything — her good looks, brains, or mercurial temperament — Catholicism defined her. The youngest of three daughters in a prominent family, Maria had a childhood marked by her father's swift financial ruin. Her two older sisters attended Catholic school. But when Maria turned six, her parents had to enroll her in public school. There wasn't enough money for three parochial school tuitions.

The decision had a lasting impact. Although she was denied a Catholic education, Maria vowed it would not hinder her in the observance of her faith. She learned what she needed at home: her mother, Rosario, certainly saw to that. Rosario said morning prayers, grace before meals, and afternoon prayers after lunch. After dark, the de la Rosas said vespers, or evening prayers. And, of course, there were blessings at bedtime. So inside their opulent church, its altar flecked with gold, there was little difference between Maria and her sisters. She knew everything they did, and could follow the Latin mass as well as anyone. She committed the prayers to memory, glancing at them in the daily missal when she needed, repeating them throughout the day, until she got them right.

During the war, the de la Rosas suffered, like other Filipinos, under the four-year Japanese occupation. Their home was the only place they felt safe, free of their invaders, and it was a virtual shrine. There were crucifixes, ceramic figurines of the saints, and pictures of Mary in her many incarnations. But most prominent was a statue of the Sacred Heart of Jesus: atop an elaborately carved pedestal sat a bare-headed Christ, a crown beside him, a scepter in his right hand. A red heart, wrapped with a ring of thorns, glowed from the center of his chest.

The U.S. Air Force bombed Manila repeatedly. The bombers aimed at Japanese military targets, which had been placed in crowded residential streets. When the de la Rosas heard the airplanes overhead, they fell to their knees before the Sacred Heart of Jesus and asked Christ for protection. Houses around them were destroyed, their inhabitants sometimes wounded. But the de la Rosas were spared. The family believed they owed their survival to the icon, the image of God's mercy and love for mankind, and to their unwavering faith.

Today, Maria Cruz is a tiny septuagenarian with a warm smile and a brisk manner. Her small apartment in suburban Maryland is testament to her devotion. The statue of the Sacred Heart, transported from her childhood home, rests squarely on the living room wall, illuminated by a large globed light. On the wall are figures of

Mary, the twelve apostles, tiny prayer cards tucked into picture frames. Photographs of Linda, Doug, Camille, and David smile from every tabletop.

Maria is a private person, reluctant to talk about her life. "What is there to tell?" she asks. On matters of her religion, however, she can go on for hours. When Maria was growing up, her mother hoped she would become a pharmacist. She could always find work that way, Rosario said. So Maria learned the trade and started at her first job after the war. But she was unfulfilled and longed for a life more spiritual than one mixing chemicals. She knew she helped people, but she sought something more. She wanted to become a nun.

Rosario sobbed when Maria spoke of her plans. How could Maria think of it? The convent was far from Manila, and Maria would be isolated there. The de la Rosas would never see her. Maria, disheartened by her mother's reaction, tearfully asked her parish priest for advice. "You cannot do it if you have doubts," he told her. She vowed to be as devout a layperson as she could be.

Months afterward, a friend set Maria up on a blind date with a young army sergeant, Ernesto Cruz. He was smitten by her and proposed marriage shortly after they met. They married in her family's church, on a balmy morning in March, and made their home on a U.S. Army base. Linda arrived ten months later.

From the moment she was born, Catholicism was woven deeply into Linda's life. It was part of her identity as a Filipina, as natural as getting dressed in the morning. From parochial school to eating fish on Fridays, Catholicism was a way of thinking and being. Linda's maternal relatives, in fact, observed customs women had practiced for centuries before them. They covered their faces with lace veils and sank to the floor to recite novenas. One aunt proceeded up the aisle on her knees in penance, a rosary draped around her wrist. Such devotion, for Linda, was part of the landscape.

Ernesto, eager to escape the desperation of postwar Manila, wanted to return to the United States quickly. He feared discrimination against the Japanese — and, in turn, all Asians — in California, where he had been raised and where his brothers still lived. Army friends lived in Chicago, and he believed he would have fewer problems there as a Filipino. So he, Maria, and Linda made their home in the city's North Side, on a leafy street near Lincoln Park, where there was a small Filipino community. Maria made a few friends within it. But she was homesick, and spent the long winters huddled in woolen sweaters, nursing colds. Everything was different in Chicago: the endless snowfall, the brick buildings, the fast pace of life. She had virtually nothing in common with her neighbors except Catholicism.

At church, everyone — Ernesto, Maria, and Linda — was happy. The Church of the Immaculate Conception, a stone Gothic structure near their house, was a lovely place. When Linda crossed herself before the life-size crucifix and found space in a pew, she was transported. Beneath the soaring arches and the watchful eyes of the gilded saints, she felt as if she were in the house of the Lord. Candles flickered in naves, and mass was said in Latin. The way the priests swooshed by in their cassocks, the brass incense holder clanging as they proceeded up the aisle — it all seemed so holy. During Chicago's humid summers, church was invigorating for the soul and the body; white marble floors kept the building cool.

As a girl, Linda found that even her free time reflected her faith. She played the organ in church, and when she invited her school friends over to play, their games often had religious themes. Once, she and her friends staged a rendition of Mary's crowning, a celebration in which children make flower crowns for the Virgin and lay them at the altar. In this case, the altar was Linda's dresser, where she kept a neat row of religious figurines. "I was pretty religious as a child," she says. But when puberty hit, her interest in her faith dropped abruptly. "Suddenly, going to church just wasn't cool anymore. I was going to Catholic high school already, and it just seemed too much."

Like all teenagers, Linda began to think about her place in the world, in her family, and among her friends. The church seemed to be the only thing she shared with her peers. In fact, Linda looks back on her Chicago childhood as the most isolated period of her life. She was an only child. Her mother worked, but her friends' mothers stayed at home; Linda went to their houses or to day care. She also suffered racial prejudice: the family of her first boyfriend, a Polish American, forbade the boy to date Linda because she wasn't white. They broke up, and Linda was devastated.

When she went to Northwestern University, she automatically gravitated toward people who, like her, were outside the Midwestern mainstream. "When I met Jewish people, they sort of appealed to me," she says. "I didn't exactly need an identity — I had one — but the people I met and became friends with after high school were always Jewish." Her best friend was Jewish. They looked alike, even spoke alike. "I don't know if I picked up her gestures, or she picked up mine," she says, "but people had a hard time telling us apart."

Linda lived at home, so her freedom was somewhat restricted — Maria kept a close watch on her. And although she longed to sleep in on Sunday mornings, she went along to mass. "My mother pretty much dragged me," she says. "By that point, I had really no interest in going." In fact, Maria wielded influence over the subjects her daughter studied at college. Maria was baffled by Linda's major, English literature, and insisted she take courses that would give her a skill. At the advice of some colleagues, Maria steered Linda toward courses in statistics and medical record-keeping. Hospitals have complex records departments and were always in need of organized minds. Study that, Maria urged. Linda reluctantly agreed.

After graduating from college — as an English major despite her mother — in 1969, Linda headed west, to San Francisco. "It was the center of the universe in those days," Linda says. She found a job in Oakland, in the records department of a large hospital. She was astonished at what she discovered in California. "It was the most freeing experience of my whole life," she says. Yet it had nothing to do with drugs, free love, or angry Vietnam protests. "There were Asians everywhere. I could walk down the street, and nobody would stop to look. Nobody would stop to say, 'What are you? Chinese or Japanese?' People just accepted you as this Asian person, and it was no big deal. In Chicago in those days, nobody even knew what a Filipino was. In San Francisco, nobody cared. It was like banging your head against a stone wall and then suddenly stopping. You didn't realize how much it hurt until it felt so good to be in California, among other Asians."

She loved her job — especially its atmosphere. She was one of a handful of women in a hospital full of young male doctors; her female colleagues, nurses and receptionists, were mostly middle-aged. "I was basically looking for a husband." She shrugs. "And I have to admit, in that hospital, it was like letting a kid loose in a candy store." She never lacked attention. She was pretty and gregarious, and made constant wisecracks. People couldn't place her accent, and guessed that anyone with so much chutzpah had to be a New Yorker. In particular, Doug Lowenstein, a resident from Detroit, found her irresistible. One day, awake for his thirtieth hour, he was in the cafeteria line, partly dazed, exhausted, and energized at once. He spotted Linda behind him and left his place among his colleagues in the queue to go talk to her. She told a joke — neither remember which one of her many — and he laughed. He sat down with his fruit salad and watched Linda bite into a taco. He was mesmerized, and so was she.

A few months later, they were living together. "We fit together like old shoes," Linda says. "I hate the way that sounds, but that's the way it was. Every relationship before had been up and down, insecure, and stormy. With him, we just fit together. We were like an old married couple — and I was only twenty-three. He was twenty-seven. I think it was because we were both raised with Midwestern values."

Doug scoffs when he hears "Midwestern values." The yelling and fighting he witnessed as a boy hardly seemed like "Midwestern values" to him. His house was full of conflict: over Doug's atheist grandfather, who lived nearby; over the lack of Judaism in his parents' home; over the upbringing of the three Lowenstein kids. A tall, broad-shouldered man, with a head of thick black curls and, incongruously, a dense white beard, Doug laughs often as he tells his family story. He insists that Jews and Judaism are distant from him, yet he dots his sentences with Yiddish. And not just "kvetch," and "shlock." He says his father knew Henry Ford before he made his fortune, back when Ford rode the streetcar like any ordinary Detroit "shmegegge." "My dad claimed he was just a shmendrick," Doug says.

His work as a research oncologist — quietly puzzling out the complexities of various cancers — seems a logical fit. Growing up, he retreated into the background as much as he could. He stayed out of his family's many quarrels and tried not to be noticed. "I got to be pretty unflappable," he says. There was so much door-slamming, and name-calling, he had to, if only in self-defense.

Doug's father, Stanley, the son of religious Polish Jews, was born in Baltimore. His job as a postal worker and union organizer took him to Detroit, where he met and married Minnie Friedman. Their marriage was troubled from the start. Stanley constantly harangued his Minnie over her lackadaisical approach to Judaism. "He was always razzing her, 'You don't keep a Jewish house,'" Doug says. To Minnie, however, this was something of a compliment.

Minnie was the favorite child of her father, George, a Russian-born Jew who fled the pogroms. She was his mother's namesake and the most like him in looks and temperament. She shared his atheism and his distaste for organized religion. While his other four daughters became devout Jews, George applauded Minnie's non-kosher kitchen and her secular kids. When Stanley insisted that Doug and his older brother Roger become bar mitzvahs, Minnie agreed only reluctantly. They celebrated Passover, Rosh Hashanah, and Yom Kippur each year, but not in their own home. Doug barely remembers those times as holidays. "I know they were, but it didn't make a big impression," he says. "We were always shlepping across town to the Jewish part, where one of my aunts lived. They were real Jews over there." Minnie avoided preparing for holidays, preferring to let her sisters cook and clean for family dinners. The one holy day the family did observe at home, with guests, was Yom Kippur. That way, Minnie didn't have to cook.

The Lowensteins, in fact, celebrated Christmas. They didn't have a tree, but they did exchange gifts. Hanukkah was a minor holiday. Once or twice the family lit a menorah. Doug seems to remember spinning the dreidel, but he can't be sure. What did all that matter? He was more interested in fitting in, both in school and in his neighborhood of Italian Catholics and German Protestants. Doug says emphatically that few of his neighbors and classmates knew he was Jewish; then he changes his mind. "Maybe they did, because of the name. And because I didn't go to catechism classes or whatever they were." He hated Yom Kippur for that reason alone: it was a dead giveaway. Why else would he be missing school?

Yet Doug says he never encountered anti-Semitism. In his early years, he tried to keep his head down: among his neighbors, in school, as a member of his family. Painfully modest, he reveals many details of his family life yet few of himself. Those, Minnie happily provides. Now eighty-seven, and living in an apartment near Doug and Linda, she glides into conversation about her husband and children. She insists she has trouble remembering, yet seems to recall old family events with ease. It is easy to see that Minnie's word, in her household, was the law. She is tall and trim, with sharp dark eyes, and her dyed brown hair is swept up with hairspray. "My walking's for the dogs," she announces when she enters the room on Linda's arm. A few minutes later, she springs up to play the piano: "I Could Have Danced All Night" and the theme from "Love Story." She sings, too, in a strong, high falsetto that belies her years.

Stanley has been dead for many years, almost a decade. But the sting of his problems with her family is close to the surface. "Achh," she says, waving her hand. She changes the subject, asking whether Doug had mentioned that he won the citywide competition for "Boy Mayor" of Detroit when he was in high school. He had not said so, as a matter of fact. "Well, he did," she says, her eyes open wide. "He didn't even tell his father and me. We found out from the paper!"

Surely it is easier to recount Doug's triumphs than Stanley's perceived failures. Minnie's relatives looked down on her and Stanley, and let them both know their feelings in no uncertain terms. "They were in show business," Minnie says proudly. Doug later translates this: the family owned movie theaters.

At any rate, Stanley was working class; Minnie's sisters were "high society," as Doug puts it. They were observant Jews; Minnie was not. Stanley, of course, wanted to be more devout — he even wanted to move to the sisters' predominantly Jewish neighborhood. Not to be near them, of course, but to be near other Jews, within walking distance of a shul. But Minnie would have none of it. There was nothing wrong with their house. She got along with the neighbors just fine, never had any trouble. Besides, her father lived close by.

Doug wanted to play football like his older brother — he certainly had the build — but Minnie put her foot down. She and Stanley argued about that. He was her studious son, and she wasn't going to have him risking injury in something so frivolous as sports. He was going to be a doctor. "He could have hurt his hands in that game," Minnie says, as if she is still shocked by the idea. "What if he wanted to be a surgeon? Not my Douggie." He didn't argue. He wanted to be a doctor, too, almost more than he wanted to play football. He liked school, and was good at it. "I was a pretty compulsive student," he confesses. The only day he missed in twelve grades was Yom Kippur, each year.

Doug's bar mitzvah, given the family dynamics, was more of a "major deal" than other events with relatives. He prepared for the occasion at a "minor-league shul" not too far from his house. For nine months he studied the Hebrew necessary to get him through the day, and for nine months he dreaded it. Minnie says Doug was such a good student, and learned so quickly, that the rabbi hoped Doug would go on to rabbinical school. Despite her nonchalance about other Jewish matters, she reveals this with great pride.

Indeed, Minnie was deeply invested in Doug's success. She shies from this interpretation, but it does seem as though there was competition: she wanted her sisters to see that her son, the Hebrew whiz, could perform as well as theirs with less than half the preparation. And she also wanted to show that she could plan a festivity that would meet their standards. When the day came, Doug recalls, his parents were actually happy. "I gave my little spiel after my haftarah reading, and it was all okay."

Things often got so bad at home that Stanley would leave Minnie for the weekend. He had a small family, two much older sisters and his parents. One sister, whom Stanley adored, lived in Chicago. On weekends, he'd pack the kids in the car and drive to see her. All the way there, Stanley would complain to Doug, then a teenager, about Minnie. During the week, Minnie spoke disparagingly of Stanley to Doug. "I just sort of listened to them both," he says.

The trips to Chicago revealed something else. Time with his aunt made Doug see how much Jewish culture meant to Stanley. They'd go to Jewish delis and bakeries to stock up on herring, lox, and bagels — all the things Minnie refused to buy. Often, Stanley spoke Yiddish to his sister. Minnie knew the language as well — she and Stanley sometimes spoke it while arguing so that the kids wouldn't understand — but to his sister, the words came out warmly, without sarcasm. On pleasant days — Stanley took the children to Chicago more and more as Doug grew up — they would sit outside on his aunt's stoop. School let out for the summer earlier in Detroit than it did in Chicago, and Doug remembers afternoons in early June when he would watch little Catholic girls, with their braids and pleated skirts, stroll two by two down the sidewalk to their school, St. Peter's. Little did he know that his future wife was among them. It was Linda's school.

During his college years, Doug lived at home to save money. Once he got to medical school, at the University of Michigan, he took to the freedom of life on his own: without tension, without constant anger. For the first time outside Hebrew school, he met Jews his own age. "It was nice," he says, and smiles. But he wasn't attracted to any Jewish women. Without being asked, he quickly adds, "My girlfriends were *definitely* non-Jewish."

After med school, Doug got a coveted internship in Oakland. "Everybody wanted to be in California," he says. "I got lucky." He loved San Francisco and did his best to be hip, part of the scene. He moved into an apartment near Haight-Ashbury with three long-haired guys. "They would light up joints at eight in the morning," Doug says. "It's a wonder I got through that internship." He stayed away from the recreational drugs of his hippie friends — his schedule left little time for recreational anything — but he certainly looked like them. He let his curly hair grow and sprouted the beard he still has. He may have had to wear surgical greens all day, but at least he could walk to work in his favorite clothes: a red polyester shirt, bell-bottom pants, and a tight-fitting leather jacket. He opposed the Vietnam War and even visited a Berkeley attorney who worked with conscientious objectors. In the end, Doug was never called into service, but he dreaded the mail every day. As a doctor, he wanted to save lives, not see them wasted around him.

"It's fair to say I was experimenting at that point in my life," he says. "I just loved it out there. I loved the fact that there were different people, especially Asians. What did I know? I liked Chinese food. That made me interested in Asian culture? Eventually I wised up, learned more about other Asian cultures. And I definitely was attracted to the women, no question."

When Doug met Linda that day at lunch, he was immediately drawn to her mane of black hair, her dark eyes, her sultry laugh. The more she talked, though, the more he realized she had something much more profound than good looks and quick wit. "She had this fast, sarcastic sense of humor. She had Jewish friends. She really identified with Jewish culture. She'd spent a lot of time with Jewish people. So she was Asian, which attracted me initially, sure. It was just so interesting, from my point of view, so exotic. But she also had this knowledge of Jews. The irony was, she was as Jewish as any Jew I'd ever met."

They moved in with each other right away and turned their apartment into what Doug says was "a cool pad." They strung plastic beads in the doorways and stalked the import warehouses near the pier for inexpensive Indian decorations: engraved brass candlesticks, woven rugs, wall hangings of elephants. Linda burned cones of incense in ashtrays.

That their son was living with a Catholic woman in San Francisco hardly fazed Minnie and Stanley Lowenstein. Doug was a doctor, and they were thrilled. "I was a little disappointed he didn't take up with a Jewish girl," Minnie says, "but then I met Linda. And once I saw how nice she kept the apartment, I couldn't complain."

Maria and Ernesto Cruz, however, were not quite so pleased. "It wasn't that Doug was Jewish," Linda insists. "It was just fine with my mom that I was dating this nice Jewish doctor. But she was livid when she found out we were living together, absolutely enraged." Sex before marriage? Linda was living in sin. What she was doing went against everything Maria had taught her. More to the point, everything the church had taught her. How could Linda do such a thing?

During their conversations, Maria would cry into the telephone, "Please, Linda, make an honest woman of yourself. Marry the man." She had other concerns, too. A fellow pharmacist who was Jewish told Maria how disappointed he was when his son married a Gentile woman. When he found out, he told Maria, he wanted to commit suicide. But he had come to know his daughter-in-law and to like her. "And he told my hysterical mother this — supposedly to make her feel better!" After Maria heard that, she told Linda her relationship with Doug was doomed. "You're not getting any younger," she warned. "He's going to leave you for someone Jewish." Linda hardly needed her mother's prodding or any extra worries. She wanted to get married, too, although she never let her mother know. Month after month, Linda would beg Doug, "Marry me, marry me."

But whenever she brought the subject up, Doug laughed it off. Marriage, to him, was his parents' miserable union: always arguing about money, about his father's station in life, about who was a good Jew. Linda thought at least part of the problem was the fact that she wasn't Jewish. She certainly expected the Lowensteins to disapprove. After her experience with her Polish boyfriend, she knew anything could happen. But Doug insisted his parents weren't like that. Their only conflicts were with each other. They liked the outside world just fine.

After four years of living together, Doug and Linda finally did get married, in a simple ceremony at New York's City Hall. Doug had an oncology fellowship in Manhattan, and somehow, at thirty-one, he didn't find the idea so bad after all. Ernesto and Maria, upset that the wedding wasn't in a church, rushed to New York nevertheless. "I was just thrilled he would marry me," says Linda. "Four years of bugging this person! I didn't care if we got married in a Dumpster at that point." Doug laughs. "It's a surprise I got married at all."

The Lowensteins moved to suburban Washington, where Doug had a fellowship at the National Institutes of Health. Linda enrolled in law school at Georgetown University. Indeed, good fortune seemed to befall Doug and Linda in all but one respect. Year after year, their hopes of having a baby were dashed. When in vitro fertilization became available, Linda "lined up at the door," she says. Doug's connections gave Linda access to top doctors. But ten years of drugs, procedures, and surgery failed. "Once you get sucked into that merry-go-round, you know all the people in the offices, all the other people going through the same thing. It becomes your social life. It becomes your identity, almost."

Throughout that sad decade, Maria implored Linda to fall back on her faith. Maybe the reason she couldn't conceive was that she hadn't been married in the church, Maria suggested. God wouldn't sanction her marriage until a priest officiated. Perhaps then she'd have a baby. Linda was desperate. She'd try anything, and arranged a ceremony in Georgetown's chapel. To be fair, she arranged for a Jewish ceremony, too. She found a rabbi who would preside, and she and Doug married, for a third time, beneath a makeshift chuppah in the basement chapel of a church.

Linda doesn't remember praying for a baby in those days, but she is sure Maria did. Maria made it clear: if only Linda would put more faith in God — and show it by going to church — God would take care of her. Sitting in the pew, Maria said, you think of God's sacrifice, his only son on the cross. Just maybe, Linda might return to mass.

Indeed, as much as Linda wanted a baby of her own, she was not drawn back to the church. Church seemed too structured, too regulated. She could have a relationship with God without going to mass. And besides, she hated always to ask God for something. That was one of the many things she disliked about her faith. "In Catholicism, you're always praying for this or praying for that," she says. "I feel uncomfortable doing that. It's one thing to thank him for giving me a nice life — I do that sometimes — but it's another to always be saying, 'Please God, let this happen.'"

She pauses. "God, to me, is more like a loving father than an angry God, telling me to go to church. The God I learned about in all of those years of Catholic school is not the God I know. That's not God, with all those rules. The whole layer — of church, church administration, hierarchy, and that whole intervening religion stuff, whether it's Episcopal or Catholic or Jewish — it's just not the way for me to go. I don't need someone telling me the rules of how to relate to God. The God I know is there, and I'll pray to him if I need him. And maybe I *should* be going to church. But I can't bring myself to say, 'Well, I should go to church; otherwise I'm not a good Catholic.' I consider myself a Catholic. My mother doesn't, because I don't go to church, but who is she to say? Whoever's in charge, in every religion, they become rigid and get hung up on their administrative rules. I think they become more of an obstacle to God than a path to God.

"I consider myself Catholic, I consider myself a believer, and I find it a very sustaining faith. When I need God, I can talk to him. But I don't feel the need to go to mass on Sundays. I don't even feel the need to go on Christmas, on holidays. This is amazing to my mother. She is devastated by it."

All that dogma, all that guilt. Who needs it? She shrugs. What about the prayers? Is anything left over from Catholicism, anything at all? There is just one little thing, she says. She doesn't particularly like to fly, and she doesn't drink. So when she boards an airplane, she recites three Hail Marys before taking off. When the plane starts its descent, she says three more. It helps calm her down, almost like a mantra. And, every year, starting on November 30, she whispers the Novena of St. Andrew — a prayer thanking God for Christ's birth — as she car-pools past the tinseled malls in her minivan. Sometimes she forgets and skips a day. But she starts the recitations with nothing but good intentions.

The Lowensteins celebrate many holidays: Hanukkah, Christmas, Easter, Passover. At Rosh Hashanah, Linda prepares a brisket, tzimmes, and apples with honey. For Hanukkah, the family eats all eight nights in the dining room, where a modern ceramic menorah rests in the window, facing the street. Linda likes to separate the holidays; they are different, and should be treated as such. Every year, she makes sure she doesn't make a bigger deal out of Christmas than Hanukkah. Although to hear Camille and David tell it, they actually prefer Hanukkah: more presents. Still, it's not fair, Linda says. How can a humble menorah compete with a sparkling Christmas tree? Latkes and applesauce are nice, but face it: kids prefer Christmas cookies and candy canes. Every year, as the leaves start to turn, Linda flips her calendar page to December. If she's lucky, Hanukkah ends a few days before Christmas, in time for her to put a tree up in the living room.

Just as rearing their children in two different faiths came to pass without planning, so too did celebrating Christian and Jewish holidays. Doug and Linda sometimes skirted the issue of a Christmas tree by visiting the Cruzes for the holiday. When Camille arrived, Linda decided they needed to celebrate the day for her. So they bought a little tree and decorated it with only lights. "We passed it off as a Hanukkah bush," Doug says, scowling. But each year the tree got bigger and the ornaments more elaborate. Although he had grown up exchanging Christmas presents with his siblings, Doug found that a tree in his own house just crossed a line.

In fact, Doug dislikes any kind of Christmas exhibit. Linda and Maria used to string lights outside, on Doug and Linda's patio. The Lowensteins live in a wooded suburb, and their house is set back far from the street. But still, such an "ostentatious display," as Doug puts it, sets his teeth on edge.

"I guess a big tree is just too much of an open symbol of Christianity," he says. "I'm not a hundred percent comfortable with it. You can see my bias. We have a menorah in the window. I mean, it's clear. I'm Lowenstein. I'm Jewish."

Linda prefers to focus on Thanksgiving, which everyone can share. Ernesto, Maria, and Minnie come over, and they all share a big turkey supper. But it's exhausting, frankly, to keep up with everything, all the holidays, all the kids' activities. Ever since Camille was born, Linda has stayed at home with the children, volunteering in their classrooms, taking them to and from music lessons and soccer practice and, now, religious school.

When Camille was in second grade, she had some trouble with learning. Doctors diagnosed her with Attention Deficit Disorder, and suggested that she might fare better in a place more structured than the crowded classroom of her public school. After many stops and starts in different private schools, a friend mentioned a respected Catholic school, St. Margaret's, where Camille could receive the extra attention she needed. With some reservations, the Lowensteins enrolled her there. "It's worked out real well," Linda says, a bit sheepishly. "It's as academically demanding as a private school, it costs a lot less, and it has a nurturing attitude the other schools don't have. Plus it has a culture I understood."

Once Camille started putting on her blue jumper and saddle shoes every morning, Linda found memories of her own Catholic school trickling back. She began to notice little things she had forgotten, like the respect parochial school students show for their teachers. When she volunteered, she saw how quiet the kids were. "You could hear a pin drop in those rooms," she says. In David's noisy public school, the kids — not the teachers — seem in control. And then Camille started talking about things like the Golden Rule. At public school, Linda thought, this would never happen. Maybe St. Margaret's wasn't such a bad idea after all. "I wasn't seeking it, but I'm glad I found it. There's no gentleness in a public school. The kids are really into being hip and cool and all that, but they're not taught to be kind to one another. Camille gets a strong infusion of values at Catholic school.

"When you're trying to adopt children, you have to go through a home study. You have to write down what you want for your children, how you would raise them. And I always said I would instill values. But it was all words. I didn't really know how I'd do that. When I see what she is getting at Catholic school, I see she's being taught moral values — not necessarily religious values. I hope some of those stay with her even if she rejects the religious part of it."

But Camille seems interested in her school. She likes it; so much so that she even wears her saddle shoes on the weekends. She has a long, lithe frame, and her skin, the hue of tea with cream, is soaked with a perfume she got for her birthday. "Did I put too much on?" she asks, waving the air in front of her. She seems to know the answer.

Camille, almost twelve, is in that awkward transition between baby sitters and boyfriends. Not a child, not a woman, she seems torn by her interests. When she describes something, she promises to show it later. She heads upstairs to fetch her treasures — a tiny plastic angel, a soccer trophy, a cardboard box of glass unicorns. When she talks about religion, she is unequivocal: "I'm Christian." She pauses. "I guess I'll end up a Christian, and my brother's a Jewish boy." She says this matter-of-factly as she fidgets with a metal contraption that changes shape with the flick of her wrist. "It's an orb." She stares in amazement. How could anyone not know?

Camille, like other Catholic children, took her first communion at eight. At seven or eight, children are largely seen as able to distinguish right from wrong, sin from good deed. They are expected to make their first confession at the time of their first communion, since at that age they are also able to express their faults. Camille remembers the event happily. It was a lovely spring Sunday, and she got to wear a pretty dress. "All white," she says, her hands sculpting the air into imaginary flounces. "It was great," she says. "We had a special mass, and we walked in a parade at school."

St. Margaret's is fun, Camille says. "Well, for *school*." She goes through the routine of her day: before the Pledge of Allegiance, her class says a prayer. They say three Hail Marys, one Our Father, and then pray for someone who is sick or needy. Over the intercom, the principal greets the students warmly, and, on Mondays, gives the "value of the week." "Sometimes it's kindness, sometimes it's responsibility, sometimes it's honesty," Camille says. "Or we hear, 'Be thoughtful. Pray for So-and-so.'" Does she? Camille nods emphatically.

On this April day, just past Easter and Passover, she is asked whether there is any confusion over these holidays at her house. She shakes her head. "I do Easter at school," she says. "We go to mass and have an Easter egg contest there. But Passover, we do at home. We read this book and we have spices and herbs and we leave an extra place for that guy. What's his name? Elijah? Oh, yeah, that's it."

David, clad in his Little League uniform, sits cuddled next to Linda on the couch. In a few years, she says, he will be self-conscious about his affection for her and hers for him. She soaks it up while she can. He has almond-shaped brown eyes, a cleft chin, and a delightful wide, gap-toothed smile. David is too young to realize the difference between his faith and his sister's. But he does know he has Hebrew school on Sundays, when Camille has free time. She is quick to remind him that she has religion class at St. Margaret's, so they're even. He grins when asked what it means to be Jewish.

As quickly as his tongue can get around the words, he answers, "*Baruch atah adonai, eloheinu melech ha'olam . . .*"
Then he asks, "Am I done, Mom?" and darts off.

Doug wonders about his children's religious separation. "If you think about it long enough, you'd have to agree there might be problems. The kids could become confused at some point. If that happens, it could put some pressure on us; we'd question whether we've done the right thing. We both feel they need something, some kind of religious background. We believe that. If it was up to me I'd do nothing, and I don't know if Linda would've done anything, either.

"I think if I'd pushed Linda, she'd have converted. But the fact is that I didn't; I left the door open. And then her mother was a catalyst. Camille now obviously identifies herself as a Christian. She *is* a Christian. Linda wanted me to talk about it before we had kids. I guess I didn't feel it was that important at the time. I do that — put things off. And by putting it off, it got done for me. The decision got made for me and for Camille. I readily admit it was a railroad job. It was certainly not my choice. But I acquiesced. I wasn't happy about it, but I didn't put my foot down, either."

Doug crosses one leg over the other and shifts uneasily in his chair. He studies his hands. And so it is that the guy who never wanted anyone to know he was Jewish, who has spent more time in church than in synagogue, who baptized his daughter, and who drives off to work on Yom Kippur, feels somehow sad about being left out of the Jewish fold.

Children change everything. The arrival of a baby forces parents to confront their religious legacies, to reconsider decisions made long ago, and to revisit the spiritual dilemmas of their own youth. For Doug Lowenstein, his interest in raising a Jewish child was sparked by the most curious of circumstances — his mother-in-law's demands to baptize his first child.

At fifty-two, near the end of the century, Doug sees himself and his legacy much differently from the way he did in the turbulent years of the late 1960s. He acknowledges the logical inconsistencies of what he and Linda have done with their children. "It's important, for me, to be Jewish. But Linda doesn't have to be Jewish. And if Linda doesn't have to be Jewish, Camille doesn't have to be Jewish. But that's contradictory, I guess, because the next kid *had* to be Jewish. Having a child pushes buttons." He shrugs. "It makes you think in ways you didn't before you had them."

EIGHT

Outside Looking In

§

E RIC MUELLER sits in his living room in suburban Chicago, steely James Bond jaw getting stiffer by the moment. A Midwesterner of Swedish, German, and Irish stock, he says the first thing that sums up his background is this: "I'm an American." The description fits. Blond, blue-eyed, tall, and broad-shouldered, Eric played football in high school and rowed in his Ivy League university crew. Raised outside Chicago, he spent long weekends playing on his grandparents' farm. His idea of exotic food, as a child, was his mother's Swedish meatballs.

"I don't think heavily about what my ethnic background is. It's just not something that's in the forefront of my mind, ever. I consider myself an American and I like to think of everybody else here as American, too, and that's it. If they're other things, that's nice, but that's subsidiary. And I've learned the hard way that it isn't that way with the Jews." His expression is incredulous.

"I have Jewish business partners who've known me for years professionally, and then somehow they find out my wife is Jewish. And suddenly I'm more accepted. It's like, 'Oh! Now you're a real person! Before I just thought you were kind of bright, but now that I know this about you . . .' I think, 'Shit, why should I be evaluated like this? Why can't I just be more accepted as a business associate?' It really bothers me. I think that's a little bit of what separates people."

He pauses, drapes one long leg over the other, and continues. "Another thing that bothers me is that all Rachel's friends are

Jewish. Why is that? Are my friends Swedish? Are my friends German? No! My friends are Italian, they're Irish, they're Jewish, they're everything. I don't even think about what they are."

Eric, a banker, has no desire to belong to any "tribe," as he puts it. He finds it baffling that his wife, Rachel, felt an instant kinship with his Jewish secretary, merely because they share a heritage. In conversations, Eric says he empathizes with the fears, anxieties, and insecurities that Jews feel as a tiny minority in a predominantly Christian country. As much as he has embraced his wife's wishes to raise their children as Jews, he himself feels very removed from the rituals and shared assumptions of even "cultural" Jews.

Eric and Rachel's union is among the most complex of inter-faith marriages. When Eric divorced his first wife and began dating Rachel, he was already the father of three children, whom he was raising as Christians. The home he left was steeped in the traditions in which he had been raised. He dressed up like Santa on Christmas mornings. On Easter, he got up early and hid the eggs his children had dyed the night before. Now, his three oldest children, Caroline, Eva, and John, live nearby with their mother and spend weekends with Eric and Rachel. The children dote on their baby half-sister, Emma, eighteen months, and newborn half-brother, Andrew, who are Rachel and Eric's children. At Rachel's insistence, Emma and Andrew are being raised as Jews. Emma had a naming ceremony when she was a few weeks old; Andrew had a ritual circumcision.

Rachel and Eric walk a logistical and spiritual tightrope. Consider a typical weekend. Caroline, Eva, and John arrive Friday evening just as Rachel, a financial analyst who works from a home office, is preparing a Shabbat meal. She says the Hebrew prayer over the candles, and the family sits down for dinner. Sunday morning, Eric or his ex-wife takes the three oldest children to Sunday school or mass. How well does this "blended family" work? Eric and Rachel wonder themselves. It seems fine for now. But what will happen when Emma and Andrew grow and ask questions about the Christmas trees, stockings, and Easter baskets that their siblings enjoy? Will a family's normal tensions and rivalries be sharpened by the difference in religion? Will either set of children ever feel truly at ease about their faiths?

Rachel, a slender, athletic woman in her mid-thirties, with blue-green eyes and straight black hair, says that her first marriage, to Sam, a "nice Jewish boy," was all but preordained. His background mirrored hers: each grew up near a big city, she in New York, he in Chicago. Each attended a Jewish summer camp as a child; each family was prominent in its congregation.

"For most of my life, being Jewish was something that was done for me," she says. "It's not something I ever had to think about." Her older sister and brother became bat and bar mitzvah with elaborate ceremonies, but as Rachel approached thirteen, she declined the experience altogether. "I just didn't feel like it." She laughs; teenage folly. "I didn't like Hebrew school." Looking back, she sees it was the one thing, in her early life as a Jew, that *she* decided.

The next Jewish milestone — her first wedding — was yet another event that went according to someone else's plan. "It was a typical Jewish princess affair with a gazillion people at a nice hotel," she says. "My mother organized the whole thing, and Sam wanted to invite everyone he'd ever known. My mother has extraordinary taste, and it was a beautiful wedding, but I ended up feeling as though I were an actress in her play. I had this big beautiful white dress and way more people than I wanted to have. I felt incredibly guilty about all the money we were spending. I was uncomfortable about the whole thing. But somehow it happened anyway, and I ended up feeling totally detached from it all."

She and Sam moved to Chicago and attended Sam's Reform temple, an ornate building along the shores of Lake Michigan. Although Rachel's family also belonged to a Reform congregation, she had become disdainful of Reform services as an adult. "They just seem so far from the essence of Judaism," she says. This one was even more "high church," as she puts it, than most. It was among the many things that led her to start doubting the marriage, because Sam didn't see her point. "In that suburb, everybody's

Jewish and really, really rich. That place kind of nauseated me, especially on the High Holy Days. I don't like going places on the High Holy Days where you feel underdressed."

Soon enough, the marriage faltered, and she and Sam divorced. She began dating Eric, whom she had met through her work. It was then that, for the first time in her life, Judaism became "front and center," she says.

Nowhere but in education — they had both attended Ivy League schools as undergraduate and graduate students — did their lives overlap. His paternal grandparents, of German, Irish, and Scottish origin, had been in the United States for generations. His maternal grandparents, to whom he was very close, settled on the harsh plains of southern Illinois as farmers, miles from the nearest neighbor. Rachel's grandparents, Jewish emigrants from Russia and Hungary, crowded into tenement apartments in New York City, where they lived alongside thousands of other newcomers struggling to make their way in their new country.

Eric's upbringing, he says, was "American." Sure, some things were rooted in Swedish tradition — what the Muellers ate at holiday meals, mostly — but Eric never saw their customs as anything but wholly American. As a child, Eric spent a lot of time with his Swedish grandfather, a weathered dairy farmer with a fondness for pickled herring and earthy dark bread. When he speaks of him, Eric's face softens. Some years ago, Eric took his grandfather to Sweden for his ninetieth birthday, in part so that he could once again see his village and in part to say good-bye. Even as an old man, ill and frail, his grandfather retained a quiet dignity and stubborn independence that made a deep impression on Eric.

He remembers fondly his grandfather's love and reverence for the outdoors, and recalls lazy summer days on Wisconsin's lakes, where his grandfather taught him to fish. When the two set out together, poles and worms at the ready, hours on the little green rowboat would pass with few words between them. "But I knew it was there," Eric says, of his grandfather's affection. One warm afternoon, Eric sat with his head dangling over the boat, waiting and watching through the clear pond. Suddenly a fat bluegill leaped at his line but darted away with the worm before Eric could pull up his pole. "Grandpa! Grandpa!" he shouted, distraught. His grandfather smiled and shook his head. He conveyed his regret silently, by pressing a bright yellow butterscotch into his grandson's palm.

Rachel always felt on the fringe of American society. Raised in a predominantly Catholic suburb, Rachel was aware, even in New York, that she was an outsider. "There was always something to remind you that you weren't a part of the main culture," she says. In elementary school, teachers asked Rachel, their only Jewish student, to go from class to class each December to explain Hanukkah. It infuriated her. "I couldn't understand why they didn't assign this to some nice Catholic kid who might just end up learning about it. It was a lazy, sloppy way to do it. They could easily have expanded the mind of someone else." Her voice is full of disgust.

Being Jewish, however, was only a part of why she felt isolated. A brilliant student, she found her schoolwork unchallenging. Several days a month, Rachel would complain of a sore throat, even if she felt fine. It was "code," she says, which enabled her to stay home and read. Her parents, who had set high goals for their children, never discouraged these "sick days." They figured that her forays into literature were more valuable than what she would be learning in the classroom. So, as a teenager, she transferred to a private school in New York City, where many of the students were Jewish. "It was full of a lot of really overprivileged kids from the Upper East Side," she says of the experience, "but to me it was nice to be around people who valued intellectual and cultural pursuits. I felt much more at home with those people."

It was their religious conundrum, and not their cultural disquiet, that consumed much of Eric and Rachel's early days together. "It had always been very clear to me that I would marry someone Jewish, that I would have a Jewish home," Rachel says. And then, suddenly, there was Eric — who not only was not Jewish, but who had already established a very Christian household. Rachel's sense of Jewishness became a focal point of their conversations. "As I recall, he said, 'Clearly this is a big issue for you, and clearly we should raise the kids we have someday as Jews. I think we should all be on the same program.'"

Eric didn't consider it much of an issue at the time. "It was no big deal," he says. "I said right up front: 'Look, we can raise our kids Jewish. That doesn't bother me at all. I'll even look into conversion myself.'" Eric's parents, a Lutheran and a Catholic, reconciled their religious differences by rearing their children in the Episcopal church. Yet as an adult Eric found a lot he disliked about the faith. "I've always had a fundamental disagreement with the basic tenets of Christianity. I've always been uncomfortable with a lot of the teachings — the necessity of believing in a certain son of God. Certain of the basic factual, historical details I just don't buy into."

He attended an introduction-to-Judaism class with Rachel at a local Reconstructionist synagogue. He liked the course and the rabbi, but he was immediately surprised by a number of things. First, he and Rachel attended services sporadically. "That's very different from the way I was brought up. In some ways that's good and in some ways that's bad; regular attendance forces a little discipline and a little thought every week. You can't let it slide or not discuss it or not think about it. If you don't go to church, at least for an Episcopalian, you're kind of missing the boat."

As a child, he adhered to a stiff Sunday schedule: he got up, ate breakfast, put on his best clothes, combed his hair neatly, and went to church. Friday evening services feel so different, occurring at night, after one of the busiest workdays of the week.

There were more remarkable contrasts, too. When they attended High Holy Day services together for the first time, Eric was shocked to learn that they had to pay for their seats. "You've got to shell out big bucks to attend the High Holy Day services. That's just standard! And then, to join a synagogue — you have to pay to do that, too. It just amazes me! The financial pressures of being a Jew are tremendous. There's a requirement, if you're going to be active in your temple: you will do this. The whole thing about money, and forcing money from the collective — it's mind-boggling to me. Maybe it's my independent streak. I rib my Jewish friends; that's where they get their liberal tax-and-spend classical Democratic stuff. I'm amazed by that.

"It's very different from passing around the collection plate, because when a plate comes around, you can choose to participate or not. It's generally a small contribution you make. And it's totally up to the individual. It's personal choice, personal responsibility. In Judaism I sense a lot less of that. There are rules; they're aggressive and you must play by them. From a financial point of view — I just don't think financial aspects should play a role in religion, but then the Vatican is one of the greatest business organizations in the world. The whole subject I'm just adamantly against. I don't think religion should mix with business."

Rachel reminds Eric that they had to pay for their seats only before they became members of the congregation. "The reason they charge is that they don't want people to come just for the High Holy Days."

"What's wrong with that?" Eric asks.

"The point is, we'll make it expensive for you to come just once a year, because we want you to come more often, to be part of our congregation year round."

"Well, forcing people into financial obligations doesn't seem to me the right way to do that. Religion is a personal thing, and if someone wants to attend a particular service, he should be free to do that. It shouldn't have anything to do with his or her financial condition."

They pause briefly and let the subject pass. But it's clear that the more Eric found out about Judaism, the less he was inclined to convert. "What I've learned is, though I thought Judaism was a religion, that's only part of it. And for many people it's just a very, very small part. The majority of it is clearly ethnic and cultural heritage, and tradition that's really not religious. And that's much harder for me. It's like changing who I am, or giving up some of my personal history. It's one thing to talk about a philosophy I'm comfortable with. I can deal with that and participate in that. But I've found that being a Jew is not converting. You're never really a Jew just because you believe in some of the principles of Judaism.

"I'm not sure I'll ever feel totally accepted, or that I'll ever feel I could truly be an insider. But then again I'm also uncomfortable giving up my ethnic heritage, where I come from and the tradition in our family. That's all just who I am. I've been surprised how much that defines being a Jew. I didn't know that before. And I don't know where I'll come out on this.

"I've learned enough about the Jewish religion that I'm very comfortable with it. But you know, you can definitely get a sense of how people are reacting, whether it's just a look of 'What's this guy doing here?'" — Eric sweeps the air over his large frame — "or 'Who's this? He's definitely not part of the program.' You can definitely feel it.

"And it feels kind of funny. I don't find it real troublesome or painful, but it does exist. I'm sure it's happened in my life before, but if it did I wouldn't have cared. Because now with Rachel and our family, I think I want more to be accepted than before. Before, if I wasn't accepted, well, I didn't give a damn. Who cares?" Eric laughs uncomfortably.

"I'm getting more and more worried about it," he says. "My secretary, Amy, is Jewish and she's real funny. I try to think what it is I like about Amy: she's bright and intense and verbal and talkative and wants to sort things out, and I need that in business. Rachel and Amy are always on the phone together. Amy always says, 'I just love talking to Rachel,' or 'Oh, just a minute, I'm talking to Rachel.' And I'm, like, 'We've got work to do; stop talking to Rachel!' I asked her one time, 'Why do you guys talk so much?' And she said, 'Because we're so simpatico,' or something like that. And I said, 'Why is that, Amy?' She said, 'Well, she's like me. We're all the same. You know, one of the tribe.' I said, 'Wait a minute, come on, that's the kind of crap that drives me nuts.'"

Rachel tries to explain to Eric why Jews sometimes feel instant connection with other Jews. "It's a cultural thing," she says. "There are women who are very outspoken, women who are very reserved, women who are traditionally feminine, and women who are more assertive. And women who are in the same part of the spectrum feel more comfortable than with women from a different part. Culturally, Jewish women are at one end of the spectrum. It's quite simple."

She elaborates, in an academic tone, "The spectrum relates to all women. But Jewish women are acculturated to, and comfortable with, being outspoken, and taking themselves seriously. Jewish women of our generation have been socialized to be comfortable with speaking their mind and registering their voice. We place a high value on education, and there is an equality between men and women that may or may not exist in other ethnic subgroups."

Eric is uncomfortable with the immediate ties Jews forge with other Jews. *He* doesn't feel especially comfortable with other Swedish Americans. Why should he? He is annoyed when Jews make the same assumptions. He and Rachel went to dinner with a long-time business associate, a Jewish man. During the course of the evening, the topic of Judaism came up, and Rachel and the man engaged in a lively discussion. Later, the man told Eric, "I feel so much more comfortable around you now than I did before." Another business associate seemed shocked to learn of the naming ceremony of Rachel and Eric's daughter, Emma. He had had no idea that Eric was married to a Jewish woman. "You're kidding!" he exclaimed when Eric told him. "Another member of the tribe? That's fantastic!" In one sense, Eric says, he likes that Emma and Andrew are embraced by strangers. On the other hand, he is made uncomfortable by this unswerving fidelity. "I'm an American, goddammit. I'm not a part of anybody's tribe, and these are my children you're talking about. I don't like that. I just don't. I laugh, but I really don't like it. I just don't get it."

In some ways Eric seems perfectly situated to get it. His marriage to Rachel has made him much more attuned to anxieties of Jews in a predominantly Christian culture, although, in fact, Eric sees Jews as clannish. He is baffled by the outsider's view of American culture, and can't understand why Jews feel community with other Jews they hardly know or may never meet. He says he learned from his Swedish grandfather the values of being independent and self-reliant.

Eric is so confident in his identity as an American, he truly can't understand how others might see it differently. Yet he is a keen observer of the casual anti-Semitism that surfaces from time to time. "I've known many people who were anti-Semitic, even good friends," he says. "They would never be overt or obnoxious about it, but I would say they probably are." Jews might see these comments as further proof of the need to protect one another. Eric draws a different conclusion. "It's just human nature, I'm afraid. But now I'm more sensitive if I'm sitting around and somebody makes an ethnic comment. It always used to bother me, and before I'd ignore it. Now I won't. I can't.

"In my fraternity, there was a Jewish guy from Chicago who took a lot of grief for being a Jew. He'd let it roll off his back, but a number of the guys would say things to him. You know, the typical comment from people who were insensitive or a little bigoted, like, 'Jews are obnoxious,' or 'Jews dominate the media,' or 'Jews are totally interested in money.' I still see that stuff coming out of people. Certainly there's a real split in the business community. I see the mainstream American side, and they think: 'If you have an ethnic background and a strong religion, get it out of my face. It's not what we're here to think about. Keep your private lives to yourselves.' And then there are people who are blatantly anti-Semitic. But this is what I'm troubled by and frustrated by and feel caught in the middle by: I see a lot of Jews who are bigoted or biased or prejudiced or chauvinist in their own ways. When I talk to them about it, when I get the chance with somebody I know, they kind of justify it by saying, 'Well, our people have been shit on for years,' and so on. I don't buy a lot of that. I think there's some truth to it, of course, but I think this whole anti-Semitism and the battles with racism — it's clearly a two-way street. The Jews, because they've been so outnumbered, have been on the receiving end of a lot of this, but it goes both ways."

How will such open doubts about Judaism shape his children's views? It seems almost inevitable that Emma and Andrew will be getting two different messages about their religion and culture. From their mother will come the unquestioning allegiance. Your mother is a Jew; therefore, you are a Jew. End of story. From their father, though, will come a skepticism and a dim view of those who cling to "tribalism." And what will Eric's older children, as well as his younger ones, think of Rachel's sensitivity toward their father's heritage? She and Eric bought a house and joined a country club in a suburb close to his first family. Before Rachel signed the papers, she says she assured herself there were at least a few other Jews in her neighborhood and at the club. "I don't want my kids thinking there's something wrong with them," she says.

In the intricate balance of holidays and faiths the Muellers have struck, however, Eric's older children at first sensed that something was deeply amiss. The first December Eric and Rachel were together, Eric's second daughter, Eva, then seven, asked why Rachel and Eric did not have a Christmas tree. Rachel explained very matter-of-factly that she was Jewish, and that Jewish families don't celebrate Christmas. "Oh," Eva said quietly, nodding. For her, the absence of a Christmas tree — and of her father from his Christmas role — had but one meaning: betrayal. "What's Daddy now?" she wanted to know. "And why isn't he what we've all been together?" The questions persisted for weeks. A child's "But why?" can be a powerful prod.

One night, Eric sat with Eva and tried to explain his religious views: that he very much respected Christianity, and that his own roots were Christian. There were wonderful things about Christianity, he told her, values he held dear: being kind to others, helping those in need. Jesus, after all, was Jewish, and Christianity and Judaism had many things in common. "But Rachel is Jewish," he went on, "and I support her very much. I believe many of the things Jewish people believe, and over time I may be making that more the religion I practice."

The talk seemed to calm things somewhat with Eva. But for Eric, there are lingering questions. Religious beliefs are one thing; cultural celebration quite another. The festivities he once so enjoyed, he now leaves behind with regret. "Christmas was a wonderful time for us, a great time for all our family. I really miss it." His angular features grow wistful. He glances at Rachel, then out the picture window to the street, where neighbors on this wintry Sunday afternoon in late November are hanging Christmas lights.

Eric's memories, both of recent Christmases and of distant ones, are close to the surface. As a child, his family made a ritual of choosing the biggest, fullest fir from the Boy Scout lot and bringing it home. Everyone pitched in with the decorations: winding strings of tinsel and lights around so that they looked just right; putting on just the right number of ornaments. Many of them the children had made themselves, inscribed with their names and the date. "It was kind of neat to bring them out of the box every year and remember," he says. "That, in a sense, was the best day. The house seemed so full and happy." On Christmas morning, the extended family gathered at Eric's parents' house. "We'd get up and have a total maniac-ripping of presents," he says, "then spend the hours until dinner playing with our toys in front of the fireplace. We had a massive feast; a turkey, the whole bit. Hot Swedish drinks, my mom's Swedish meatballs and Swedish cookies."

He sighs. "I partly miss Christmas morning, seeing the joy on my kids' face when I was dressed up as Santa Claus. But it's also the whole season. The whole time when wreaths start going up and lights are getting hung and carols are being sung. It's the whole process. I feel kind of left out, not having a tree or a wreath."

Rachel looks at him quizzically. "It's funny that you say that, because I've always missed those things, too. Christmas tastefully done is tremendously beautiful. The rituals are beautiful." She frowns. "I've always loved other people's lights, and I've always been jealous. I've always felt bad that we can't decorate. Last year we talked about it. I can't see what's wrong with that, actually. I'm not sure there's a lot of religious significance in having electric lights in your bushes.

"From my earliest experience, I always looked at Christmas as something fun. I wished we could do it, too. On the other hand, I think it's a little crass to appropriate the external aspects of a holiday when you don't really buy into the idea. And I think it's very confusing for kids having Christmas and Hanukkah, although I guess if it's something Eric really felt strongly about, it would be okay. I guess you have to be comfortable with what your family traditions are, with what you're doing. And we're just starting to map those out."

While Eric and Rachel may well be working out their religious plans, some patterns are solidly in place. Take Eric's traits as a father, for example. He has a firm approach to discipline, sending kids to time-out or to their rooms if they act out or mouth off. He is not opposed to spanking on rare occasions, either, if they fail to respond to warnings. And why not? It didn't hurt him as a child. Sometimes, kids just need to know their boundaries. When he was growing up, kids did — especially when his Swedish grandmother was around. "She was *harsh*," he says, resting on the last sound. He, however, lets kids be kids. "I really believe in that. They're not young for very long. I don't restrict a lot of things. But there have to be limits. If you don't eat your dinner, you don't get dessert."

Rachel's childhood environment was vastly different. Her mother, whom she describes as "very bright and very intense," put her career as a writer on hold while her children were young. Her father, who managed a large company, pampered his wife and children. Rachel describes him lovingly, as a kind, unassuming man. To hear Eric tell it, Rachel's dad spoiled her and her siblings. "He's very soft. He's one of these people who might meet an obnoxious person who says terrible things, and afterward he'll say, 'Oh, it's okay.' People take advantage of him as a result, including his wife. She's like an attack dog. I mean, the stuff he takes, I wouldn't take for two seconds."

"They've been married for forty-five years, Eric," Rachel says, bored. She has to agree, though. As a child and in her first marriage to Sam, Rachel felt as though she most often got her way. The sense of being indulged doesn't exist so readily with Eric as it did with her father or with Sam. "He'll always be there and will always take care of me," she says. "But it's not the same."

Indeed, theirs is a marriage of quick retorts and bold remarks. Rachel defers to Eric, who is five years older, but only a little. There is a push and pull in their relationship that seems just below the surface. She took the name Mueller when she married Eric; in her first marriage, she had kept her maiden name. "With my first husband, it was a big deal for him that I didn't change my last name. I heard, 'Our kids won't know who their mother is' — that kind of stuff. But I wanted to keep my own name, although it somehow seemed a bigger deal before than after. When Eric and I got married, it was different. I didn't want his kids to feel I wasn't one of them. I didn't want it to be one more thing that would keep us apart."

Friends describe Rachel as assertive, confident, smart, and organized — the kind of person who can cook, get top grades, exercise, tutor young kids, and still have free time. Rachel has always seen herself as capable, but perhaps never quite so much as now, when she realizes that it is through her determination that the links to her faith and culture will be transmitted. She faces it as a responsibility, with a solemnity with which she never before regarded Judaism. Certainly she never saw it in quite such stark terms in her first marriage. "I pretty much took it for granted," she says.

"Part of being a child and a young adult is that you don't step into the role of making things happen in your family. Now my sister and I take responsibility for Passover, for doing the whole thing. I joined a synagogue on my own, with Eric, which was a very big thing for me, because it was the very first sort of adult thing, Jewish thing, that I'd done."

When they discuss the quotidian details of their lives together, they start talking fast, as if they are eager to expose — affectionately — the habits of the other.

"Rachel, when she's upset —" Eric shakes his head. "It's just unbelievable."

Rachel scoffs. "Food and eating: those are the really big differences. One of the things that's important to me is sitting down for dinner together. When we first became involved, it didn't occur to Eric that he often had dinner alone or just grabbed something when he came home. It really didn't matter to him. But in my culture, food is love. At least Eric is responsive to my ideas about it. In his first marriage, he and his wife wouldn't even eat dinner together, and he was home at six-thirty. That's not even late. To me, that's just awful, eating dinner without your spouse. When I was growing up, we were always waiting for someone to get home so that we could sit down and eat together. Having a big meal together — it's part of being a family."

Eric shrugs, and contributes this: "I eat butter that's been sitting out for ten days. She's hyper about stuff going bad. She's always saying, 'We've got to throw that out. It sat out overnight.' She smells leftovers and wonders whether they've gone bad after two days."

"Scandinavians eat butter warm! It's disgusting."

"And Rachel and her family are much more hypochondriacal than I am. If they have colds, they call her sister — she's a doctor — and she prescribes all this medicine. For a cold! In my house, we didn't go to the doctor unless there was a lot of blood."

Perhaps the biggest difference comes when they disagree. When Eric was growing up, his family didn't display much emotion — about anything — and he links the lack of affect to his Swedish roots. "I went to Sweden as a college exchange student," he says. "I'd always thought of myself as a pretty laid-back guy, but compared to the rest of the Swedes, I was, like, hyperactive. Those people are unbelievable. Nothing could get them upset."

That is in clear contrast to Rachel, Eric says. "She screams so much, it's amazing. Sometimes I'll say to her" — he changes his tone to a stern stage whisper — "'Rachel, please listen.' I tend not to be a yeller. I hold things back, and I'll talk slowly and intensely, but softly. I'll say, 'Rachel, I asked you to do so-and-so.' And she'll scream: 'Stop yelling!' And the fact is, you'd have to be listening hard to even hear me, but it's the intensity and the tone of my voice that really make her stop and listen. She accuses me of yelling all the time, but I don't. I never yell. We had no yelling growing up. There was no yelling, no yelling."

"The way Eric really drives me bananas is by not agreeing to argue," Rachel says. "That's how he really gets me. He doesn't engage me if he doesn't want to when there is a disagreement."

"I'll say, 'Stop it. I'd really like to hold a conversation with you, but when you're screaming or in one of your moods where there is no rationale, it's pointless, in my opinion.'" He pauses. "And she'll just want to keep going to sort it out. I'll say, 'Let's pick this up again when we can talk about it in a less heated way.'"

Rachel protests. "I've either been newly married, pregnant, or just given birth during our married life. It doesn't count!"

"Okay," Eric says, impassively.

"He does this." She waves her hand toward him accusingly. "He does this thing where he doesn't respond. So I'll cry."

"She cries all the time. By my standards, by the people I know, you cry a lot."

Rachel rolls her eyes. "I cry a lot?"

Where Eric sees pointless bickering, Rachel sees a cultural chasm. To most Jews, she says, quarreling is a finely honed skill — among children and their parents, wives and their husbands. She sees it as a given fact of Jewish life, and paraphrases a sociological paper on the subject: "In Jewish culture, arguing is a highly developed form of loving interaction, and it is very specific to Jewish culture. This is obvious to anyone who has spent time with Jews, who may be able to argue vociferously and yet not get upset by what the other person is saying. It is a culture in which interrupting is not a tremendous insult, and speaking loudly is not impolite. Abrasiveness is sometimes desirable, and one's ability to argue one's point is highly valued."

But after several years together, she says, she and Eric are growing more aware of each other's perceptions of things. "Maybe he's yelling a little bit more, and I'm yelling a little bit less. I'm trying to be a little more aware of the caustic power of my voice. In a rush to get out the door the other day I mistook my daughter for my dog, and spoke sharply to her. She burst into tears, and I was depressed all day."

Spending weekends with their father, Eric's older children have experienced something entirely new: Shabbat dinner every Friday night, and Hanukkah every December. This comes in addition to Christmas, Easter, and Sunday school each week. Last year, just before Andrew was born, Eric, Rachel, and Emma spent the last two weeks of December in Florida with Rachel's parents. The day after Christmas, the three older children joined them, and although Hanukkah had just passed, they celebrated eight days of it all over again. "We figured, 'What the hell?'" Rachel says. "I'm sure it wasn't quite kosher. But Emma had sixteen nights of Hanukkah."

Both parents say they don't want to confuse their children. Yet both acknowledge the evident clash of cultures.

Eric says: "I want the kids to have a consistent philosophy. I want to limit attendance at temple services until they're a little bit older and can deal with that in a more mature way, although we do light candles on Friday nights and exchange Hanukkah gifts. My ex-wife feels much more strongly than I do that the kids shouldn't get confused, religiously."

Rachel sees this new exposure as a plus for Eric's older kids, whom she almost unfailingly calls "ours." "We make a big deal out of Hanukkah, and it's certainly a fun holiday for our children. In the long run I think it's good for kids to have a sense of other religions. Being Jewish, you certainly learn about them — you really don't have a choice. But I think it's not so many Christians who have had exposure to Judaism."

He nods. "I'm a big believer in that kids, when they're eighteen or twenty, make up their own minds about things, but in the early years they should have consistency and be taught a philosophy. Later, they can sort out how much more they want to accept. That's one of the reasons I've continued to support my three older ones in their church activities."

Eric's older children and his younger ones — particularly his younger ones — will undoubtedly question why some siblings get Christmas and Hanukkah gifts, the others only Hanukkah presents. They will wonder why their older siblings attend church, and they attend synagogue. "Emma already misses them when they leave for Sunday school," Rachel says. "She really fusses. How it will all play out as they get older, I don't know."

NINE

Different Loyalties

§

R OBIN LEONARD is Jewish, devoted to her synagogue and
the Jewish people. Lee Ryan is a Christian, active in her
Anglo-Catholic church in San Francisco. When they became a
couple fifteen years ago, that difference was one of a catalog of
distinctions between them. Robin is gregarious and extroverted;
she measures her free time in hour-long increments between com-
mitments. Lee is reserved and introverted, and likes almost nothing better than coming home from work to read. Robin comes
from an emotional family: "My mother's opinion is, you always
express anger, constantly, even when you're not angry. You always
make sure you're angry at something or someone, and you always
express it." Lee's relatives, on the other hand, are more subdued.
"In my family, we don't bring up difficult things if we can possibly
avoid it," she says.

Robin and Lee met as students in 1980 and became a couple immediately. They were convinced that love and commitment
could help them surmount the wedges between them, from their
views on socializing to the way they discussed their problems. They
never imagined that what seemed so fresh and unique could become so vexing and irritating.

They do have, they point out, a lot in common: a devotion to
feminism; to their intellectual careers in law and publishing; to
civil rights. But when it comes to religion, they live in utterly
separate worlds.

Since childhood, Lee has been active in her parish. On Sunday mornings, she gets up early, calls her parents in Indiana, eats a bowl of cereal, and sips a cup of tea. She throws on a pair of jeans — "I only have to look nice from the ankles up," she says — and gets into the car. San Francisco is at a standstill on Sunday mornings, and she gets to her church in twenty minutes. Today, she is an acolyte and is more than an hour early for the eleven o'clock mass. She climbs the steps to the empty church, opens the door, crosses herself, and kneels in a pew to pray. She is alone, it seems, with the large wooden crucifix that dominates the altar.

Lee rises and retreats to a small vestibule, where she sheds her overcoat for her black cotton cassock and begins buttoning the small buttons that reach from her neck to the floor. She tosses a white lacy mantle over her neck — from afar, it looks as though she is wearing a doily — and goes about her duties. On this day, she prepares the altar for the celebrant and holds the pages of the prayer book open as he reads. A shy person, Lee doesn't initiate much conversation. When she does engage someone, she nervously brushes her short brown hair away from her slender face. Once the service begins, Lee stands at her place in front of the church, listening intently, her voice softly reciting the responsive prayers. The sun pierces the stained glass windows, dappling the floor in front of her with amber light. Once, she laughs out loud at a joke the rector tells. She smiles a warm, enveloping grin that seems to take her serious features by surprise.

Fridays are always a little rushed for Robin, even though it is her day off. She takes her responsibilities as a Jew seriously and chooses the end of the week, just before the Jewish Sabbath, to fulfill the obligation of tzedakah, or caring for the needy. All afternoon, she is home baking cookies. As soon as they are cool, she slips them into boxed meals from a food bank and spins up and down the hills of the city's Castro district to deliver them to people with AIDS. She races home for a Shabbat dinner, and by eight o'clock she is back in her black Toyota, winding through Golden Gate Park on the way to synagogue.

A small, gregarious woman with short brown curls, Robin

smiles in greeting as she makes her way to the door. Once a president of the congregation, she recognizes almost everybody. "Hi, Howard," she calls out. "Shabbat shalom." She waits beside the door as she spots a friend down the street: "Gail!" she cries. Like a small child, Robin waves with her whole arm. She embraces Gail warmly, and they chat quietly as they make their way inside. Then she sits down and closes her eyes. For the first time all day, Robin feels calm. "Put me in a service with a lot of Hebrew, and I'm a happy little kid," she says. "I don't understand all of it, but it's important for me to hear it."

Friday after Friday, she finds herself mesmerized by the ancient melodies the cantor intones at services. Just a few years ago, she made it to synagogue only occasionally. Now, she wouldn't miss it. Most of her friends are Jewish, and so are her activities. She belongs to a Torah study group, serves on various committees at her synagogue, attends the Reform movement's conferences. The more she learns about Judaism, the more she yearns to know, and at thirty-six she is thinking seriously of going to rabbinical school. When she reads about women who stay at home to raise kids, then at fifty decide to go to medical school, Robin tells herself she could make a similar leap from her job as a book editor.

In fact, rabbinical school doesn't seem such a distant notion. And not only Robin has taken note of this surge of interest in her faith; she was awarded a grant from a prestigious foundation to study Judaism with a group of her peers. Designed to educate Jewish lay leaders beyond their bar and bat mitzvah studies, each group meets weekly for two years and ends with a trip to Israel. The seminar spans Jewish history, art, and law. Robin is thrilled by the prospect of learning more about Judaism, and feels that the program will tip the scales — one way or the other — about rabbinical school. "It may be exactly what I was looking for, or I may want more," she says. At any rate, she can't quite believe her good fortune.

As she waited to hear whether she would be a fellow in the seminar, she had the same sick sense high school seniors feel in the spring as college acceptances trickle in. With her heart thumping in her chest and her hand trembling, she would open the mailbox. The letter arrived while Robin was out of town; Lee called her in her hotel room to say what she had hoped to hear: "It's here, and it's thick." Lee had barely opened the letter before Robin started to cry. "I was so happy, I didn't even hear past the first sentence," she says.

Gay interfaith couples have the same disputes and difficulties as their straight counterparts. They agonize over Christmas trees. They have cultural misunderstandings about voice levels during arguments and the amount of food needed for entertaining. They don't entirely understand each other's parents. But for gay couples, there is something beyond even all that.

Religion among gays is a particularly touchy issue. Many feel shunned by the faith of their youth. Traditionalists from Southern Baptists to Orthodox Jews denounce homosexuality as unnatural, a sin. Some members of the clergy have been active in the campaigns to pass legislation that openly discriminates against homosexuals. But despite this antipathy, many American gays and lesbians are yearning for a spirituality they feel they can find only in organized religion.

"In the gay community there's a lot of antireligious sentiment," Lee says. "I certainly understand why, although I think that sometimes the anger is so diffused that the less oppressive religions are included with all the others. And to have some support in the household, albeit from someone of a different tradition, is very helpful to me. I'm easily intimidated; I wouldn't have made a great martyr in second-century Rome. So to have somebody who doesn't sneer at Western religious traditions and who's interested in grappling with how we can apply these to our lives — as lesbians and as people of the late twentieth century — has been a great encouragement."

It is no surprise that Lee's conversation slides easily from allusions to ancient Rome to thoughts about the place of gays and lesbians as the millennium nears. She is an extraordinarily erudite person, driven by a voracious intellect that devours stacks of books each year. A student of Latin and Greek, she is as familiar with the Hellenistic period and the Bible as she is with last Sunday's book review. She speaks in perfectly formed paragraphs, delivered with a diction so staccato that they sometimes take a moment to process. She is as apt to quote the Torah as she is the New Testament. "You shall love God with all your heart and your soul and your might," she says, sitting up, as if recitation of the shema (the most common Hebrew prayer) is part of every Christian's daily repertoire.

Her world extends beyond the cerebral. She is soft-hearted toward animals and cries easily, even at television commercials. She was reared in college towns from suburban Boston to Bloomington, Indiana, as her father pursued his career as a consultant to universities. Lee calls herself a "yellow-dog Democrat" and says, with evident pride, that both of her parents are "real liberals."

As the Ryans migrated from town to town, the one constant was the Episcopal church. Lee was confirmed at twelve and became an acolyte. She was a member of her youth group and attended church every Sunday. Aware early on that she was a lesbian, she didn't feel at odds with the church or its teachings. "I never felt I was doing anything wrong," she says. "The Episcopal church isn't really hot on the trail of pursuing homosexuals and making their lives miserable." (The church's heresy trials over the ordination of gay priests, however, are another matter — one Lee says is too painful to discuss.)

Lee's father was a member of their parish board and became "soured," she says, by church politics, an evolution that prompted dinnertime discussions of organized religion. "My mother always said, 'Well, Judaism, now, there's a religion. They let you ask questions.' So that's the stereotype I grew up with."

In college at Yale, sleeping in on weekends suddenly seemed a better idea than getting up to go to mass. But years later, one frigid Sunday morning when she was in law school, Lee woke early, just in time to go to church. She missed the hymns, the prayers, the liturgy. So she dressed warmly, hopped on her bike, and slipped into New Haven's Anglo-Catholic church, Christ Church. Accustomed to the Episcopal liturgy, she was both drawn to and hesitant about the emphasis Anglo-Catholics put on Roman Catholic tradition, and the amount of Catholic dogma in the service. But she immediately liked the rector. "I made the transition from a kid's Sunday school understanding of what this religion was all about to an adult's understanding of it," she says.

Indeed, faith is never far from her mind. "What I think — intellectually — that makes me a Christian is being baptized. But beyond that, and why I'm not lapsed, I guess, is that I believe the core message. Fact is, I can read the apostles' creed and I mostly believe it. I mean, I'm accepting of the incarnation and resurrection as true events. I don't want to get into what's 'true' and what's 'literally true'; that's a different matter. True is much more than God created the Earth in six days. I don't see myself as any kind of fundamentalist."

Discussing the Trinity, she lays it out as logically as if it were a geometry lesson. "There's the Father, the Son, and the Holy Ghost." Without a hint of irony, she says, "The Father created the Son, and then created the Holy Ghost. There's not three, there's only one! The whole thing is a *mystery!* You're not supposed to understand it. It's totally incomprehensible. What kind of human being would think of this? It's a way to remind people that you can't comprehend God. And yet, on balance, I'd much rather there be a God than not."

Her adherence to tradition is so great that she seems piqued by the attempts of some to tailor religion to current mores. "I hate the secular Christmas," she says. "I just hate that it starts at Halloween and goes on and on. I can get on my Anglican high horse and say, 'It's Advent! It's penitential season! Christmas should be celebrated on the twelve days of Christmas!' But of course on January first we have to have Valentine's Day things out." She rolls her eyes.

When it comes to Judaism, she is no less dogmatic. "It's amazing that in Reform temples there's even a debate about Christians going up to the bimah," she says. "That's inappropriate! Read from the Torah? Are you kidding? Me? That's for you guys. There are boundaries here. I have my own shtick. If you're that drawn to Judaism, convert. I think it's disrespectful for me to expect the rules to change just so they won't hurt my feelings."

It is late one Sunday evening in August, and the cool damp of the city's fog hovers outside the windows of their large apartment. Robin wanders around, pointing out each Jewish item: a mezuzah on every doorpost, two kiddush cups perched among Jewish history books, a seder plate from Israel, a havdalah set, and hand-painted wooden candlesticks. On the wall is a large photograph of the couple from their kiddushin — Hebrew for "holy union" — embracing under a chuppah. "Lee lets me be Jewish," she says. "She lets this home be — at least to all appearances — a Jewish home."

The reverence in which Robin holds her Judaism has rapidly deepened in the past few years, a change she cannot attribute to any one thing. "My involvement started out as very local, but now I have a more communal sense of purpose," she says. She used to get "irritated," she says, when people wished her a merry Christmas. Now, she says she couldn't care less what people tell her in December. Her Jewish holidays have become so sacred, she says, it really doesn't matter what others do or say. "Let them enjoy what's theirs," she says, "and I'll enjoy what's mine. My holidays are a marker for me, of who I am, and how I distinguish myself from others." She giggles. "Certain people in my office are always kind of aware of the High Holy Days, and struggle to find the right greeting. Someone this year looked at me, then hesitated before saying, 'Happy Yom Kippur.' I appreciate that — it's an effort, at least. So I used it as a way to explain about the day."

Her attitude toward Judaism stems in part from her parents, who always proudly identified themselves as Jews in their predominantly Catholic New Jersey town. As a child, her only difficulty as a Jew came when she began to ask her rabbi questions about homosexuality, which Judaism historically condemns. The rabbi was mortified, she recalls. "He said, 'Put it out of your head.' I just knew he was someone I wasn't going to get information out of, and I didn't pursue it. I was always self-assured and had enough chutzpah that my response was not to go too deeply into his answer, not to feel ashamed, but to get my information elsewhere."

And so she did. Although she became a bat mitzvah, she felt the gaps in her knowledge of Hebrew and Judaism were so great that she wanted to continue her education. She and other Hebrew school friends signed up for classes at a private Jewish school. "We were so poorly educated that we were laughed out of the class," she says. She winces. "We knew nothing. So we stopped after a semester. We were thirteen, fourteen, and it was very painful. It's a tough age to begin with — you have acne, you have cramps, you feel awkward, and you're trying to fit in. And at that point I was fairly aware of my sexuality, and I was trying to come to terms with it."

When she was growing up, her parents kept their menorah in their living room window year round. It was more than decoration: it was a declaration to their Christian neighbors. But it was not an entirely welcome message. When she was in the seventh grade, Robin and her Jewish friends had pennies thrown at them. "You're so cheap," the classmates shouted, "here are some pennies for you to count." In high school, a German American in Robin's chemistry class often hooked a hose up to a Bunsen burner, then pointed it at her and other Jewish students. He would turn on the gas, and say, "Too bad Hitler didn't get all of you!"

Life at New York University was much easier than it had been in high school. Robin was surrounded by other Jews, both as classmates and residents, and she reveled in the atmosphere. She found everyone in New York City "a little bit Jewish," even if they weren't technically so. "Culturally, ethnically, it's all there — you're surrounded by Jews and Jewish things: food, mannerisms. The Jewish holidays are days off for practically everyone." Indeed, with the omnipresence of good bagels and lox and the Yiddish words that even the tabloids used in their screaming headlines, Robin felt at home. But once she was out of the city in law school upstate, she looked to organized religion for communion with other Jews. There, she helped to form a loose congregation with other Jewish students and looked forward to the time she spent in their company. Aside from that, the synagogues she attended put her off.

They were either too Reform — "No Kumbaya on the guitar for me" — or too dominated by gay men, who seemed insensitive to the historic absence of women in the Jewish liturgy.

Robin was starting her law school education as Lee was finishing hers. Once Lee graduated, she was offered a job as the law librarian at a San Francisco law school, and the couple moved there straightaway. Almost as soon as they moved, Lee found San Francisco's Church of the Advent. She liked the priest, she liked the parish — it is 60 percent gay — and soon found her spiritual home. A quiet woman with a devastating sense of humor, Lee finds comfort in solitary pursuits. "I'd just as soon come home from work and read than do anything else," she says.

For Robin, however, the transition to San Francisco was not quite so smooth. She had transferred from law school at Cornell to Berkeley's Boalt Hall, but felt awkward among her classmates, who had formed friendships during their first year. Outgoing, she needed more than just Lee as support in a new city. "When we arrived, I was twenty-four. It had been eleven years since I'd had any formal Jewish ties, and I was a cultural Jew yearning to be a more religious Jew. Cultural, meaning that I take the social responsibility of Judaism seriously. In New York, I was surrounded by Judaism on an informal level. It was comforting. But when I got here, I wanted something more than that. One day I picked up a gay newspaper and saw an ad for a gay synagogue. I thought, 'Well, here's a way to meet people, and I am Jewish.'" But she was leery. As a lesbian, she had found previous gay synagogues wanting. Indeed, as she entered Sha'ar Zahav ("Golden Gate," in Hebrew) one Friday night ten years ago, she had a list of check-offs: it had to be traditional, but with gender-neutral language. Women had to be involved in the liturgy. Yet it couldn't include so much Hebrew that it was inaccessible to Lee. And it had to be welcoming to interfaith couples. She was bound to be disappointed: how could any one place answer all of those demands?

But Sha'ar Zahav did. An older man stood at the back of the sanctuary, his hand thrust out warmly in greeting. It seemed to be his job, just saying hello to people. "He was so gracious. I think the first words out of Lee's mouth were 'I'm not Jewish,' and he said, 'That's fine; there are so many members here whose partners aren't Jewish. You're welcome to be a part of our family. Come in and join us.'" The gentleman, a Holocaust survivor and a long-time member of the congregation, made them both feel at home instantly. "It was unlike anything I'd ever seen," Robin says. "We felt so welcome."

Lee had attended services with Robin from time to time during their commute between New York and New Haven, and was always interested by what she observed. "I like the feeling of a synagogue. It's warm and welcoming and spirited," Lee says. She straightens her back and lifts her head high on her neck. "Episcopalians *are* God's frozen people. It is absolutely different in a synagogue. I have a warm spot in my heart for Sha'ar Zahav because I got a much, much warmer welcome there than from any Episcopal church I visited when I came to San Francisco. I persevered only because I'm an Episcopalian and I'm not going to go anywhere else. I'm not about to change my entire religious belief structure just because certain people were friendly and other people were standoffish, at least for the first five or six years you know them, after which they warm up a little bit. So I always liked that, the social aspects, before and after, talking with friends.

"I have a real attraction to the whole personality of Jews. But I believe the core message of Christianity, I really do, and that's what draws me to it. If I didn't believe it, I wouldn't be a Christian. And I don't imagine not believing it."

Robin, however, does not share Lee's ecumenical sense. Although she says she has never been threatened by Lee's faith, she has never been drawn to Christianity. She appreciates Judaism for the same reasons Lee does: its warmth, the emphasis it places on ritual in the home. "On Sunday Lee is up and out of here and on her way to church. She gets a lot out of it; it intrigues her intellectually, but she also struggles with it. She doesn't just go along with it because it's easy, because for her it's not so easy. She wants to put it into context and a place.

"Lee is a very private person, and her Christian life is in many ways the most private aspect of her life. Part of it is out of respect to me as a Jew. The basic belief system — despite the people out there who refer to Judeo-Christian ethics — Jews and Christians are very different. Lee comes to synagogue with me and can integrate most of what we say. We may be waiting for a messianic time — and they're waiting for the second coming — but going to a Jewish service is not a problem for her. And the opposite is true for me. But she'd never expect me to integrate Christianity into my life."

Robin, in fact, feels wholly uncomfortable in church. On the few occasions she has gone, she found herself flipping through the hymnal when others were singing or glancing at her watch in the hope that time was passing quickly. Just about everything made her uncomfortable — the crucifix, the mention of the saints, the many prayers for forgiveness. "I just don't feel I belong there," she says. "It's clearly, clearly not my tradition."

She sighs. "I do wish I could share more with her. In the back of my mind I probably have a fantasy — not so much that Lee would convert but the fantasy that suddenly she's Jewish. Maybe the fantasy is that thirteen, fourteen years ago she didn't walk into Christ Church in New Haven but instead into a synagogue."

Lee and Robin's sense of separation is underscored by their religious calendars. One observes her faith on Friday nights; the other on Sunday mornings, each orbiting politely around the other. Their calendars collide only when the first night of Passover coincides with Good Friday. (The New Testament establishes Christ's death near Passover; unlike other events in the Gospel stories, it is the only occasion specifically dated.) Lee fasts on Good Friday, as required by Christian tradition; sometimes the same day Robin prepares for a seder.

"There are chickens roasting and kugels baking and gefilte fish stirring, and what am I doing?" Lee asks. "I'm fasting!"

"I feel sad to be at a first- or second-night seder and Lee's not there because it's Good Friday," says Robin. "I miss her, and I want to be celebrating a hundred percent of my Judaism with her. I obviously don't insist that she come to a Jewish seder on Good

Friday and celebrate — that would be totally inappropriate. But that's about the only time I sit and think, 'Gosh, I wish she were here. It's such a happy time.' We're here with our friends; we have a good circle of Jewish friends, with four little babies. I just wish she could celebrate it all, and at the same time I respect her choice and her faith and what she's doing, and also that she doesn't expect me to compromise my own life."

Indeed, Lee does more than just that. Respectful as she is of Judaism, and schooled as she is in Christianity, she feels anguish over the bitter, tangled past of the two faiths. Many interfaith couples tend to emphasize the tenets that Christianity and Judaism have in common: the Ten Commandments, monotheism. But not Lee; she feels a collective guilt for the history of Christendom.

"Every time one of our Jewish friends has a kid, I just rejoice," Lee says. "Ah-hah! Another one! Here's one in your eye, all you people who tried to wipe this nation out. That's how I feel."

Their separate realities were perhaps most evident when the couple traveled to Israel with a group from Robin's synagogue. Their first night there, Robin could hardly contain her excitement. She felt victorious and proud, comfortable and happy. Lee, on the other hand, was deeply uneasy. She was aghast at what she found at Christianity's holiest shrines.

As she and the group wound their way through the narrow streets and alleyways that make up the Via Dolorosa, Lee held forth for her Jewish friends, years of New Testament study yielding fruit. "She provided Christian color commentary for us," Robin says.

Finally, they reached the site where St. Helena is said to have discovered the remains of Christ's cross, the vast marble stones that are the foundation for the Church of the Holy Sepulcher. When she entered the church, the heavy smell of incense stinging her nostrils, Lee paused for a moment as her eyes adjusted from the bright sun of the Jerusalem afternoon to the dim light of flickering candles. She did not like what she saw.

This beacon of Christianity, the supposed site of the crucifixion, was an architectural and factional chaos. It lacked the melancholy piety she had envisioned. In fact, priests of every sect —

Greek and Russian Orthodox, Coptic, Latin, Armenian — elbowed one another on their way to prayer. "Oh, typical," she thought. "Here, too.

"I couldn't believe it. It was so disappointing. This sect was fighting with that sect about how many square feet each should have, and who had the best space. And I thought, 'You can't suspend this, for anything?'" She answers her own question. "Not here, not anywhere."

She laughs. "I was so grateful to be in Israel with a Jewish group because the Christian side of it was so depressing to me," Lee says. "First, it is not my nice via media Anglican spirituality — the people who have custody of the holy shrines are either Eastern Orthodox or Franciscans — and it ain't my tradition. And kitsch? Kitsch? *Ongepotchket!* I learned a new Yiddish word, 'overly decorated.'"

Just about every site they visited, whether Christian or Jewish, made her feel worse. At the entrance to the Museum of the Diaspora, Lee was transfixed by a large book called *The Scrolls of Fire*. In it, Lee says, were fifty-two literary depictions — art and poems depicting incidents of anti-Semitism in world history.

"You look at it and read all about how Christians — or people who were at least in the Christian cultural tradition; whether the message stuck with them or not, I don't know — did nothing but persecute Jews for two thousand years. I thought, What a wonderful advertisement for my tradition!"

"Lee was in many ways more offended by the book than many of the Jews on the tour," Robin says. "It's there for synagogues that wish to integrate it into a kaddish service each Friday night." She looks at Lee, and shrugs. "Fifty or fifty-one of the fifty-two were done in the name of Christianity. We began looking at the book together, and it became clear to me that this was something Lee needed to deal with on her own. I went on ahead while she stayed behind, read every one of them, and bought the book. I think the anti-Semitic message that has come from Christianity in many ways has more deeply affected her than me."

"It's a perversion of everything I hold important about my faith," Lee says. Her languid pose, which has become even more relaxed after several cups of herbal tea, suddenly becomes rigid, and her face flushes. "I'm convinced that the source of Christian anti-Semitism is everything that's evil. And all of it is base slander. It really bothers me. It really angers me."

A few days later, in Tel Aviv, Lee took a walk alone on the beach. "Here's what I saw in Israel: Christians fighting over sacred spaces, and evidence everywhere of inhumanity to Judaism. And I asked myself, 'Have we done a single good thing in two thousand years? Would the world be a better place if Christianity had never existed?' I wondered, 'Were we a net gain to humanity, or a net loss in the end?'"

Living, as they do, in San Francisco, where they are active in their religious communities, Lee and Robin have attended the funerals of many young people. The topic of death comes up in conversation a number of times: gay people living in San Francisco in the 1990s face it every day. With other interfaith couples, however, it is usually a difficult subject to broach. Many in their thirties and forties haven't yet thought about how to deal with the death of their mate; often, parents are still alive, and the topic has simply not arisen. Few are aware that non-Jews cannot be buried in Jewish cemeteries. People often joke that they will be cremated together and have their ashes spread in favorite places: mountains, beaches, even off the Brooklyn Bridge. Many have been surprised to learn that cremation, in fact, is forbidden by Jewish law, and until only recently was frowned upon by the Catholic church.

Returning from funerals of friends, Robin and Lee would often talk late into the night about what they envisioned for themselves. "Even if you're not a gay man or not religious, you think about death a lot," Lee says. "The issue is kind of forced. So I've thought a lot about what would happen if I were to predecease Robin." She has it all planned: she wants a solemn requiem mass at her church.

"I think Robin has to have an opportunity to do whatever will give her comfort. That's paramount. Any of my rituals" — she pauses here — "well, I wouldn't know about them, would I? I'd be dead, so who cares?"

Robin's synagogue shares space with another Reform congregation at a cemetery in Colma, a town just outside San Francisco; bodies can no longer be buried in San Francisco because of the sanitation problems posed by the earthquakes that plague the city.

"In the mid-1980s, members started dying. We had a few points that we wanted to negotiate and put in our contract with the other synagogue. One was to permit same-sex couples to be buried together. The other was to permit non-Jewish partners to be buried there, too. And the other congregation said okay. It's weird; many of our rabbis won't marry you, but nevertheless they want you to be in the congregation, and then they say you can't be buried together. The inconsistencies are so great. But in terms of burial, in the gay community it's very important not to be excluded one more time.

"I believe that when I'm dead and gone, I'm dead and gone. The afterlife is not an issue for me. If after I'm dead and gone, I happen to meet up with people here again — whoa — what extra icing on the cake! I'm a very here-and-now sort of person. There are some elements in Judaism that are mystical — kabbalistic Jews are concerned with the afterlife. But not me. I think we've got one life to live, and we're here. Just do it. It's a very traditional interpretation."

"As much as it's not my custom," Lee says, "I think sitting shiva is a wonderful thing. It recognizes mourning, that you should get more than your seventy-two hours of leave. You should get the seven days, the thirty days, the annual remembrance of the yahrzeit candle. I think one of the great things about the Jewish tradition is that it recognizes that grieving is never really complete, and that it goes in stages."

She sighs. "I don't tend to focus on the afterlife a lot. I kind of hope it's true. But again the most important thing is to live now.

After you're dead, you're dead. What Robin believes and what I believe doesn't have anything to do with it, in a sense. If I'm right about it, I'm universalistic. Everybody'll be there. I don't buy this God-rejected-the-Jewish-people business. I think that if there is an afterlife, we won't be separated. It's likely to be a bigger and better San Francisco. I don't think it's a sort of surrealistic thing with people traipsing around on clouds with harps or anything. When Jesus talks about the kingdom of heaven, he's talking about justice and mercy being carried out on earth. It's like tikkun olam: to heal the world."

In the end, however, it was details, and not death, that separated Robin and Lee. Although neither could predict it, their relationship would end after nearly sixteen years.

They made a life together, of course, each more than a bit wistful that she could never share the essence of the other's faith. There were problems, of course, and trouble in communicating was one of them. They had recognized those gaps years earlier and sought counseling. (In fact, they saw a family therapist who specialized in interfaith couples.)

But ultimately, they could not overcome many of their differences, and they dissolved their domestic partnership at a courthouse in San Francisco. Ask them why they broke up, and they mention conflict about some of their choices — buying a condominium together, arguments over the responsibilities of a "challenging" dog — as well as an underlying tension about their different styles of expression. Religion, they insist, did not pull them apart. "It had virtually nothing to do with it," Lee says.

But it comes up again and again. They say now that they did not foresee their own break-up, but there certainly were hints. Robin didn't so much wish that Lee would convert to Judaism as that Lee was "suddenly Jewish." And once she won the grant to study Judaism more seriously, she wondered whether the two halves of her life would fit together. How could she be a Jewish spiritual leader and yet have as a partner a Christian woman? "It's scary," she said then. "We are similar in so many, many ways. We have so much love and respect for each other. We're not competitive. We're content to let the other do what she needs to. But this scares me. What will happen to us if I go to rabbinical school? Would our relationship survive it?"

Lee had the same worries. At the time, however, she never let on. "I wondered about us; I wondered what would happen. I wondered how it would all play out. I'm a kind of a one-day-at-a-time person, though, and it never got that far." She laughs uncomfortably.

Long before they broke up, Lee was sad about their religious obstacles. "We see eye to eye on so many big things: politics, money, sex. But not when it comes to religion. I'm really sorry we can never make aliyah together [read a Torah portion at the lecturn, or recite the blessings that precede or follow it]. I'll sit and kvell when she does, but that's about it." She spoke slowly, deliberately. "I'm sorry that I'll never internally understand what it is to be a Jew, what it is to be born a Jew. If you come to it as an adult, it's not the same, I think, even if you do convert." In small ways, they seemed to prepare for their eventual separation, even if they weren't aware of it. Whenever Lee would discuss her admiration for the warmth of Jewish ritual and culture, she seemed clear that it was not — and would never be — hers. "If I no longer had Robin," she said on several occasions, "I'd miss it a lot."

Before they broke up, things had deteriorated so badly that Robin and Lee were barely even speaking. "And I guess, to some extent, who we are culturally has something to do with that in a tenuous way," Lee says. Robin's busy schedule, between her work, her seminar, and her synagogue, made Lee feel left out. "It got to the point where I could see her between nine and nine forty-five on Wednesdays," says Lee, "and I wasn't very happy about that." She grew resentful. And, Robin says, silent.

"It got so that I didn't hear anything more than 'This item in the newspaper really makes me angry,'" Robin says, "or 'I've got stuff going on at work that I don't want to talk about.' It made it very difficult, very frustrating, and ultimately very lonely."

In the end, as Robin puts it, "We didn't interact and share many things, on a profound level."

For the first time in years, Lee Ryan found herself at home with a book on Rosh Hashanah. Three months earlier, she and Robin had sold their condominium, divided their belongings, and moved into separate quarters. It felt strange not to be at synagogue with Robin, not to listen to the rabbi's sermon, not to hear the wail of the shofar. Instead of a feast with roast chicken, challah, and apples with honey, Lee ate yogurt for dinner. "It felt odd," she says.

At Christmastime, Lee put up a crèche, something she was reluctant to do when she lived with Robin. She had, once or twice, put it up in a corner of their apartment. But this year, Lee put it on her mantel, in the center of the room. She gets up on Sundays now without having to tiptoe. She doesn't have to rush home from church.

By coincidence, Lee moved back into the building where she and Robin had once lived, into the former apartment of an Orthodox Jewish family. For months, Lee received mail addressed to her old neighbors. What came, mostly, were the third-class documents that slipped past the postman's notice: community bulletins and flyers from kosher food companies. For the longest time, Lee says, she took them inside and read them; it seemed normal that she should keep abreast of Jewish activities in San Francisco.

"Then all of a sudden I thought, 'Wait a minute. I shouldn't really be getting stuff from Kashrus Connection. This isn't really a part of my life anymore.'"

And yet it is. Like the apartment she now inhabits, Judaism, in no small way, inhabits her. "It enriched my life," she says.

TEN

Sushi and Gefilte Fish

§

A DELA RABINKO and Teru Kawamoto never met. But if they had, they might well have compared notes about the anguish they endured during World War II. Young Adela, a Polish Jew, fled her village for the dubious refuge of the Soviet Union, where she toiled in labor camps for thin gruel and stale bread. Teru, who had left her native Japan for Hawaii in the early 1920s, watched as the FBI dragged her husband away on December 7, 1941, to be put in an internment camp on the outskirts of Honolulu.

Their talk could have well turned to privations of life during wartime, the loneliness of being isolated from family, and the parallels of injustice on two continents. Strange, how a teenage girl fleeing Hitler's armies in Europe might have links with a young Buddhist mother in the middle of the Pacific.

One thing is certain. Whatever they could have discussed or imagined, they would probably never — not even in their wildest imaginations — have hit on what they would one day share: family.

Indeed, the union of Teru's granddaughter Ann, a photo archivist from Honolulu, and Adela's son Morris, a banker from New York, is a highly unlikely one. As longtime friends of the couple would say, years later, at their wedding, "They are as different as sushi and gefilte fish."

When the Germans rolled into Poland on September 1, 1939, they overtook the ill-equipped Polish forces in a matter of days. Their intention was that the country's flat plains would become *Lebensraum* — living space — for ethnic Germans. Poles were to be Germany's labor force.

When the Nazis reached the southwestern Polish town of Sosnowiec, Adela Levanthal and Zalman Rabinko, young sweethearts, were taken by surprise. Like millions of other Polish Jews, they had little inkling of what was to come. "The Jews," Adela recalls wondering, "what could they want with us?"

Although the systematic annihilation of Europe's Jews in concentration camps was yet to come, the Nazis began mass killings in some villages immediately. Their agenda was clear from the outset of the Polish invasion: railway cars used to transport German troops into the war zone were painted with crude pictures of Jews with hooked noses and the inscription: "We're off to Poland — to thrash the Jews."[1]

No sooner had the Nazis marched into the town square than they began rounding up Jews. Among the first were thirty men from Zalman's apartment building. The men stood in horror as the Nazis shoved them into three rows of ten. Zalman was first in line. He was twenty-one years old.

During the commotion, Zalman's older brother, Shloime, who was standing behind him, grabbed Zalman's collar and pushed him into his own place. He then took Zalman's place at the front. "You're younger than me," Shloime said. They were his last words.

"They didn't want to use up bullets," says Adela, "so they threw grenades." Now seventy-six, she tells the story matter-of-factly in her Miami apartment, a thick Yiddish accent adding to the drama.

Most of the men died instantly, including Shloime. Zalman, in fact, wasn't at all sure he himself had survived. Bleeding, face down, with the acrid smell of the grenade burning his nose, he opened one eye when the blast had ended. He was alive, but he kept still, careful not to budge. Any move could be fatal. Better, he thought, to act as though he were dead, at least until dark. He closed his eyes and took shallow breaths as he lay among the corpses of his brother, his friends, and his neighbors.

Late that night, with all quiet, Zalman slipped through an

open basement window in his building and stole up the stairs to a bathroom. Later, he managed to get the attention of other residents, his sister among them. He was covered with blood.

A Catholic neighbor ripped the shirt off his back and tore it into strips for bandages, dipping them into the toilet so as not to arouse suspicion by running the faucet.

Days later, Zalman met with Adela. "I was on the run with my mother and father, and Zalman said he wants to go, run some more," she recalls.

The two set out alone, afraid but determined. Adela felt she would have the chance to live beyond her nineteen years if she fled east with Zalman, and bade her parents farewell. Weeks later, the couple was married in Lvov, Poland. A rabbi officiated, but not in a synagogue; that would have been too dangerous. With a simple gold band on her finger, Adela accompanied Zalman eastward, following the banks of the Volga.

When Adela speaks of that time in her life, she recounts the details as though they had happened to someone else. She is reticent, and not very convincing, when she says that the devastating events which marked her early life are not important today.

In the plains of Central Russia, Adela and Zalman worked in labor camps. It was the only way, she says, that they could be sure of a meal — a piece of bread, a potato, or perhaps watery soup. In the wartime Soviet Union any food at all was a blessing not to be questioned.

Time passed in a blur. Each day unfolded like the day before: waking at dawn to chop trees and cut them into firewood. Backbreaking even for those with the hardiest constitutions, it was perhaps most grueling for Adela, who discovered early in 1940 that she was pregnant.

The pregnancy advanced, but not well, as Adela continued with her work: transporting loads of wood by the armful. She was ill, undernourished, and exhausted; the weight of her belly and her arduous work exacted a heavy toll. Dizziness overcame her frequently. She walked for miles to the nearest village in search of a doctor. Fluent in Polish and Yiddish, Adela tried frantically to understand the Russian of the peasants who surrounded her, but in vain.

"I was terrified of them," she says. "Here I was, a poor pregnant Jewish girl, and I couldn't understand a word they said except for 'Bozhe moy,' my God. They were crying. I was so scared, I didn't understand them. I thought they were going to kill me. But then they gave me food. And then I understood they were crying for me."

Weeks later, she gave birth to twin girls. Born prematurely, they did not survive the bitter winter. Another daughter was born four years later, in Tajikistan. "Always we were running," she says. "When it got dangerous, we ran."

But Adela was lucky. She, Zalman, and their daughter lived through the war. Her parents and one sister perished at Auschwitz; of Zalman's eight siblings, only two sisters survived. His mother was killed shortly after Zalman fled with Adela; the Nazis shot her in her bed. After the war, Adela, Zalman, and their small daughter moved to Paris, where Adela gave birth to another girl. The Rabinkas left Europe for New York in the 1950s; Morris was born in Brooklyn three weeks after they arrived.

Once in America, Adela and Zalman tried to put their years of suffering behind them. "We used to make jokes, my husband and I. He always said he was ten years younger than he really was. Whenever I asked him why, he would tell me he didn't count those years in Russia, those years in France. He didn't want to remember them." Adela sighs. "I went through hell in my life, it's true. And I could say I'm going to curse the Russians, curse the Poles, curse the Germans. But in every nation, in every religion, there is good and bad. You can't say until you know the person."

Halfway across the world, Teru faced problems of a different sort. News of the bombing of Pearl Harbor hit the Japanese community in Honolulu early and hard: most, like Teru, her husband, Yasubei, and their seven children, shuddered to think what would happen to them in their adopted land.

The Kawamotos, who had arrived in Hawaii as agricultural workers, had struggled to succeed. Over the years, they salted away enough money for a small grocery store and an apartment building. When the first bomb struck Pearl Harbor, they knew it could only spell havoc for their lives. The family must stick together, Yasubei said. One daughter, Wini, was forbidden to honor a commitment she had long kept: teaching Sunday school at a nearby church.

Instead, the family rushed to board up the store; looters were rumored to be already in action. Almost as soon as they returned home from their shop, angry English voices shouted through the door. "Open up," they cried. Two stern FBI officials waited impatiently. They were there, they said, to take Yasubei away. His crime? Being born in Japan. "Foreign alien," the men muttered.

Yasubei was soon released; he died of cancer in 1944. But the internment camps held great indignities for thousands of Japanese Americans. From Hawaii to Arizona, and in many other states, they languished in crowded, dirty conditions. They slept in shacks or dormitories on mattresses stuffed with straw and shared latrines with hundreds of others. Guards scrutinized their moves from watchtowers; at night, searchlights pierced the darkness.

The Kawamotos' trials did not end with Yasubei's death. For the duration of the war, Teru, who had also been born in Japan, was required to report to the FBI for humiliating weekly interrogations. Crippled with rheumatoid arthritis, she walked with great difficulty, and then only in soft Japanese slippers. So eager was she to appear Western that she forced her deformed feet into leather shoes for the agonizing trip to the bureau. One of her children always came along to translate, since Teru did not speak English.

"She took it all in stride," says Wini Kawamoto Toyota, Teru's daughter. "There was no getting her dander up."

That is only partly true. Friends, after all, had spent the war in the internment camps her husband escaped only by virtue of his terminal illness. The family's bank assets were frozen. Teru insisted that her children adapt to their new nation more thoroughly than she had, and instructed them to banish any obvious traces of Japan from their home. They destroyed all books written in Japanese. Some of her children even abandoned Buddhism and Shintoism. Wini, in fact, joined a Methodist church as a teenager. "I wanted to be all American," she says. "On anything that smacked of Buddhism, I turned my back."

When Morris met Teru's granddaughter Ann in New York, during the boom years of the 1980s, they were in their early thirties. Ann was in Manhattan on a year-long stint as a housesitter for family friends; Morris was working long hours as a banker. Both were lonely, and complained to mutual friends that they needed someone to go to the movies with, if nothing else. Their friends set them up on a date.

Morris, forty, says he had a "regular" childhood in Brooklyn, playing ball with the kids on his street, going to the movies, studying Hebrew with his chums. Much to his mother's dismay, he brought pizza and submarine sandwiches into the kitchen she endeavored to keep kosher. The neighborhood was ethnically mixed, but the Polish, Irish, and Italian kids who lived nearby attended Catholic schools; the elementary school Morris went to was filled with other Jewish students. His surroundings were so Jewish, he says, that he was almost an adult before he realized that Jews were a minority.

The only son, born six years after his younger sister, Morris was doted on by the family. "I grew up thinking I was the messiah or something. I at least thought I could walk on water. It was terrible when I got out into the world, because nobody ever thought I was that great again." Surely others thought highly of him, though; Morris's talents in banking and languages — he speaks nine — have moved him around the world for his work, from Russia to New Caledonia.

As a teenager, he excelled at the Bronx High School of Science, one of New York's most prestigious public schools. In high school and college in the early 1970s, he became active in the student protests that marked almost every campus. "I didn't define myself so much as a Jew," he says, "but just as a member of my generation in the United States."

The fight for social justice and against the Vietnam War seemed only natural at the time. But in retrospect, Morris looks at his foray into radical politics as a channel for his rage at the world, at the injustices heaped on his family. Most of his fellow marchers were Jewish, too, although they, like their parents, were born in the United States. "They were interested," he says, "but when I look back I think my involvement had perhaps a greater urgency. I had all this anger. And it wasn't really at all at the Vietnam War."

Adulthood brought his faith into focus. Morris had not given serious thought to Judaism since his bar mitzvah. When he was in his late twenties, though, religion began returning to his life, if only by merit of his address.

In the 1980s, he lived in Manhattan's Upper West Side, home to many prominent Jewish writers and intellectuals. Kosher restaurants and bagel shops line the streets; some grocery stores post signs in English and Yiddish. Many of his friends were also the children of Holocaust survivors, and, like him, spoke Yiddish. Morris was struck by that: forty years after the war, he was surrounded by people whose mother tongue was a dying language.

Although he had rarely been to services since his bar mitzvah, organized Judaism began to beckon. He and his friends went "shul hopping," going from synagogue to synagogue on Saturday mornings to find a suitable spiritual home. "It felt sort of 'with it,' cool, to do that," he says. "It was the mid-eighties and most people were club hopping."

During a stint as a commodities trader in Moscow, Morris visited Israel twice. After college, he had worked briefly on a kibbutz. But now, he was astonished at how emotional he became, even just landing there. What also surprised him, given his views on the Vietnam War, were his feelings about Israel's militarized society. Sipping passion fruit juice in his Honolulu kitchen one January afternoon, Morris searches for the right words.

"I thought the whole — just to see — Jews in uniform, fighting . . ." His voice trails off; he clears his throat. "I felt proud, you know, to have a nation. I've spoken to other people about that experience — just coming in and looking down and seeing a nation that Jews built." He smiles, revealing two rows of dazzlingly white teeth. "It felt really good."

Indeed, the "regular" childhood Morris insists he had was so only in some respects: he had two parents and two sisters, and all of them lived together. His father supported the family on his tailor's salary. Morris did typical kid things; he went to public schools, played sports, read comics. But the extraordinary experiences of his parents perhaps permeated his life more than anything else. He was always aware of the suffering his parents had endured, even though they rarely spoke about it.

And sometimes, late at night, Morris would find his father sitting in the living room, silent and alone, the embers of his cigarette glowing softly in the darkness. He often wondered what his father might be thinking, but there was a tacit understanding: you didn't ask.

When Ann recounts her childhood in a lush Honolulu valley, a smile crosses her face. Her childhood memories are happy ones, a broad mix of Japanese, Hawaiian, and American customs. At Thanksgiving, the roast turkey was accompanied not only by stuffing and mashed potatoes, but by sushi and sashimi, too. She was close to her younger brother, and her many cousins were never far away. There were always big celebrations to look forward to: Christmas, New Year's, Easter, and the Japanese children's festivals, Boy's Day and Girl's Day. Her mother, a professor of education, taught at the experimental lab school Ann attended. Free time, when not spent playing, was devoted to Sunday school or Girl Scouts.

"As far as the Japanese thing goes, it's sort of like being Jewish in Manhattan. It's all around you. Even though I wasn't Buddhist,

at most of the important family events, like a funeral something, the Buddhist thing was always there."

A petite woman with thick black hair cut like a doll's, Ann wears round glasses and simple cotton dresses. She is forty but could fool strangers into thinking she was twenty-five.

Like Morris, she was so surrounded by her own ethnicity that she took it for granted. But she was also aware, as are most Hawaiians, of everyone's ethnic make-up. "In New York you're sort of aware of who's Jewish. Here you know who's Chinese, who's Japanese, who's half Chinese or half Japanese and half haole," she says.

But in Hawaii, unlike New York, ethnicity does not separate the many groups. Everyone, Ann says, celebrates everything: from the lunar New Year, which is welcomed as much by Caucasians as it is by Asian Americans, to St. Patrick's Day. "There are hardly even any Irish here," she ventures, "but people in Hawaii just love to party." Christmas trees covered with fake snow appear just as early in Hawaiian department stores as they do on the mainland.

When Ann went to college in upstate New York, she was in an almost all-white setting for the first time in her life. Her parents had attended New York University in Manhattan, and were eager for their daughter to get the kind of education they felt she could not get at home.

A good student, Ann nevertheless felt out of place. She was unprepared for the cold, despite the blankets and sweaters she had brought. Classmates saw her as exotic, snacking on macadamia nuts she carted from home and wearing thongs in midwinter. Her looks and customs prompted plenty of inquiries. "I'd go to frat parties and hear things like, 'What kind of money does Hawaii use?'" She was also noted positively for her differences. The Black Women's Society made her an honorary member; like its members, she was an "other" at a traditionally white school.

Together in New York, this unusual couple — one cerebral and Jewish, one carefree and Japanese American — soon became inseparable. Before their friends introduced them, they told Ann that

Morris was "Jewish, but not really Jewish." Morris takes offense at this. "They said I wasn't really Jewish?"

"Well, what did they know," Ann says. "You didn't have payess [the Orthodox sidelocks] or wear a yarmulke." In fact, their religious differences were apparent on the first date. Morris, who had studied Zen Buddhism in college, was disappointed to learn that his Japanese-American friend had been raised a Methodist. "When he asked me questions about whether or not I was a Buddhist, I kind of thought, 'Oh, just another stupid haole,'" she says.

Although they partook of New York's assets — restaurants, plays, museums — life in the city also had its pitfalls. Ann was no stranger to cold after her four years upstate, but winters in Manhattan seemed more intolerable. It was dangerous, too: Morris was mugged in the lobby of Ann's building, and the Central Park jogger's rape, which made national news, had the city — and Ann — deeply frightened. She couldn't imagine a place more emotionally or physically different from Honolulu.

And so, after a few years together, they agreed to move to Hawaii, in part to be close to Ann's father, Ralph, and mother, Wini, who, like her mother Teru, had become ill with rheumatoid arthritis. They knew they would eventually get married, and they wanted to start a family. Sue also wanted their children to know at least one set of grandparents. Hers is a large extended family; Morris's few relatives were scattered from California to Israel.

Agreeing to go to Honolulu was easy. To be sure, it was remote, but Morris didn't want to deny Ann the proximity to her parents. Zalman by now was dead, and Adela lived in Miami near one of her daughters.

Negotiations of another sort were under way, too: Morris had asked Ann to convert to Judaism. Their friends believe the move was a compromise — I'll move to Hawaii for you if you convert to Judaism for me — but the couple insist it just worked out that way.

On a sunny Saturday morning in January, Morris and Ann drove to services in their gray Toyota. Their baby daughter, Zara Hiromi, named for two grandfathers, sat snug in her car seat, eyes wide, her breakfast of avocado sticking stubbornly to her hair.

Looking out at Honolulu's palm trees and sun-splashed streets, it was hard to imagine a more unlikely setting for a rich Jewish community. On shuttle buses from the airport, the talk is of seeing Don Ho at his evening lounge show. Tourists wear purple orchid leis until the petals are wilted and brown; the garlands are replaced later in the week by hulking hibiscus blossoms bobby-pinned into tightly permed curls. Impressively round visitors, dangerously pink, amble down famed Waikiki Beach.

It is America, but it is not: the sonorous tones of Hawaiian balladeers and the soft, tinny sounds of ukuleles replace Muzak on hotel elevators. *Asahi Shimbun,* the largest Japanese daily, awaits buyers in plastic boxes on Waikiki streets alongside the *Los Angeles Times.* Miso soup is listed on breakfast menus. And as they near the rainy valley that houses the synagogue, they pass Buddhist temples, Shinto shrines, and church steeples.

At Sof Ma'arov — Hebrew for "the End of the West" — Ann plunks down with the baby in the foyer. Zara-chan, as she calls her, using the Japanese diminutive, can explore the stairs without disturbing others. (Morris calls his daughter Zarale, using the Yiddish diminutive.) A half-dozen Eurasian children scurry around the entrance of the converted mansion that is home to Sof Ma'arov on Saturdays, a Unitarian church on Sundays, and an art gallery during the week. The parents of toddlers fish through their diaper bags for Tupperware containers of papaya and mango chunks. Pineapple juice is stored in pitchers for the Oneg Shabbat, the gathering after services that is often held in American synagogues.

Sof Ma'arov is a participatory congregation with no head rabbi, and its members pad up to the bimah in Birkenstocks and bright Hawaiian shirts. Brooklyn intonations mingle with the soft lilt of Hawaii natives in responsive readings. The Rabinkos attend almost every Saturday. "It really connects me to history," Morris says. "When some people find out I go to services every week, they say, wow, he's really religious. But my going to synagogue isn't just a religious experience. It's really just feeling part of a whole long tradition."

Morris strikes an unusual figure in Honolulu, where he is vice president at a large bank. Self-deprecating, with a sharp sense of humor, he has few of the traits that mark native Hawaiians, who move to the rhythms of a more relaxed schedule.

In fact, Morris does not sit still. Back home after services, he keeps moving in his kitchen. In midsentence, he stoops down to pick up some of Zara's toys, which he has discovered under the table. Raindrops strike lightly on the windows. He looks at his daughter, who has just learned to walk. Holding out his hands to her, he says, "We started going out and I guess maybe I wasn't totally honest with myself because at first I thought, 'Oh, it doesn't matter as long as I'm Jewish, we can raise the kids Jewish, and the Reform movement would recognize our kids as Jewish.'" Zara toddles off.

He pauses. "I thought about all of that stuff. But I wasn't really being honest with myself. Because Judaism is a community, not just a religion, and I wanted my kids to accepted as Jews. It really wasn't enough just for *me* to think they're Jews." He taps his chest. "It took a long time for me to realize that it was important. At first it wasn't important. But the more I thought about it, it was. So I asked Ann to convert, and she really found it offensive. She thought it was no different from a kind of forced conversion. But I was just saying, 'Jews don't say the whole world has to be Jewish. I'm not out trying to convert the whole world to Judaism. I'm just talking about my wife, my house.'"

Ann, for her part, was very upset. When she pressed Morris to explain why her conversion was so important to him, he wasn't able to answer. Some gall, she thought; he was asking her to make an enormous life change, and he couldn't articulate why.

"I wanted to know what it was Morris wanted me to convert to, and all he could tell me were these vague things about his religion, his experience," Ann says. She became adamant: if Morris couldn't explain it, what was there to discuss?

They fought. Although they had settled into a comfortable routine — movies on Saturday night, bagels, coffee, and the *Times* on Sunday morning — they froze on the topic of Judaism. "We talked it to death," Ann says. "We would get mad when it came up, and it did, a lot. It would just be a dead end." They spoke of breaking up.

"The tension was awful," Ann recalls. "He was saying, 'I love you, I want to marry you, I want to be with you the rest of my life, but you have to convert.' It was a big blow to me to realize that I wasn't good enough as is. And it was a huge, huge commitment." There weren't going to be any changes, she said. Period. "I wondered if he was just doing this to push me away. He said he wasn't, and Morris is a straightforward person, so I had to take what he said at face value. We were lost. We just didn't know where to turn. It was a really unhappy period."

Morris and Ann turned to others for guidance. Finally they found a course at New York's 92nd Street Y, the Derech Torah, a Jewish education class. "We took this class, and then some things started to click." She amends her sentences. "A lot of things clicked, but a lot of things didn't. The class clarified what about Judaism was important to us," she says. "We saw what was possible instead of arguing or discussing things we didn't know about."

Morris and Ann's conversations about the role of Judaism in their lives, often stymied by anger, are typical of those of many interfaith couples. When faced with questions about their traditions or religion, secular Jews are often unable to explain. Non-Jewish partners are baffled by the deep attachments to culture and religion that seem to touch their partners' lives only occasionally.

If you care so much about being Jewish, they wonder, why don't you go to synagogue more often than just at Rosh Hashanah and Yom Kippur? What's to squabble about, since you're hardly "religious"? (In Morris and Ann's case, these questions were particularly evident around Christmastime. Ann couldn't understand what harm there was in celebrating Christmas. To her, it was a secular holiday, one she had shared growing up even with Buddhist family members.)

Because Jews outside Israel are surrounded by a majority culture, they are automatically familiar with its basic beliefs and rituals. They may not be educated about Christianity, but Christmas and Easter, for example, require no explanation. Most Gentiles, on the other hand, know little about the tenets and traditions of Judaism. And often they do not understand the distinction between Jewishness and Judaism: a partner may *feel* Jewish yet not be religious. The Christian partner is left scratching his head. What do you mean, you *feel* Jewish? Then why don't you ever *do* anything about it?

The explanation of Jewish law — that you are Jewish if you have a Jewish mother, regardless of your level of devotion to ritual — is foreign to many non-Jews. Because Christianity requires *seeking* the covenant — getting baptized, going to church for the sacraments — the idea of being born into a faith is unfamiliar. Without exposure to Jews and Judaism, many Gentiles are unaware that Jews see themselves as a people, a nation, a tribe, not just a religion.

Those couples who make the effort to educate themselves about Judaism and its many meanings — religious, cultural, ethnic, and historical — learn to maneuver around some of the natural misunderstandings.

In the end, the class at the Y prompted Ann to convert to Judaism. But Morris, she says, underwent a conversion of sorts, too. "Once he figured out the kind of Jew he wanted to be, we both mellowed our viewpoints," Ann says. "Before, it was all sort of threatening. Everything was black and white. I'd say things like, 'If you really loved me, you wouldn't ask me to convert.' I didn't understand it at all when *he'd* say things like, 'If Israel ever got attacked, I'd go over and join the army.' The class helped clear up so much of that."

Indeed, Morris discovered that the cultural aspects of Judaism were much more important to him than the religious ones. "When it comes right down to it, it's more being a member of a tribe than even being a member of a religion, even though the religious aspect is what ties the traditions of the tribe together. But it's more just being part of a chain — it's almost like being a member of a family.

On the one hand I don't know who my great-grandparents were, and I don't know my family genealogy. But this connects me to feeling, a part of a family that is five thousand years old. And that has a great purpose and a meaning."

Once in a while, someone makes a wisecrack about Ann not being a "real Jew," and it makes Morris angry. "Some people may not think Ann is really Jewish, but that's their problem. Their Jewishness becomes questionable, because they're outside the tradition and the law. The rules of the game in Judaism are that you're supposed to fully accept converts as Jewish. If you convert, you're Jewish, and if you don't accept converts as Jews, you don't know your religion very well." Indeed, Moses Maimonides wrote, "A convert is a child of Abraham, and whoever maligns him commits a great sin."

Morris looks up. "Her parents came from Japanese immigrants; I came from immigrants. Her parents can speak a foreign language. I could identify with that more, and feel more comfortable with that, than I could with some mainstream WASP family."

Once they moved to Hawaii, Ann and Morris found that things fell swiftly into place. The couple moved into the home in which Ann was raised. The house, perched on a hill overlooking a valley, has a splendid view of the ocean. Although gray clouds hover menacingly above, sunlight glints off the Pacific to the west. Cruise liners and barges shuffle across the horizon. In the garden, lemon and lime trees border palms, and tiny green geckos, Hawaiian lizards, dart about.

It is here, Ann says, with the class behind her, that she felt prepared for the changes conversion would bring. "I learned so much about the Jewish way of life," she says. "I came to feel as though I was converting not to a religion, but to a way of thinking." She associated religious order with the rigid code of conduct to which she was accustomed in Japanese society. She begins to list just the superficial observances: you address those older than you with one greeting, those younger than you with another; you bow, in deference and in respect, when saying good-bye. If you are a woman, you are expected to speak in a high-pitched voice. The rules, unwritten or not, go on and on. Automatically, she assumed that Jewish culture would have similar strictures. For example, she thought that she could never become a "good" Jew if she didn't keep a kosher home. And no matter how attracted she was to Judaism, she wasn't prepared to take that step. Her lifelong diet of sushi and sashimi included almost daily portions of shrimp or crab. How, she wondered, could she give up her favorite foods? Sacrificing those, she thought, would be like giving up part of herself and her heritage.

So it came as a pleasant surprise to her that, though no one discouraged her from keeping kosher, no one would reprimand her if she didn't. "I found out that Judaism encourages you to make the decision that's right for you," she says. "You can question things about Jewish law and arrive at your own answer."

Once she established that, conversion seemed less overwhelming. But being in Honolulu helped, too. Once there, Morris and Ann set out to find a congregation, and ended up at Sof Ma'arov. Soon enough, they were engaged in synagogue life, and Ann began her conversion study. The couple set a date for their wedding.

The splendid September day, a few days before the Jewish New Year, had many undercurrents. Their families gathered around the chuppah on the grounds of an elegant hotel, with the ocean lapping just a few feet away. Dark heads of hair, predominantly Japanese, wore white yarmulkes. From a distance, they looked like dots on a blackboard.

At the reception, Ann's brother Kenneth gave the traditional Japanese toast, leading the guests in hearty cheers of "banzai" — long life and happiness. A Hawaiian band, women dressed in muumuus, men dressed in aloha shirts and white slacks, sang soft island melodies accompanied by ukuleles. Morris and Ann wore garlands of fragrant maile leaves, which Hawaiian legend promises will yield wearers good health and prosperity.

The copious spread of food ranged from a giant loaf of challah to trays of sushi. Morris addressed the guests in Japanese, thanking them all for coming. Ann spoke in Yiddish, admonishing the assembled not to be ashamed of their appetites. "Ess, ess, ess!" she said.

Other cross-cultural rituals did not flow quite so smoothly. One of Morris's sisters marched up to the microphone with her husband and began belting out the words to "Hava Nagilah." Morris joined in the singing, but the guests sat still in their chairs, clapping along politely.

Standing beside the chuppah next to her son, as the familiar sound of Hebrew floated past, Adela Rabinko wore a pained smile. Happy as she was to see Morris married, she grieved for Zalman, who had died the year before. He had lingered painfully for months, slipping in and out of consciousness with a series of strokes. Zalman had little understanding that Morris and Ann were engaged, even though they had told him.

"He liked Ann," she says, hesitation in her voice, "but he didn't really know her." She sighs. "Let's face it: he would've liked it the other way. After everything he went through, he thought pretty soon there wasn't going to be any more Jews."

She brightens, eager to put the best face on things. With characteristic bluntness, she adds, "I wanted him to marry a Jewish girl — I wouldn't lie to you — but I wanted first a person. And Ann, she's a wonderful girl."

She is pleased that Ann converted to Judaism, if only because she believes it is important that a child have one faith. "I didn't care if he became Christian or she became Jewish. It's not a joke — you should have one thing. If you have a child, the child shouldn't get mixed up." She sighs. "Morris isn't a baby anymore. How am I going to tell him who he should love? If he's happy, who am I to tell him who's good for him?"

The Toyotas, however, were less sanguine about their daughter's relationship before they met Morris. Wini Toyota, Ann's mother, speaks authoritatively, like the former teacher she is. Debilitated by her illness, she relies on her husband for the slightest of motions. She can still, she says, turn pages by herself, and spends long hours reading. Late one warm January afternoon, her face glows softly in the sunlight that streams through her apartment window. She smiles widely and often, even in what is obviously chilling pain.

The Toyotas' apartment is spare and tidy. Fuchsia bougainvillea creeps along the terrace, and a large Japanese panel, stark and beautiful, dominates the living room. A crib for Zara's sleepovers monopolizes a wall; the Toyotas spare nothing for their only grandchild.

Wini reflects on her own religious choice: attending Sunday school as a young girl. "I just wanted to," she says, "even though I do remember my grandfather worshiping at a Shinto shrine." Much like the sons and daughters of Jewish immigrants who endeavored to shed the ways of the shtetl, Wini wanted to blend into her environment. Her looks may have tagged her as Japanese, but she could move beyond the physical boundaries of her circumstances into a more amorphous realm: the mind.

Because, perhaps, Wini was so eager to embrace Western religion, the idea that her own daughter would in turn reject it came as a bit of a shock. Ann's father, Ralph, who, like Wini, attended the Methodist church despite his Buddhist roots, says Ann's conversion came "as a total surprise."

"We were aware of the fact that because she went to school on the East Coast, the possibility of her marrying outside her race was great," he says. "So when she told us about Morris, it wasn't just American culture, which we know. It was totally different. The Jewish thing involves religion and food habits, things we didn't know about."

Some of the Jews the Toyotas did know, they say, did not leave the most favorable impression. To the reserved Japanese, the forthrightness of the Jews with whom they were acquainted came across as rudeness and disrespect — great taboos in Japanese society. "I hate to admit it," Wini says, "but a few Jewish people we know in Hawaii personify the worst kind of stereotype: pushy, loud . . . When we met Morris, we were very pleased. Here was a quiet, restrained fellow who was not at all like the stereotype." Wini laughs, and recalls taking her elderly sister to see *Fiddler on the Roof* some years ago. As they exited the theater, her sister turned to her and said, "I don't know why they're making such a fuss about Jewish and not Jewish," she said. "You're either haole or you're not haole!"

Ann and Morris have embraced each other's culture. Ann has found great solace in the Jewish "way of thinking," while Morris has explored Eastern thought. Since moving to Hawaii in 1990, he has studied Japanese, meditation, and tai chi. To the untrained ear, his proficiency seems great; he modestly insists that he "struggles along" with the language. (Ann recognizes only a few words.)

Morris hopes one day to be fluent enough in Japanese to teach Zara the languages of both sets of grandparents. He loves Japanese food, a fact that earns great respect from his parents-in-law. "He is more Japanese than our son," Wini says. "Our own son cannot be without his hamburgers and catsup. He puts catsup on rice!" Ann has shelves of Jewish cookbooks; she is as apt to prepare matzoh ball soup as sukiyaki.

Morris sees it this way: "I remember thinking that Jews were supposed to be a light unto nations. If Jews stay insular and marry within Judaism, then it's just going to be like a black hole, with no light getting out. Those Hasids who try to keep it all within aren't radiating light. But we're like rays of light."

ELEVEN

Chicken Soup

§

A S SHE PUTS IT, Clara Frost is your average Jewish mother. She worries too much. She prepares more food than guests at her table could possibly eat. And anyone who is sick within Clara's orbit is likely to get a great deal of attention. "It's just awful not to feel well," she says, no stranger to illness herself. "You should be as comfortable as you possibly can. You need fluids and plenty of chicken soup. And I'm not kidding about that," she adds. "Millions of Jewish mothers can't be wrong."

All fine and good, of course, except if you are her husband, Jack. When he is sick, he wants to go to his room, draw the shades, crawl into bed, and sleep. "And that means I don't want anyone, not even my loving wife, sticking her head in the door every half-hour and asking if I'm all right. I want to be left alone!"

But when Clara is ill, Jack doesn't return the favor. "It would be nice to be fed after three days in bed. And forget chicken soup. I'd settle for a glass of water."

Jack shakes his head. "I can't tell you all the times I've caught my breath thinking Clara is about to die. And when I find out it's really nothing — that she's stubbed her toe instead of having a heart attack — I get angry. But it always happens."

Clara wags her index finger. "You know, doctors make assumptions on the basis of their patients' last names. They take the complaints of Jews and Italians least seriously, WASPs most seriously. Did you know that? Studies have been done on it."

This repartee is typical between Jack, a county judge in Albany,

Oregon, and Clara, a French teacher, who have been married for nearly forty years. It is who they are, they say: an Ohio Protestant and a Jewish New Yorker whose lives, backgrounds, philosophies, and even political orientation differ dramatically. Still, the marriage is successful, fueled as much by intelligence and respect as by emotion.

Throughout the Frosts' long marriage, their home has been predominantly Jewish; major holidays are greeted with the traditional trimmings. They recognize Christmas, too: a tree goes up in mid-December, and Clara prepares a special meal. When their daughter Lisa was small, Easter was also a part of the Frost family calendar: they marked the day with an egg hunt and a big Sunday supper. Conflict arose — and then only with meals — when Easter and the first night of Passover fell on the same day. Jack belongs to no church; Clara is a member of a small Reform congregation.

Jack, whose family tree spans from the poet Robert Frost to settlers who reached America 250 years ago, is the eldest of six children in a prosperous family. A man with no formal ties to any faith, he has been supportive of Clara's Judaism throughout their marriage. In fact, he considers himself a "Jew with a green card," someone so familiar and comfortable with Jews and Jewish customs that he feels he has become a resident alien among them.

Indeed, when the Frosts were first married and living in Japan, where Jack was serving in the army, Clara realized on the first night of Hanukkah that she had forgotten to pack a menorah. Despondent and homesick, she burst into tears. Jack took his coat and hat from the rack and slipped wordlessly out the door. An hour later he returned with a hunk of wood, sat down at the kitchen table with his pocketknife, and began to whittle his bride a menorah. Over the years, he has contributed generously to Jewish causes, even spearheading a renovation fund for the synagogue where Lisa got married. In fact, his affinity for the Jews is so great that if he believed in converting to a religion, he says, he would have chosen Judaism long ago. But he says conversion — to any religion — is not something he endorses.

Clara, the second daughter of two Russian Jewish immigrants, grew up on Long Island, where her father, a psychiatrist, ran a mental hospital. As a child, she was surrounded by other Jews: a large extended family, neighbors, classmates, friends from the Conservative synagogue she attended.

Once she married Jack and moved to Oregon, Clara maintained her ties to Jewish culture in earnest. Within a few weeks of arriving, she discovered, to her horror, that matzoh meal and bagels were nowhere to be found. She asked her mother to send the ingredients necessary to prepare her favorite foods. She even taught herself to make challah; her first loaf was so pretty, she wouldn't let anyone eat it.

Like all people who've been married for years, Clara and Jack know each other's stories, but, more out of enjoyment than politeness, still laugh when they hear them told. They interrupt each other, gently, to admonish or correct; when describing past incidents, Jack occasionally looks to Clara for a Yiddish word. Their home is warm and spacious, and tabletops are crowded with pictures of their daughter growing up. Displayed most prominently is a large photograph of Lisa smiling, in a bridal gown, her dark hair laced with flowers. She stands with her husband, Mark, who is also Jewish, under a chuppah.

In Clara's Long Island neighborhood, Jews and Gentiles were segregated. Not surprisingly, so was her socializing. She dated only Jews, either from her synagogue or high school. "I never, ever thought or planned to marry a Gentile," she says. Her memories of growing up are happy ones. When she talks of her family, her big brown eyes take on a distant gaze. "It was just wonderful growing up in a Jewish home," she says. "Just wonderful. And it wasn't Jewish in a religious sense, because my parents weren't very religious. It was cultural. It was a social thing, being with other Jews, doing Jewish rituals. That's what made it so nice. I think it's fun to be Jewish. Even though, God knows, we've had an agony-filled history."

When Clara was little, her grandmother, a tiny woman who spoke only Yiddish, took her by subway to Brooklyn on Fridays to do the Sabbath shopping. "The smells! It was another world." They'd stop first at the chicken market, where her grandmother would squeeze and sniff the dead birds to make sure they were fresh. She would haggle with the butcher in Yiddish, then stop at the deli, where Clara would peek over the tops of giant pickle barrels and take in the pungent scent of vinegar, garlic, and dill. Clara liked the fishmonger's the least; there, the carp and whitefish glistened on their beds of ice, their glassy eyes scary and unseeing. The last stop was at the greengrocer, to pick the perfect tart apples for an apple strudel. Her grandmother labored over that dessert; she rolled the dough until it was thin enough to stretch the length of the table. Once, when the grandmother wasn't looking, Clara's older sister wrapped the dough around her neck and wore it as a cape.

Passover was Clara's favorite holiday. Although her grandmother lived in a one-bedroom apartment in Brooklyn, she insisted on having the entire family for the seder. The many card tables she put end to end snaked from the kitchen to the bedroom, where the children always sat on the bed. "We weren't a religious family, but I did grow up going to synagogue every Friday night. I can't always go now because I can't see to drive, and Jack's tired, but I've always enjoyed it. It did something to the end of the week. It was like tying a bow on a package; it made it complete."

An olive-skinned woman with threads of henna running through her short-cropped dark hair, Clara, in her early sixties, still has the pixieish looks that first attracted Jack to her. An extrovert, she wears a lot of red. When she laughs, which is often, dimples puncture her cheeks. She has picked plums from her garden and brought a chocolate cake home from the bakery. Demurring, even though it is just past dinner, is simply not allowed. "Well, won't you have some coffee then? Sure you don't want some cake? We'll talk a long time; you can eat it later. I'll cut you some, so if you change your mind, you'll have it." She places the full plate, with fork and napkin, on the table as if it had been requested.

When the conversation is over, she turns on the lights that illuminate the walkway, even though there is plenty of light from the street. "If you were any younger, I'd make you call me and tell me you got home all right," she calls out in the darkness.

Jack is plainspoken and funny; the judiciousness he brings to his work can be seen and felt in all aspects of his life. Black horn-rimmed glasses, in vogue now, dominate his face, but not because Jack is trendy: the frames are identical with the ones he sports in his wedding photograph. His thick hair is mostly silver, cut short, like a marine's, and he wears starched white shirts. His vowels are Midwestern, flat and tonal, despite his thirty years in Oregon. His approach — to marriage, to religion, to child-rearing — is practical, matter-of-fact, a product of his Ohio roots.

Growing up, Jack was a rebel. There was no trouble with drinking, fast driving, or girls, nothing like that at all. But he did think differently. And in the 1940s and 1950s in Findlay, Ohio — the town where Jack's father was an executive at the town's main industry, a rubber company — thinking differently was a big deal indeed. He defied his father's wishes to follow in his footsteps, choosing instead to study law. He was the first person in his family to attend college; in Findlay, you were expected to join the company after high school. Even though Ohio State was only ninety miles away, Jack's father insisted he attend the University of Michigan. Business friends had suggested either Michigan or Harvard as top schools for law. Harvard was out of the question, but not for financial reasons. "Too many pinkos," Jack recalls his father saying.

"When I was a kid, my family was always pretty well off. We didn't live in the fancy part of town or have new cars, but by the time I was in high school, lo and behold, my old man was a big shot. All of a sudden I was being invited to all kinds of things — low-level debutante parties, that sort of thing. I sure got a taste of that early on, and I found out quick who my real friends were.

"In all that, we used to tell jokes about the Irish, the blacks, the Scotch, whoever," Jack says. Clara interrupts the story: "Scots, Jack. The term is Scots or Scotsmen."

"Oh, Clara. I'm Scotch. That's what I grew up with, and I'm

not changing it. Scotch." He says this loudly, as if he is correcting the pronunciation of a difficult foreign word.

"At any rate, we told jokes about others — not because they were threats, because they weren't. It was because there were differences, and you could see that in some ways people of other backgrounds were like you, and in other ways they were different than you. I just grew up with the idea, I guess from my father, because he was the big influence on my life, that it's stupid to try to categorize people on the basis of their race or their color or their creed. Clara always trumps my father up as prejudiced —"

"He was!" She laughs.

"— and I guess in a sense he was. But at the time it was very Midwestern to make comments about Jews or blacks or whatever. And around Clara, well, sometimes he just said things to get her excited. Because somehow he conveyed to me that it was stupid to be that way about people. He was backhandedly admitting that, to the extent he was that way, it was stupid."

When Jack was a boy, his parents did not attend church, although his maternal grandfather was an evangelical minister. His paternal grandparents, however, were not religious at all. Jack says one of the first conversations he can remember was with his paternal grandfather; the topic was death. "He talked about it very practically. I remember thinking, 'My God, people die! They go away and they don't ever come back!' It made a big impression."

Jack's evangelical grandfather died some years after that discussion. His grandmother soon moved in with Jack's family, and tried to bring some religious order to the house. It was Jack's job to mow the lawn, a task he generally put off until Sunday. When his grandmother arrived, however, that all changed. Once she heard the blades moving, she charged out of the house and scolded him. "This is the day of rest, young man! This is the Lord's day! You put that lawn mower away."

Jack was never drawn to the tenets of Christianity. He was, to borrow the term often used about Jews, a "cultural" Christian. A Christmas tree? Wouldn't be December without it. Memories of his boyhood holidays are storybook perfect: snowy moonlit walks with his father on Christmas Eve, waking up to a living room resplendent with a tree that had appeared magically overnight. But he had a deeper skepticism about the events at Bethlehem.

Perhaps it was Jack's indifference to religion that prepared him for life with Clara. Devout Christians married to observant Jews, with their fundamental disagreements about Christ, heaven and hell, and baptizing children, are apt to struggle much more — particularly in raising a family — than do couples in which at least one partner is shy of faith. And Jack was a religious cynic, he says, from the start.

This, he says, is the legacy of his grandfather, who doubted divinity of any kind. He thought people were better off concentrating on their lives on earth. Growing up, Jack often heard that being naughty, acting out in any way, could exclude you from heaven. Midwesterners of German and English stock took their faith seriously. "If you didn't get on the stick, you wouldn't be going," he said. "Work hard, keep your head down, you'd get there." Jack's grandfather took issue with that, and always told him, "Jackie, it's too bad people just can't live and let live." Jack was twelve or thirteen at the time, and had begun to wonder about this mythical place, this life everlasting. What was it like? he wanted to know.

The old man had a gravelly voice, and when he described heaven, he let Jack know he had his doubts about the place. The weather was always nice; everyone was always in a good mood. You're with God and Jesus above the clouds, he said. "You mean when you go up there, everything's wonderful? No problems?" Jack asked, incredulous. "Yep," his grandfather replied. "Least that's what they say."

"Well, doesn't it get awfully boring? I mean, after a year or two of that, aren't you ready to leave? Wouldn't you be bored to death? You'd probably start doing bad things just to get outta there." "Yep," his grandfather replied, nodding.

As a teenager, Jack briefly attended a church across the street from his house. "Did I go there because it was a particular denomination? Did I go there because it was the church across the street? No! My girlfriend went there, that's why."

"That's one thing about Gentiles I'll never understand," Clara exclaims. "They're always changing. They do! 'Well, we decided we didn't like this church so we became that, but then we found this church and now we're this.' To me, it's inconceivable. How can people switch back and forth when churches have such fundamentally different philosophies?"[1]

Jack shrugs. Indeed, when his father was promoted to a higher mangement job, the family began attending the Lutheran church. He reports this wryly, suspiciously. "Is that a social climb-up?" Clara asks.

At the same time, his parents insisted that Jack enroll in religious classes. He was not thrilled with the demand, to say the least. "I don't want to be unfair to my parents," he says, "because I don't really know — they may have had some psychological or spiritual need or felt something was missing. But my feeling was then and still is that my dad had reached this social status. And suddenly they come home and say I've got to take catechism. It was one of the few times in my life that I was told I had to do something."

He was the only high school student in the class; all the other kids were twelve or thirteen. The minister, a kindly, gentle man, was the father of a friend. Jack questioned almost everything the minister said. He drove everybody crazy, he says, by being a smart "you-know-what." Not long before he was supposed to be confirmed, he went to see the minister. "You know," Jack said, "I've got a problem." "What, son?" the pastor asked. "Look," Jack replied, "I think Jesus Christ was a great man who had a lot of influence, but I don't think he's any more the son of God than I am." Jack groans with the memory, rubbing his broad hand over his face. "Poor guy."

Their discourse continued, the minister arguing why Jesus was God's son and why Jack should believe it. Jack never changed his mind. "It's no big deal," he told the pastor. "It *is* a big deal, and you really should believe," the minister replied. Moments before the confirmation ceremony, Jack told the minister that he would be convinced of Christ's salvation only if God produced a bolt of lightning on the altar. "With this kind of thing going on, what could the guy say?" Jack asks. Lightning did not strike, but Jack felt no reassurance.

Jack's first exposure to Judaism came in college. A Jewish student who roomed on the same floor invited Jack to spend a long weekend with his family in Detroit. It was a strange trip. "I thought, 'Boy these people do a lot of talking and hugging! And they eat very well.' I liked it." He thinks about this a moment, then grimaces, as if the recollection was not quite correct. "Well, I didn't not like it, but it was kind of hard to deal with people who came on to you so fast. They'd get right into it: 'What are you going to school for?' et cetera, et cetera. You know how Jews are."

Clara slaps her hand on the table. "Hey! That's a prejudiced remark!"

"In my mind, it's only prejudice if you categorize people with something that's not characteristic of them, or put them down and say, 'This is what's wrong with them.'"

"But Jews come in every color, from every background, from all over the world!" Clara says, her voice rising.

"Oh, come on, Clara. It's easy for you to say, 'But she just has to be Jewish. She looks Jewish; she acts Jewish.' I'm saying there was something Jewish about these people's conversations, the way they related to each other. And it's not only Jews who do that — there are other groups this behavior is typical of — but it's certainly not typical of Midwestern WASPS."

"It's not funny, though." Clara's face looks hurt. "If you're Jewish, and another Jew comes up and says, 'Oh, he looks Jewish, and that one has a Jewish name and of course she is, and oh, I know he is, he has to be,' it's all right. But if somebody else does it, we don't like it. Not even if it's our husband."

"That's one thing about the Jews. They're very sensitive that way. I'm Scotch," he says defiantly, looking at his wife. "But the point is, I don't take offense that people talk about how cheap the Scotch are. But if you say something about anything that might be indicative of Jews, many Jewish people are immediately offended. Why? Because they've been persecuted throughout the ages, and hearing it from someone else, however unseriously, is just too much."

In this exchange, these lifetime partners have summed up a large dimension of an interfaith marriage. There is the mythology, of course: "I married you, and we're not really that different." Then there is the reality: "Sometimes when I least expect it, you sure say some baffling things." Layered on top of that are particular sensibilities, of which Jack seems well aware. Much like siblings who freely point out the foibles of their parents yet smart when their spouses do, Jews feel at liberty to talk about who acts or looks Jewish. But, as many non-Jewish spouses find out, woe to anyone outside the circle, even resident aliens, who dares make the same point.

Jack Frost met Clara Schein at the University of Michigan. He was twenty, Clara nineteen. "Somebody else had told me she was Jewish," Jack says. "I couldn't have cared less. She was good-lookin'; that's what I liked. In fact, I don't recall us ever having a face-to-face chat about her being Jewish, me being not. Clara was a rather popular lady on the Michigan campus. She was a go-go-go girl. She was pretty and attracted a lot of attention because she was a lot of fun. She was a very vivacious person." Jack glances at his wife, whose eyebrows are arched in anticipation. He adds, "And intelligent, too.

"The whole point is, when you're young and when you're picking a partner, one of the first things that counts is attractiveness. She appealed to me because she was intelligent and bright. She was also very sure of herself. When you get to know her, she has insecurities like everyone else, but she was — and is — a lot of fun."

Wedding plans came into the picture immediately. Both Jack and Clara believe their marriage reveals little more than meeting the right person at the right time. They married because they fell in love, not because they rejected their families. Indeed, the formula was quite simple: they met a decade before the era of free love and living together: men and women married in their early twenties, much as their parents had done before them.

When Jack met Clara, he didn't give her Judaism a second thought. The issue of faith has never much entered into their life together. "I think one of the reasons we married and got along so well for all these years is that even though culturally Clara is very much into being a Jew, neither of us had strong religious feelings one way or the other. It might have been tough if we had."

Jews in the late 1950s and early 1960s were in the midst of crossing the social boundaries that had existed for their parents and grandparents. Like Clara, they were attending colleges with diverse student bodies. The trend had begun when Jewish servicemen returned from World War II, and, with the GI Bill, went to universities far from the traditional Jewish schools in New York. Like the Scheins, many Jews had crossed the suburban frontier, leaving behind the ghettoes of New York City and Chicago. Backbreaking sweatshop jobs were largely a thing of the past.

Indeed, Clara's family was something of a Jewish prototype. In his best-selling book on American Jewish immigrants, *The World of Our Fathers*, Irving Howe writes that 55 percent of the Jews employed in the United States, according to a 1957 government religious survey, were "professionals and technical" and "managers, officials and proprietors," as compared with slightly over 23 percent of Americans as a whole.[2]

Family therapists often classify couples by their "appropriateness" for each other. They gauge similarities in age, class background, education, even hometowns when evaluating the "appropriateness" of partners. In interfaith couples, of course, religion is added to the mix, often throwing otherwise fitting matches askew. Clara and Jack, like most interfaith couples, seemed well-suited partners. But their parents at first discounted the fact that they were both intelligent, college-educated, and ambitious. What mattered more were their differences.

"Our parents, like any parents, felt that maybe it wasn't the right thing for us socially," Jack says. "In those days, what we did was like a black-white marriage today: both sides of the family are

going to say, 'What are they doing? They're going to alienate themselves from both groups, and put their kids in a tough position.'
They figured life is hard enough; why take on this extra —" He
squeezes his eyes shut, thinking hard, and snaps his fingers. "I can't
think of the Yiddish word I want. Help me out, Clara. What is it I'm
looking for?"

"Tsouris," she replies, the Yiddish word for "troubles."

Clara's parents, Rebecca and Gabriel Schein, indeed had reservations about the marriage. Dr. Schein, a compact man whose spectacles loom over his small face, is now in his mid-nineties. Years ago,
he moved from New York to Portland, Oregon, to be near Clara.
When he looks back on her marriage to Jack, he recalls vivid
doubts.

In the early part of the century, pogroms forced Dr. Schein and
his family from what is now Belarus. His only memories of his
shtetl, Neszvizh, are sad ones. A small regiment of Cossacks was
based nearby, and a rumor spread that they were coming to wipe
out the town. "So my grandfather took precautions," he says in his
soft voice. "He put all the heavy furniture against the door to
prevent them from breaking in. Fortunately it was just a rumor.
But we were always on guard after that, and I remember my grandfather saying, 'Let's run to America.' My father was already here,
working in New York to make money. I was only five years old at
the time, but it made a big impression."

Once in America, his family settled in the Brownsville section
of Brooklyn. It was little different from Neszvizh. In fact, he can't
recall anyone in his neighborhood who wasn't Jewish. Everyone
spoke Yiddish, and on Saturday all the stores were closed. He
received a traditional Jewish education, at a yeshiva, but says life in
the New World, no matter how Jewish his surroundings, had an
inevitable effect on his Jewishness. "As I grew older, my connection
with my faith became more watered down," he says.

All his friends were Jewish, but they spoke English to one
another and their siblings; Yiddish was reserved for parents and
grandparents. "Our concerns were those of people living in Amer-

ica. I wanted to be American as soon as I arrived," he says. "My memories of Russia were very negative, connected with pogroms, and I could never forget them. We lived in terror."

Growing up, he didn't take religion seriously. Dr. Schein says, in fact, that his ties to the faith were "feeble." But culturally, Dr. Schein grew up with no doubt about who he was: he was a Jew. "It's not that complicated." He shrugs. The pattern followed into marriage. Holidays were family affairs, even if they were religious celebrations, and the Scheins were never particularly devout about attending services at their synagogue. "As far as I was concerned, it was more a matter of getting together with friends."

Even so, the Scheins were surprised when Clara brought Jack home. "We just didn't know how it would come out," he says. "We were a bit skeptical; it would even be fair to say we had strong reservations. It was just that it was our first experience with such a thing. It was unusual; none of our friends or relatives had experienced anything like it. But it was by no means a scandal. As far as religion was concerned, I found it hypocritical to raise objections, because I didn't observe any Jewish precepts. But it didn't take long to accept Jack fully. In a short time, we were very happy with the marriage."

An uncle who was a devoted Zionist and prominent lay teacher, however, refused to attend their wedding. Clara learned of this years later, after the uncle died and her father refused to attend the funeral. She had always thought her uncle hadn't come to her wedding because of travel restrictions on the Sabbath, but she learned at his death that he had voiced his objections loudly — particularly by not coming. To him, Clara had ceased to exist.

To be sure, when Jack and Clara were married in 1956, only a small percentage of American Jews chose non-Jewish mates. There were so few others like them that the Jewish community didn't know what to make of the phenomenon. Many, like Clara's uncle, wrote off Jews who married outside the fold.

Her uncle's disapproval came as a surprise to Clara. So did the comments of Jewish classmates in college, who admonished her for marrying Jack. "'How *could* you?'" she recalls a dorm-mate asking.

All of it struck her as elitist and exclusionary, traits she found repugnant and wholly incompatible with Judaism.

Reactions similar to that of Clara's uncle are rarely so bold in non-Jewish families. But he was not alone in his disappointment. Jack's mother once told Clara that no one had to know about Clara's background. "It's all right, dear," she said. "You don't look Jewish." Clara laughs this off, but Lisa, her daughter, tells the same story, wide-eyed. "I know that stuck with her for a long time," Lisa says.

Some of the most vociferous critics of intermarriage belong to the generation of Jews who lived through the Second World War, defying the odds of surviving in Europe, or those who went about their lives in America, aghast at the reports of Hitler's atrocities. So it is especially surprising to hear someone who suffered the ruthlessness of Russian anti-Semitism take an open view of intermarriage. But Dr. Schein does. He doesn't see it as negative, and he has strong advice for those who do. "My response to those who say that intermarriage is the American Holocaust is this: if a Jew feels so closely connected with things that are Jewish, there's only one place for him to go, and that's Israel." Dr. Schein's speech detours from its usual calm path at this point. "Israel is the place they should go," he says, waving a hand as if to the Middle East. "Really."

America, he says, is indeed a melting pot. But it is a melting pot of mostly Christians. "When you come down to it, it's a matter of choice: you go to live in Israel, where there is no problem, no conflict with regard to Jewish culture. Or you live here, where the non-Jewish influences are apt to predominate. And in our daily living, actually, how do we differ from our non-Jewish friends? We speak the same language; we do not speak Yiddish, we do not speak Hebrew. In our daily lives, professionally or otherwise, we are not Jewish. There are many of us who do not observe halachah, kashrut, and so forth. There are few of my Jewish friends who would abstain from bacon because it wasn't kosher, even though many grew up in kosher homes." He pauses. "It doesn't bother me that my grandchildren, my great-grandchildren, are and will grow up more American than Jewish. If one wants to live a hundred and-one percent Jewish life, Israel is waiting for you. You're accepted there fully as a Jew. I'm not saying America does not accept us as Jews. I'm just saying we can't divide our lives into being Jewish and American. It doesn't work that way."

Despite his tolerance toward his daughter's marriage, Dr. Schein says he was pleased to hear that his granddaughter Lisa was engaged to a Jewish man. "I looked at it this way: it was a case of 'getting together.' It was good that there were no barriers: Jew — Jew." He places his hands parallel to one another on the sofa where he sits and pauses. "Jew — Jew. There is an understanding between people of the same culture, the same background." The main problems, he says, come from family members. Jack's family, for example, did not take too kindly to the news that Jack was engaged to a Jewish woman. "They were somewhat uncomfortable," Dr. Schein says slowly. "The families did not have much in common culturally."

Indeed, it was not — and is not — religion that separates Clara and Jack. Much as with their philosophy of illness, whether their own or their partner's, they diverge on tradition. What has been more of a challenge is the contrast in temperament and manner, for both Jack and Clara and their families. And perhaps nothing demonstrates that quite so well as Jack and Clara's wedding night. Jack kept his plans for the evening a secret to everyone but his father, and shared them with him in case of an emergency.

Jack made reservations at the Waldorf-Astoria. It was going to cost him a fortune. "Ninety-eight bucks!" he says. Rebecca Schein kept asking what they would do that night, but Jack never told her. "I didn't see any point."

Jack's parents spent the night after the wedding at the Scheins'. They were uneasy about it, not because the Scheins were Jewish, but because they weren't the "stayover type," Jack says. "They even stayed at a motel when they came to visit us, for crying out loud," Jack says. "They weren't mixers." But the Scheins insisted, so the Frosts spent the night with them.

Jack's dad woke up the next day at dawn. He put his robe on and went downstairs, only to find Rebecca already in the kitchen. "Oh," he said, thinking he was being polite, "another early riser!" "Early riser?" Rebecca cried. "Early riser? I've been up all night! I didn't sleep a wink!"

"My dad just couldn't figure it out," Jack says. "'What do you mean, you didn't sleep a wink? What's the big problem?'"

Rebecca was on the verge of tears. "Those kids, they go off to New York City, and they don't even have a hotel room! Anything could have happened to them!" Jack's father tried to calm her down, still keeping his son's secret. Finally he said, "Look, I don't want to tell you this, because it was a surprise. Calm down; my son got a room at the Waldorf-Astoria." "The Waldorf-Astoria!" Rebecca cried. "You mean to tell me all this time you knew they have a room at the Waldorf-Astoria, and I've been thinking they slept on a park bench!"

Jack says, "My dad was real nice to her the whole next day because he felt sorry for her. He was very surprised by the whole thing. He didn't know, and I didn't know. We didn't think about how others would react. But it was sure different, especially for him. Clara's mother would explode like that, and two minutes later she'd give you a big kiss. If someone made my mother mad, you wouldn't hear from her for a week. In my family, if, once in a blue moon, someone got even half as excited as Clara's mother did on a daily basis, they'd get their nose punched."

Clara shakes her head. "I don't know how we ever got together," she says. "I always kid Jack's family about the Frost family reunions. You get the older ones sitting on the porch. No one talks except about the weather: 'Well, it's sure sunny out. Sure gonna ruin that grass out there in front. It's gonna get all brown.' Or if it's raining: 'Well, there goes the rain. I guess my joints will start aching now.' In my family, there's no such thing as silence. One cousin's in the corner having an argument with another cousin, and in another you've got two more locked in a heated debate. You've heard the joke — fifty Jews, a hundred opinions. That's my family. Sure, we express ourselves, especially when we're angry, but we kiss a minute later and the whole thing's forgotten."

When Lisa was born, Clara was determined to raise her with an understanding and appreciation of Judaism. On the other hand, because they were so far from a strong Jewish community, neither Jack nor Clara wanted her to feel isolated as the only Jew. So they celebrated both Christmas and Hanukkah, Easter and Passover. Clara felt particularly strong about honoring Jack's traditions, since he had been so welcoming to hers.

Unlike many Jewish parents in interfaith marriages, Clara didn't have the slightest worry that a Chistmas tree and Santa Claus would dampen her daughter's enthusiasm for Judaism or "make" her a Christian. "Nonsense," she says. "I knew Lisa was Jewish the moment she was born. I looked at her and said, 'This kid's a Jew.' It's something inside that just burns all the time. And with her, it was there the moment I saw her."

Lisa's arrival in 1963 didn't change Jack and Clara's household rituals, but it did enhance them. Because Lisa was the only Jewish student in her grade from elementary school to high school, Clara made an extra effort to educate both her and her classmates about Jewish holidays. When Lisa was in the first grade, Clara visited the class to talk about Hanukkah. She arrived loaded with dreidels, hot latkes, and gold-covered chocolate coins. The children, of course, loved the festivity. And until Lisa was in the sixth grade, her classmates always "voted" to have Hanukkah as well Christmas parties. "I was never made to feel different or as though I was an outsider," says Lisa. "In fact the other kids were always jealous because I got presents on both holidays.

"When I look back on it, I see my mom did a good job of making sure I felt proud of my Jewish heritage and knew the importance of keeping Jewish traditions. But my parents also made me feel enough a part of the Christian tradition that I wasn't totally isolated."

Clara wanted Lisa to have a Jewish community, but the nearest congregation was in the adjacent town. "My mom took me to the temple's Purim parties, Hanukkah parties, whatever event was going on. But she kind of dragged me, because I didn't know these people. They weren't my neighbors or my classmates, so I always felt kind of funny. And I have to admit, there is a little bit of a sense about me that I really don't belong to either group totally.

"I feel now, though, that I much more belong to the Jews. But even with Jews sometimes I sense a little distance. They don't direct it at me at all; it's just my own feeling. And I'm sure it's because they know more than I do. Which is my problem, of course."

As Lisa neared thirteen, Clara began taking her to Hebrew school. Lisa balked. "My mother says it was my one rebellion in all of growing up, but I don't agree with her. My side of it is this: I was a little girl, and my mom asked me, 'Do you want to get up every Sunday morning and go to Hebrew school?' Of course I didn't want to do that. It wasn't that I didn't want to learn Hebrew; it was that I didn't want to get up early and go study. If I'd been older I think it would've been different, but really, it was quite simple: I just didn't want to get up. It's an unfortunate coincidence that at eleven, twelve, and thirteen — difficult ages — Jewish kids are faced with Hebrew lessons. And they'd rather go out and play with their friends."

Now an attorney in Eugene, Oregon, Lisa is a soft-spoken woman with her mother's small size and her father's fine features. On a mild afternoon in late summer, she sips a 7-Up at a trendy coffeeshop. This being the Northwest, where even gas stations are fully equipped with drive-up espresso bars, Lisa's decaffeinated choice seems out of place. Even cops come in and order double lattes. She looks calm, with enormous teal eyes, a quiet voice, and a gentle manner, but insists she is not. "That's why I don't drink coffee," she says, pointing to her soda.

Her friends always accepted her as Jewish, Lisa says, although when she was in the second grade someone asked whether she believed in Jesus Christ. "Everyone else did, so I figured I'd better, too, and I said yes. I didn't understand. I wasn't educated. And that frustrated me later, because I wish I'd known more about my religion. I suppose I should give myself a break: I was only seven or eight. But when I got older, I remembered what I'd said and wished I had known more at the time."

In high school history class, Lisa watched a film of a Nazi who refused to shoot Jews and was thrown into the line of fire himself. When the teacher prompted discussion afterward about courage, a classmate expressed incredulity about the incident. "They were only Jews," the girl shot out. Lisa said nothing, but the remark stings still.

When Jack and Clara were married in 1956, not many Jews would have predicted that their children would consider themselves Jewish. After all, Lisa was raised with two faiths and grew up distant from other Jews. But she was also raised to feel a part of both worlds. When she left Albany to go to college, she was even unaware of the clues Jewish students in America rely on to recognize other Jews. "I was only vaguely aware of what was a Jewish name and what wasn't," Lisa says. "It wasn't something I thought about. And besides, it didn't matter: I was Jewish, yet I didn't have a Jewish name. Now I'm learning to pick up clues about who might be Jewish or not — my husband points out certain mannerisms or ways of looking at things in television or movie characters. But before, I wouldn't have noticed it."

For the past decade, Lisa has spent her free time in a range of liberal social causes — environmentalism, women's rights, criminal rights. Indeed, she believes her sense of duty to the world stems from the Jewish tradition of tzedakah, the obligation to be compassionate and charitable. It is the part of her heritage she values most.

There are times, though, when she feels as though she is not completely accepted by either Jews or Gentiles. She says she felt awkward as a child among some of her mother's religious relatives because her mother didn't keep kosher. "They sort of made me feel like a second-class Jew," she says. "I totally respect the kosher tradition if someone wants to demonstrate their faith that way. That's fine, but I think God intends for me to spend my energy helping other people."

Lisa got her sense of involvement from both parents. Though they are political opposites — Jack is a Republican, Clara a Democrat — both are passionately engaged in the world around them. Clara insists that her daughter's civic awareness grew from her training in tzedakah. She herself has been involved in a number of civic organizations, from Hadassah to historical societies to the school board. Lisa, Clara says, has a very Jewish sense of justice in the world. "Lisa has never, ever been a Gentile child. Now I don't know what makes me say that, but she never has been. I don't know how I know, but I know. Part of it is social, and there's a sense of — and I'm not saying this is superior to Gentiles or anything like that — but Jews have a feeling about society and the world and justice and responsibility, and it's just in you. You look at life a certain way, and other people don't see it the same way. I can't even put my finger on it."

At this, Jack pulls back from the table, impatient for his wife to finish. He, after all, has spent decades as a public servant — first as a district attorney, now as a judge. "I think Jews look at it that way, but I'm sitting here thinking, 'Geez, Clara, what the hell do you think I *do?*'"

"I can't decide," she says. "Maybe partly the Jewish factor drives you, too." He shakes his head but smiles.

What is striking is that Lisa feels she has learned more from her Jewish husband in the six years they've been together than she ever did growing up. "And that's not because my mom didn't try," she says, "because she did. But a lot of being a part of the Jewish community is cultural, and I simply wasn't exposed to much of it." Because of the distance between Oregon and New York, Lisa saw her mother's family only about once a year; the rich Jewish world her mother experienced existed only in Clara's stories of her girlhood. Nevertheless, Lisa as an adult has discovered the warmth of a greater Jewish environment: her husband Mark's family and childhood community in Brookline, Massachusetts, a suburb of Boston with a substantial Jewish population.

In contrast to Lisa, Mark grew up surrounded by other Jews. While Lisa did have contact with her mother's family as a girl, they weren't a powerful influence. "I've been to several big Jewish events in his family, and it's really a wonderful experience: the joyousness, the warmth — all of it makes me happy to be a part of that community. And it's something I've become more attuned to since meeting Mark. I'm learning a lot from him the more we're together."

She contrasted her own wedding, where a klezmer band played lively folk music, to a Christian ceremony she attended some months later. "It was somber by comparison," she says. "Mark said later it was more like a funeral than a wedding. We just kind of looked at each other throughout it; it didn't seem to be a very happy occasion. Of course the families were happy, but it wasn't quite so evident as it was at ours. Everyone got sweaty dancing the hora at our wedding, even people who had never seen it before.

"I've always felt lucky that I was Jewish, because it's something different. But now I feel even luckier, because I'm learning more." When she and Mark have a child, she says, she hopes to study with that child as he or she approaches thirteen. Her own Jewish education is lacking, but she feels she has no one to blame but herself. Others, though, might blame intermarriage.

And so it is that Judaism, for the Schein family, will likely be carried into four generations in America. For Jews concerned with intermarriage, the Frosts' story seems almost an interfaith fairy tale: too good to be true.

Clara looks at it this way: Jews take intermarriage all too seriously. Granted, her own daughter married a Jew. But she had the passion to keep Judaism alive in a conservative rural town with only two or three other Jewish families. Judaism is much more tenacious, she thinks, than people give it credit for. "Jews who look at their children's intermarriage as the end of their family history only alienate them," she says.

"I look at our history: we never should have survived the

Holocaust, the pogroms, the Spaniards, the Syrians, the Persians. We've been persecuted by so many people in so many countries.

"Intermarriage isn't such a bad thing, because we're always getting more people who are sensitive to Jewish issues and how Jews feel about Judaism itself. We're also getting people who want to join the faith. I just don't think people should be so panicked about it."

TWELVE

All-American

&

THERE WAS nothing remarkable about David Brown's bar
mitzvah in 1961. It was a warm morning, the sun bright as
lemons, and his extended family gathered inside a modern synagogue in San Francisco. Joining him on the bimah were his father,
the rabbi, and his mother's brother, Joseph Gold, who had been
asked that morning to read a Hebrew prayer. Each wore a black
satin yarmulke specially printed for the occasion.

When Joe Gold stepped to the pulpit, he looked at the rabbi,
who gave him a nod. With a deep breath and a glance at the open
page before him, Joe began reciting in flawless Hebrew that echoed
through the cavernous temple.

The congregation would hardly have known it, but Joe hadn't
spoken a word of Hebrew — or in fact even attended a Jewish
service — since his own bar mitzvah, twenty-five years earlier. His
recall of long-ago words and melodies was all that was left of his
Jewish upbringing. Joe had married a Lutheran woman, Barbara,
and converted to her faith more than a decade earlier.

"I don't know how it happened, but as soon as I looked down
at that page, it somehow all came back," Joe says. "God was with
me, I guess."

Barbara remembers the day well. She sat with their two children, Todd and Wendy, fretting that Joe would embarrass his
nephew with a string of mistakes and gibberish. Judaism was so far
from their lives. How could they expect anything different? "Those
words just came out of his mouth like velvet," she says. "I was so

proud." The children, however, were shocked. Wendy leaned across her brother's lap and whispered to her mother, "Did Jesus talk that way?"

Not only the service was unfamiliar, with no cross and no robed choir; the whole occasion was strange. At the luncheon after the ceremony, there were trays of food Todd and Wendy had never seen: lox, gefilte fish, chopped liver, and pickled herring. Some people greeted the children by saying they were aunts, uncles, or cousins. Yet they had never met — and they lived only miles apart. Even the voices were louder than what they were used to. "It was almost as if we had gone to a foreign country for a day," Wendy says.

The family Gold's journey from shtetl to Christian conversion spans just two generations. Joe's father, Avram Rabinovicz, arrived from Romania with fervent hopes of success in his adopted country. His children eagerly embraced his wish to be all-American. Joe and his siblings shrugged off their immigrant mother's admonitions to eat only kosher food, preferring instead the ham and cheese sandwiches of their Catholic friends. Joe became a college basketball star, married Barbara, and converted to Christianity without, he insists, regrets or second thoughts. The decision to abandon Judaism was straightforward. "There wasn't any competition between becoming a Christian and what I'd been born, because there had hardly been any Jewishness in my life."

Indeed, Avram Rabinovicz had begun assimilating the moment he arrived in New York. As family lore goes, the opportunity presented itself before even Avram could have guessed, when a customs official stumbled on the syllables of his surname. "Rabinov? Rabinovich? Rabinovick?" The official sighed. Avram could barely recognize the shortened vowels, and worried that his name would somehow thwart his new life. Out of nervousness, he dug his fist deep into his pocket, and grasped a small gold coin someone had given him in the Old Country for luck. The official saw the coin, and gestured to it. "Gold," he said. "You're Abe Gold." Abe

Gold dropped the coin back into his pocket. The coin was lucky, he told himself. His new name would no doubt bring him prosperity in his new land.

But his was something of a dream deferred. He settled in Brooklyn, where he met his bride, Malka. Three children were born in four years.

Brooklyn was hardly better than Bucharest. Abe felt trapped there, as if it were only a bigger shtetl. He had learned English quickly and wished his children would do the same. But in this environment, he doubted they would: everyone spoke Yiddish. Families were crowded into tenement apartments, trying to scrape by. Even Malka had no need to learn English. Some America, he thought. This, he could have had at home. So Abe struck out West, to San Francisco, in 1906, the year of the great earthquake. Malka and the children followed shortly after.

Abe set up a dry-cleaning and hat-making business in the city's downtown, which was in the midst of rebuilding after the disaster. The family settled in the city's Richmond district, home to many new immigrants, most of them Italian and Irish. Their house, Joe recalls, stood in the shadows of the great stucco churches nearby. The struggle to feed the Gold children — who eventually numbered eight — was great. But World War II gave Abe's business an unexpected boost. The military's demand for hats and caps surged when the United States entered the war. Even Malka was drafted to work, running a ribbon business that flourished as soldiers became more decorated with each passing battle.

Growing up in the 1920s and 1930s when xenophobia was mainstream thought, Joe tried to be as "American" as possible. He counted few Jews among his friends; those who did live near were "rich kids," he says, people with whom he had no common ties. Instead, he mingled mostly with his Catholic neighbors, played sports with them, ate their pasta and potato stew, even stopped by their houses on Christmas Day to see what Santa Claus had left.

The Judaism of Malka and Abe Gold would likely have raised

eyebrows among those living in the Jewish hubs of Brooklyn and the Lower East Side of Manhattan. When Malka tried periodically to make her kitchen kosher, one of the children or her husband would undermine her attempts. "She always said she was going to do it, but then she'd complain about how hard it was with all the kids, so eventually she gave up," Joe says. She wouldn't go near bacon, ham, or the red crabs fishermen brought in from San Francisco Bay. "But my father sure did," Joe says, "although my mother didn't know about it."

Like most immigrant Jewish women, Malka Gold had no formal religious education. She did not regularly attend synagogue, but knew prayers for household ceremonies. Her Jewish knowledge was mostly limited to domestic rituals, surely challenged by the tensions of living in the United States. Christian neighbors — her children's schoolmates — ate treyf, or non-kosher, food. Soon enough, the Jewish Sabbath, Friday night and Saturday, changed from a day of reverence to a workday, nothing special. Malka's cries to keep Shabbat holy were laughed off by her children. There were basketball and football games to watch, they said as they headed out the door. They saw her edicts, both in the kitchen and for the Sabbath, as archaic, a set of rules that existed for another place and time.

In the Old World, Jewish education was a male domain, as were synagogue services. In the shtetl, the synagogue was a central feature of life. In the New World, concerns for many Jews were more secular. And Abe Gold followed a typical pattern. Work came first, family second, tradition last. America worked on Saturdays; so did Abe Gold. It was as simple as that. Who had time for synagogue? No one in the Gold family went regularly.

"The only time I went was to study for my bar mitzvah," Joe says. "After that I never went back. My father would drop me and my brother Dan — he was sixteen months older — and Dan would stay for five minutes, then go off to the park. I stayed, but I don't remember learning anything there. It was important to my family that I be bar mitzvahed, but not to me. I didn't know whether my bar mitzvah was a candy bar or what."

"I didn't like Hebrew school; I only went because I had to. I don't even really remember my bar mitzvah. I said a few words, did what I had to do. When it was over, I felt great. And the only reason was that it meant we didn't have to go to Sunday school anymore." He scoffs. "About the only Jewish thing in the household was my mother reading the *Jewish Forward*."

Joe had a different religion, of sorts, one that was entirely American: basketball. He didn't have any girlfriends, Jewish or otherwise, but it is unlikely that they would have made a difference in his social life. He was poor and didn't have the money to go on dates. "I had lousy clothes," he says, "so I just went to the gym and played basketball." He spent as much time practicing as he could, from early morning until late at night. His trim seventy-two-year-old frame reveals his lifelong devotion to the game. Clad in a golf shirt, slacks, and black Converse tennis shoes, Joe has a torso as taut as a washboard. He looks up, his blue, almost violet eyes peering out brightly from behind spectacles. As he speaks, in his gentle voice, he punctuates the air gingerly with arthritic fingers. "I don't remember being home much, actually. It wasn't a very pleasant place."

In 1947, Joe met Barbara Jones, and it changed his life forever. Barbara, a regal, handsome woman with startlingly blue eyes, is direct and businesslike, every bit the former phys. ed. teacher. Erect and lean, she says she owes her appearance to the hour-long walks and stretching routines she makes a part of her day. "I was into exercising before it was 'in,'" she says. Her blond permed hair gives the impression that she stands inches above Joe, or Joey, as his friends sometimes call him. But they say in stocking feet they are the same height, five feet seven.

Impeccably dressed, make-up meticulously applied to a face that appears younger than its seventy-three years, Barbara is frank and engaging. Dangling earrings brush her cheeks, and a set of filigreed gold bracelets tinkle softly, faint as far-off wind chimes, as she speaks. Her handshake is firm, her house neat; Barbara is the type of person who likes to see fresh vacuum marks, not footprints, on the powder blue carpet of her home in San Bruno, a modest suburb just south of San Francisco.

Barbara's upbringing could hardly have been more different from her husband's. She was born in a small town at the foot of Oregon's Coastal Range, lush green hills that, anywhere but the American West, would qualify as mountains. Her family traced its roots in the state to some of the first pioneers along the Oregon Trail. Roads and nearby towns were named for some of her ancestors, and Barbara grew up thinking she never wanted to leave. Her neighbors were similar. Barbara had never met anyone unlike her own relatives until a Catholic family moved to her town, Bell Fountain, when she was in high school.

Most of the men, like Barbara's father, made a living logging in the great forests and farming some of the nation's most fertile land. The Great Depression was in full swing, but Barbara never knew it. The Joneses' root cellar was full of the potatoes, carrots, and onions that grew in their garden, and the pantry was lined with great blue jars of the tomatoes, beans, pears, and peaches Barbara and her mother canned each summer.

Neither her parents nor her three brothers were religious, but Barbara attended a community church regularly with a neighbor girl and her mother. Her own parents, she says, didn't pay much attention to her churchgoing; soon, she was a fixture of the congregation. She liked the music, the stories, and the warmth inside the little parish.

Barbara and Joe laugh frequently as they recall their years together. Sitting at their round glass kitchen table, Barbara giggles over memories, recited with great panache, and Joe fills in with unexpected punchlines. Sometimes, just as it seems that Joe has heard the story too many times to still be engaged, he will look you straight in the eye, deadpan, and deliver a biting riposte. "I was raised on zingers," he says. "I ought to know how to use them every now and again."

The Golds say they have lived a good life over their half-century together. By all accounts, theirs is a successful companionship, full of its share of joy and struggle. When they were younger, friends so admired their marriage that four sets of them named Barbara and Joe as guardians of their children in their wills.

The couple met in a short line for transfer students at Oregon State University, in Corvallis, a small town a few miles from Barbara's home. Joe had just returned from duty in World War II; he had been stationed in Germany and was now a student at Oregon State on a basketball scholarship. Barbara was finishing her degree after two years at a small teaching college. The line moved slowly; romance, on the other hand, took off at once.

"I thought he had the cutest, most vivacious smile," Barbara says. Soon, Barbara and Joe were a couple, and in between their studies and Joe's basketball schedule, they went out on dates, going to the movies and stopping for ice cream afterward.

Joe liked Barbara right away. "She was a real nice girl," he says, "real pretty, real American." It was obvious that she wasn't Jewish, mostly from her looks and her name. "But I didn't keep it in my mind," he says.

A modest man, Joe didn't tell Barbara he played basketball. When she asked about his long hours at the gym, he told her he was the team water boy. "I didn't know if I was going to be good enough to make the team," he says. He was a starting forward nonetheless.

As soon as the season started, Barbara reveled in watching Joe on the court. Though short, he made up for his lack of height with his keen peripheral vision. "It sounds crazy to talk about now, but back then people didn't really use their vision like that," he says. "It was one of the team's secret advantages." His record for assists, as well as his knack for passing the ball behind him as he dribbled forward, quickly made him a star player and a crowd favorite. He and his teammates were nicknamed the "Thrill Kids."

Jews first arrived in Oregon in the 1840s to work as merchants in the growing cities along the Willamette and Columbia Rivers. Joe, however, had no contact with any Jews, from anywhere. He doesn't recall a single Jewish classmate during his college years. "And one thing's for sure; I was certainly the only Jew on the basketball team."

As Judaism figured only nominally in Joe's life, the topic never surfaced early in their courtship. But one day Barbara got a call from her brother. "Sis," he said tensely, "I gotta ask you something. I was just at the dentist, and we were talking about basketball. He called Joey 'the little Jew.' I said, 'Hey, watch it, that's my sis's boyfriend.' Is it true? Is Joey Jewish?"

"I almost fell off my chair," Barbara recalls. "It never occurred to me to identify anybody, let alone Joey, with labels. So I said, 'Search me, I don't know. But I'll ask him.' I did, and he said yes. He wanted to know if it would make any difference with my parents, who liked him very much. And I told him I didn't think much of people who change their mind about people if they find out they're different. I said, 'I don't think so, but if it does, I'll tell them to go to hell.' I wouldn't have been able to reject Joey just because he was Jewish. I couldn't have conceived of doing such a thing."

Even if Barbara was reluctant to tell her parents that Joe was Jewish, it was not something she could keep under wraps for long. By the time the Joneses were getting to know Joe, everyone in town knew about his heritage; local newspapers referred to him as "the Jewish guard from San Francisco." Her parents, Barbara says, couldn't have cared less about Joe's religion. "They adored and idolized him," she says. Joe agrees. "I felt very accepted by everybody. Her brothers would come to the locker room after games. I enjoyed Barbara first of all, but I got along with her folks real well, too."

Joe and Barbara had come of age at a time of virulent anti-Semitism. Between the World Wars, antipathy toward Jews — as well as Catholics, blacks, Southern and Eastern Europeans — was perhaps at its peak. Quotas prevented Jews from gaining entry to many colleges and universities. Jews were barred from apartment buildings, hotels, even professions. Job ads in one New York newspaper requesting only Christian applicants appeared at a rate of a hundred per thousand in 1937, up from three per thousand in 1911.[1]

Some politicians even blamed Jews for the Depression. Father Charles Coughlin preached anti-Semitism on his radio show. The broadcast became popular with unemployed auto workers in Detroit, as well as with other industrial workers elsewhere who had little hope of finding jobs.

When it came time for Barbara to meet Joe's parents — often an anxious experience even for same-faith couples — the disparity between their backgrounds, their parents, even their meals, loomed large. On Christmas break from her first job — organizing physical education classes for a school district — she took the train to San Francisco. Within minutes of the first handshake, Malka Gold ushered Barbara into her kitchen. Her face just inches away, she began whispering to Barbara, her thick Yiddish accent obscuring the words. "The very first time she met me, she started in on me, and she never, ever let up," Barbara says. She pauses. "Never, ever.

"She took me aside and told me she was afraid her son would marry a Gentile, and that that would upset her very much, because she had a nice rich Jewish girlfriend all picked out for him." Joe interjects, "I had never heard of such a girl, of course." Barbara goes on, "She told me — and by this time, I was in tears — that because I wasn't Jewish, I wasn't welcome."

Joe was deeply embarrassed. He had tried to warn Barbara of his mother's strong views on the topic of intermarriage, but it made his fiancée's introduction to Malka no less bitter. After the disastrous encounter, Joe took Barbara's arm wordlessly and left the house. Outside, he apologized for his mother's behavior, his voice barely a whisper. He took Barbara to the nearby house of his oldest brother, Irving. Irving had married a Catholic woman, Betty, who assured Barbara that "no matter what, I had support in the family. All I had to do when Malka — we called her Bubbe — got after me was to look around and see who married whom," Barbara says. "Only one of those eight kids married a Jew and stayed married to a Jew."

Barbara was distraught over the meeting with Malka. But almost as confusing to her were the Gold family dynamics. "Here I was, from this farm, where everybody just pretty much got along, and where everybody was polite. Then I was a guest for five minutes in this woman's house, and she starts insulting me. I was totally unprepared emotionally for this sort of thing; how vocal people were, you might even say disrespectful. It wasn't just his mother. Whatever it was, they wore their emotions on their sleeves, whether anger or love. I just couldn't cope with all that. I couldn't believe it."

Despite Malka's ill wishes, Joe and Barbara were married in June 1948; a judge conducted the ceremony, which was entirely without fanfare. Neither had particularly wanted a religious wedding. "The whole thing was no big deal," Barbara says. "It was just a legal thing. I didn't — and don't — consider marriage a sacrament."

The couple moved to San Francisco immediately after the wedding, and Joe went into business with his brothers: the import and export of pet supplies. Every Friday night, Joe and Barbara were expected at Abe and Malka's house for dinner. Malka's cooking wasn't the greatest, and Barbara wastes no words describing it. "She cooked her peas so long they were like raisins," she says, "and her chicken was as dry as sawdust."

"How do you think *we* felt?" Joe asks. "We'd had the same thing every Friday night growing up."

A year after the wedding, Barbara became pregnant. They had discussed their religious differences before they got married and had agreed on a single faith for their children. "I knew Judaism really meant nothing to him, as far as the religion was concerned, and I told Joey I wanted to raise our children as Christians. He said fine, and that was that."

And so when Todd was born, Barbara began making baptism arrangements at the Lutheran church she had joined. Joe voiced reservations. "I asked him, 'Don't you remember? We have an agreement.' He was afraid of his mother."

"That was part of the reason, sure," he says. Much as Joe had avoided his mother's wrath as a child by playing basketball, he avoided it as an adult by not confronting her. Nevertheless the baptism took place, well shielded from Malka.

Whatever the occasion — the dreaded Shabbat dinners at the Golds', anniversary celebrations, birthday parties — Barbara steeled herself for facing Malka. Regardless of the event, Barbara says, Malka found something about her daughter-in-law to pick on. She would comment on the children's behavior. Barbara mimics Malka's Yiddish accent as she tells the story. "'Are those new shoes? How much did they cost my son?' Or, 'Why don't you watch your son so that my son can eat?'" She turns to Joe. "I'm not exaggerating, am I?" she asks. Expressionless, Joe shakes his head no. Barbara looks at him, then away, disgust showing clearly on her face. "You never stood up to her; you never stuck up for me."

Joe responds, quietly, "Barbara, there just wasn't any standing up to her."

"Well, I resented it," Barbara says. She attributes many of the difficulties in their marriage to her mother-in-law's intrusion in their lives and Joe's inability — or lack of desire — to confront her. Barbara had a constant stomach ache, which doctors diagnosed as psychosomatic. She was anxious much of the time, knowing she would have to see Malka. "I was really angry with myself for allowing her to do this, but I was fighting her hard and I needed his help. And he just didn't get it. Even the kids were aware of it. I bitterly resented the fact that Joe didn't tell her to go to hell. Just like I'd have told my family if they'd made a fuss over his being Jewish. It was my life, my choice, my husband."

Joe looks outside for a moment at the bright garden he has cultivated over the years. The smell of sweet jasmine drifts through the screen door. He clears his throat, then says: "I don't know why I didn't do it. I did some things later on, like when I'd take the kids to see her without Barbara, and she'd start telling me how bad Barbara was. I'd just take them and leave, without a word. She knew; don't think she didn't; she knew."

"But you never told her in words," Barbara says. "There was something in your whole family that just didn't want to confront your mother. Nobody ever did." Barbara's relationship with Malka became almost a caricature of bad feelings between a Jewish woman and her son's Gentile bride. At times, it bordered on the absurd.

Barbara says it took many years for her to get over the bitterness that Malka planted. Even though Barbara insists she has left it behind her, it seems doubtful that she has. There is an edge to her voice when she recounts Malka's endless stream of insults, and her eyes cloud as she speaks, as if the incidents had occurred last week. "In retrospect, I know I should have pitied my mother-in-law, not thought of her the way I did. I was so submerged in my own desperation that I didn't think about where she was coming from, which was ignorance. It took a long time to get that perspective, but I have it now. Sometimes I even wonder if Joe chose me because I wasn't wishy-washy. I'm a strong woman, like his mother. You can't push me around. Maybe he admired that in me, in the same way he may have admired — and loathed — it in his mother. I know it must have been difficult for her. She and Papa were immigrant parents, living their culture in this culture, and I know it must have been a tremendous conflict. It certainly was for the children.

"I've tried to live my faith through my relationships with other people. I'm wrestling God to the floor all the time. All of us have a little meanness in us. I see God in everybody, but she was one person I didn't look to for him."

The interfaith troubles between Barbara and Malka were exacerbated by many things. Each came from an isolated environment with little exposure to people whose ways differed from their own. Both were stubborn and dug in their heels for a tug-of-war, with Joe in the middle. Malka, smarting because seven of her eight children had married outside her faith, must have felt guilty, hurt, even ashamed. Barbara, unaccustomed to vivid displays of temper and emotion, reacted in ways not altogether becoming.

Today, most couples with in-law problems as grave as the ones Barbara and Joe encountered might seek therapy to help cope with such cultural rifts. But therapy in the 1950s, outside a few privileged circles, was something almost unheard of, even in California. Barbara laughs at the idea that she and Joe might have gone for outside help. "You'd just as soon flap your wings and fly," she says.

Nevertheless, Joe was determined not to relive the marriage of his parents. "All they did was fight," he says. "Mostly my mother yelled, and my father would mumble something back."

The Golds say they don't argue. They discuss things, sometimes spiritedly, but rarely with raised voices. It is not as if they never lose their tempers, Barbara says. She, for one, is quick to confront those who anger her. And she readily admits that she was overtly hostile to her mother-in-law. When Wendy was born, Barbara gave her daughter a small gold cross. She made sure it was in plain view, resting outside Wendy's collar, before visits to the elder Golds' apartment. Sometimes, on Sunday afternoons, Malka and Abe would drop in unannounced. "Mom and Pop are here!" Joe would cry out as they drove up. "When he said it, it was as if someone had hit me in the stomach with a vicious blow. It was a pain so intolerable that I would put Wendy in the stroller and leave just so that Bubbe couldn't pick her up, so she couldn't even touch her. And I let him visit with them. I didn't want to be a part of it. Joe never talked about it, never discussed it with them. But it wasn't a matter of talking or discussing. You could talk all you wanted to about it. I wanted him to do something."

Once, after a particularly bitter incident — neither recalls what it was — Joe suggested that they move to Portland to avoid further trouble for both families. Barbara was in tears. But when she heard that, she shot up from her spot on the couch and declared, "Never. Never, ever, ever. I am not a quitter. *She* is *not* going to drive me out of this place."

She acknowledges that "it was probably one of the best things he ever said to me, on one hand, because it made me sit up and stop feeling sorry for myself. But you also see that instead of confronting the issue, he wanted to move away, distance himself. And I said, 'Never.'" (It is a word she likes to use.) "I am bigger than she is.

I know that up here" — she taps her skull with her index finger — "and also in my heart." She touches her chest with her fist.

After Wendy's baptism, in 1952, Joe approached Barbara with a proposition as she and the children returned from church. He told her that he would like to become a Christian. "I looked at him and asked, "Why?" I told him that when I met him, he was probably one of the most Christian people I'd ever met. He was the one who most personified what I had learned that a good Christian should be: loving, caring, forgiving, accepting. So what was the difference?"

Joe pushes his glasses back up on his nose, and says, "Well, there was only one thing further that I could do, and that was accept Christ. Which is what I wanted to do."

Conversion to any faith is a momentous step. It requires much thought, study, and time, and the move is often greatly misunderstood by the convert's relatives. Why, they wonder, would anyone want to turn away from long-held family tradition and practice?[2]

Joe insists his conversion had nothing to do with his mother. "I did it to make our family stronger. It was really what I wanted," Joe says. "We had never made any attempt to integrate anything like Passover into our family; it just wasn't important to me. I thought my converting would really improve things."

He pauses. "I thought it would improve our family, for sure, but I also wanted it for myself. It didn't improve our family fifty percent or anything like that, but it did make me feel we were more together. And we were. Still are. We go to church every Sunday and are very involved with our congregation."

The Golds acknowledge the irony in their choice of church, considering that Martin Luther's views toward Jews were hardly sympathetic. But Barbara says the church's liberal views mirror her own. An ardent Democrat active in California politics, she believes the Lutheran church is a "good fit."

Yet Barbara and Joe never denied Joe's roots to their children. Barbara bought *The Diary of Anne Frank,* and insisted that Todd and Wendy read it when they were adolescents. When World War II became a topic of discussion in history classes, Barbara and Todd had long talks. When Todd became involved in the protests against the Vietnam War, he and his mother locked heads over pacificism, which Todd endorsed. "I asked him if he would have been a pacifist during World War Two, too," she says, her voice rising with the memory. "When I pointed out that we all would have gone to the gas chambers — his dad for being born a Jew, Todd and Wendy for being half-Jewish, and me for marrying a Jew — he changed his mind a little."

Barbara and Joe do maintain ties to Jewish issues, however remote. They are charter members of the Simon Wiesenthal Center in Los Angeles and the Holocaust Museum in Washington. Their Jewish friends embrace Joe as "one of them," he says.

To be sure, there is nothing Jewish about them. They had their children baptized, and they in turn had theirs baptized. They go to church on Sundays. Not given to introspection in the first place, Joe doesn't even think about the Judaism he left behind. Even so, there is something just below the surface, much as there was in Spain for centuries after the Inquisition, when the children of converted Catholics lit candles on Friday nights without really knowing why.

And so it was that one afternoon a few years ago Wendy Gold Jackson, a teacher in New Mexico, found herself shouting as she explained to two seventh-grade boys why a swastika was an inappropriate symbol for an art project.

"I called them in," she says. "I was just furious. The swastika is an ancient Sanskrit symbol, but everyone knows what it's come to represent. I asked these kids if they had any understanding of its recent historical meaning. 'Well, no, not really,' they said. One of them said he had 'kind of' heard about Jews being killed during the war. 'Oh, you have, have you?' I said. And I started preaching. I just started preaching. I said, 'Six million Jews were killed during the war, only for being Jewish. Hitler used the swastika as his symbol; it struck fear in every Jew. And they weren't only killed. They were mutilated. They were gassed. Their bodies were burned in crematoria, and their skin was used for lampshades.'

"I just went on and on and on. After a while I looked up, and my teaching partner had these wide eyes and said, 'Okay, I think you've said enough.' But you know something? I felt I'd hardly covered it."

Joe never told his mother of his conversion. His mother, he says, eventually found out from one of his siblings, but he never mentioned it. "She would have hollered and screamed, and I just wasn't up for that," he says.

There was really only one concern about Joe's conversion, and that was what would happen if he died before his parents. "I agonized over it," Barbara says, "because I would've had a Christian funeral for him. And that would've made a lot of people uncomfortable."

It was not the last time the subject of Christianity surfaced at death. When Abe Gold became ill, he went to a Catholic hospital for care. Barbara, who was fond of her father-in-law, went frequently to visit. One day just before his death, Abe lifted his pillow and drew out a rosary the nuns had given him. Although they never discussed it, Barbara thought Abe was trying to send her a message: that he had doubts about his religion, too.

When Abe Gold died, Malka tried her best to observe Jewish mourning rituals: removing the cushions from chairs so that family members would not be too comfortable; tearing her garment as a testament to her grief; serving hard-boiled eggs and round rolls, symbolic of eternal life. But the seven of her children who had left Judaism behind had no patience for such things; they began to ridicule her. "I'm not making excuses, because what happened wasn't the nicest thing," Joe says softly.

Irving, Joe's oldest brother, came downstairs and said, "Ah, I found Papa's will." He began to read a make-believe will, which stated that Abe had bequeathed all his earthly possessions to his beloved daughter-in-law, Betty Gold, who was Catholic.

"Betty and Malka hated each other," Barbara explains. "Betty didn't even come to the funeral, because it meant she'd have to see

Malka. So Irv was standing there, pretending he's reading Papa's will, and he makes out that he has bequeathed everything to Betty. Bubbe was watching her son do this, the day they buried her husband. All the kids were just rolling on the floor — I was laughing, too, I have to be honest. But it was really insensitive."

Joe says he and his siblings were laughing because his brother was making light of his mother's animosity toward Betty, not because they were mocking her rituals. But the afternoon's events certainly revealed the depth of the family's conflict over love, and over tradition.

Even Malka's death did not salve the bitterness she had left in her wake. When she died, Barbara didn't go to her funeral. "It would've been hypocritical of me," she says. "Despite the fact that she was my children's grandmother, she meant nothing to me and nothing to them." She pauses. "Even Joey didn't shed a tear."

"Enough Jewish"

❧

F OR NEARLY three years, I asked people questions about their relationships with God, in part because I wondered how people of different faiths dealt with their spiritual dilemmas in a marriage. I was curious, to be sure, about the figures in a national survey: was interfaith marriage as large a loss to American Judaism as much of the community believed? But I have to be honest; my reasons were also selfish. I wanted a glimpse of the future. What was it like for couples like my husband and me? A Jew and an "honorary Jew," who was by emotional predilection an "associate of the tribe." I wanted, I suppose, to prove to myself that my choice — to live on the outskirts of Judaism, a suburb of it — was okay. I had toyed with the idea of conversion. But I was not convinced that a convert could ever be a full member of the tribe or partake in the sense of community Jews all over the world share — in birth, in marriage, in mourning, in joy.

Hanna Krall, a Polish-Jewish writer who miraculously survived the war, had begun to raise these questions for me when I moved to Poland in the first year of my marriage. Her father was taken by the Nazis during the invasion of Warsaw; she never saw him again. Hanna and her mother, however, underwent a complete identity change. A Catholic friend, Maria, arranged for false papers. She also insisted that Hanna, a black-haired, dark-eyed child who looked distinctively different from her blond Polish peers, attend parochial school. Like any other good student, Hanna learned Catholic doctrine, songs, and prayers, from novenas to the rosary. But Hanna and her mother were betrayed by someone who knew their secret, and the Nazis stormed their apartment one night to arrest them. The religion of Jewish males could be determined by finding out whether they had been circumcised. Women, however, bore no physical sign of their faith. In Poland, though, which was almost 90 percent Roman Catholic before the war, there was one easy way to tell: a knowledge of Catholicism.

And so the police demanded recitation of prayers as proof of the Kralls' Polishness, their Catholicism. Five-year-old Hanna passed the test; her mother, despite her fair hair and blue eyes — otherwise "Aryan looks" — could not. The police were disgusted. "One of you is a Jew; the other is a Pole. It is up to you to decide who is who during the night." Maria discovered their absence and blustered her way into the police station, saving them both. Later Hanna would tell me, "Here I was, a small Jewish girl, and I really *was* praying to Jesus' Jewish mother Miriam — Maria in Polish. It seems she heard me."

As a journalist, Hanna devoted her life to the Jews who had disappeared. Her best-selling book about the Warsaw ghetto uprising, *Shielding the Flame,* turned her into an overnight celebrity in Poland; her subsequent books sell briskly throughout Europe. Yet she married a devout Roman Catholic, Jerzy, and did not raise her daughter as a Jew. Every year, Hanna and Jerzy erect a tiny Christmas tree in her living room. "Why not?" she asked me, puzzled that I should ask.

I began to see Hanna somewhat as a mentor and a mother figure, with mine so far away. Because her own daughter and grandson were in Canada, I sense she felt a kinship with me, as well. Almost a year after we met, I invited her and Jerzy to a Passover seder. "You will help me with gefilte fish?" she asked, a command more than a question. It was a two-day process, and the result bore no resemblance to the unappealing congealed pink globules sold in American supermarkets.

I had a lot of questions for Hanna about Jews, about Poland, about Poles and Jews, Jews and Catholics, Jews and Christians. "I don't know everything," she would tell me. Once I asked her whether she found odd my interest in Judaism and my tenuous ancestral connection. "No, no, no," she said, scowling. "In Poland, you must think about these things." She paused. "And for you — even with one Jewish grandparent, Hitler would have wanted you. For me, you are enough Jewish."

The year I returned to the United States from Poland, I thought a lot about what it was to be "enough Jewish." The birth of our daughter made the question of faith and culture more pressing. In Poland, I *had* been "enough Jewish." At services in Warsaw's only synagogue, which was Orthodox, I knew about as much as anyone else. Which is to say virtually nothing; only a few elderly Jews could keep up with the visiting rabbi. Upstairs, in the women's section, hands fluttered through prayer books, and necks craned to see if neighbors had guessed at the same page. No one understood the Hebrew; ignorance was democratic.

It was not quite so simple back home. Here, I wasn't enough anything. I wasn't Christian, since I didn't believe in Christ as the son of God. As much as I admired Judaism and embraced its way of thinking, I had great reservations about converting. I'd heard the stories of those who had become Jews in adulthood: the mothers-in-law who criticized Passover haroseth for not tasting right; the conversations overheard about conversions "not taking." I didn't need that, I figured. I could raise my kids as Jews and fit in with a Reform congregation, where my children would be accepted and I would be welcome. I wouldn't have to shed my identity in the process. But what was my identity, exactly?

I had hoped, of course, to find some clues, some distant ties to Judaism when I visited my great-grandparents' Polish hometown; none existed. After returning to the United States and beginning work on this book, I have asked dozens of historians, Jewish and German alike, who shrug their shoulders. The circumstantial evidence is overwhelming, they all say: my great-grandfather was very likely a Jew, my great-grandmother possibly so. But those facts, even if true, were not enough to resolve my spiritual quandary. My having nineteenth-century Jewish ancestors, if that is what they were, did not have much bearing on my late-twentieth-century problem. I could radically change my religious moorings; people did it every day. The question really was: did I really want to?

In the first year of doing research for this book, I had no idea how that question would come out. I made it clear I had no formal ties to Christianity, except that I liked Christmas — not for its religious content, but for what it meant to me personally. My husband, Stephen, had made it clear that he wanted to raise our children as Jews. Whenever I would broach the topic of conversion, he would shrug it off. "That," he would say, "is something between you and your God. Do it for yourself if you want. But for Ilana Engelberg? You've got to be joking. That kid's a Jew." Without realizing it, he was evoking the negative sense some American Jews have about a Jewish surname, and with it the sense of "belonging," whether you want to or not. I wanted something more for me and my children, something more positive than a distinctive name. Yet as the Gentile partner in an interfaith marriage, I had a sense that I was a stranger in a mystical tribe that lived by a set of written and unwritten rules no outsider could ever learn or understand. Those feelings only deepened as I began to interview vocal opponents of intermarriage, and to read some of the existing literature on the subject.

The implicit argument — one that can be felt in subtle and not-so-subtle ways in many families and synagogues across the country — is that intermarriage must be stopped by any means necessary. In truth, that battle has already been lost. The assimilation of American Jews and their ensuing success in this country mean that intermarriage is here to stay. Even so, the hostility toward it persists in some quarters, in families, and within mainstream Judaism. The attitude, I observed, often makes interfaith couples less enthusiastic about exploring the Jewish faith and culture. Why join a synagogue where we're not really welcome, people ask. On the other hand, I came to understand why some Jews treat the strangers to their tribe so harshly: their history as a persecuted minority; their qualms about the American melting pot; the implications, for Jews everywhere, of carrying on in the decades after the

Holocaust. Gradually, I realized that what Jews thought about me really did not, and could not, affect my own choice about religion.

In my work for this book, I met Jewish thinkers on both sides of the intermarriage debate: rabbis and therapists, sociologists and writers — each of whom had a point of view. The person I felt perhaps most drawn to was Egon Mayer, a sociologist and co-founder of the Jewish Outreach Institute, an organization promoting the Jewish welcome of intermarried couples. Mayer sees intermarriage as a historic opportunity for the American Jewish community to safeguard its heritage — something, he notes, it failed to do during the Holocaust. As a sociologist specializing in religion, Mayer stepped to the forefront of intermarriage studies in the early 1970s, when the first National Jewish Population Survey was released. He has remained there ever since, and has written a book as well as countless studies on the trend.

I was intrigued by his view, of course, especially in light of his background: he is an observant Jew born in Central Europe to Orthodox parents. Disarmingly charming, with deep dimples, Mayer is a product of a bygone era. He drinks tea from a glass and leaps to his feet in the presence of any woman. The lilt of his native speech lingers still — every so often, his *w*'s become soft *v*'s — but his allegiance to Hungary ends there. His parents, from Budapest's educated Jewish elite, had narrowly escaped the gas chambers of Bergen-Belsen, using gifts they had received for their wedding as bribes for the Nazis. They fled Hungary for Switzerland; Mayer was born in a displaced persons' camp there in 1944. After the war, the Mayers returned to Budapest and made their home in a modest flat in the hills outside town. Their lives were uneasy ones: as Jews and as former bourgeois, the Mayers were constantly watched. Even minor violations of Communist law could land a person in jail for decades. During the revolution of 1956, the Mayers left Hungary once again, this time for good. They transplanted themselves to Brooklyn, where Hasidic cousins helped them take root.

Mayer arrived in America — the land of the free, he thought — with the fervent belief in the individual's right to set his own course. The factors that had shaped his young life had nothing to do with him personally, and it is hard to say which left a deeper impression: his birth and survival as a Jew during World War II in Europe, or the monotony of communism and its elevation of the state as the source of political and social power.

In New York, surrounded as Mayer was by other Orthodox Jews, tradition wielded more weight than it ever had in Hungary. He learned Yiddish as well as English, and attended yeshiva instead of public school. It was exhilarating at first, naturally — in Budapest, he was always the outsider, and once punched a boy for calling him a "dirty Jew." In Borough Park, however, there was conformity of another kind. The yeshiva's crossing guard tried to block him from entering an ice cream shop said not to be kosher. Mayer simply pushed the boy out of his way. "You can do what you want," he told the boy, "but I'm going to have my ice cream." Years later, he recalls the incident in his office at the graduate school of New York's City University, staring out at window washers. "I was getting the same crap from people in black hats that I'd gotten from people in red scarves," he says, hands raised in exasperation.

When intermarriage first became an issue in the Jewish community, Mayer was sympathetic. "I identified with people who were looked at askance because of some perceived infraction of formal rules that have nothing to do with their inner lives," he says. "They weren't there when the rules were made, but they know they're in trouble." His defense of intermarried Jews prompted rumors that his wife wasn't Jewish and that his children were being raised as Christians. What else could explain such a position? In reality, however, his personal life — on paper — couldn't have pleased Jewish traditionalists more. He was married to a woman whose Hungarian Orthodox background mirrored his own, and they were raising their daughter as a Jew. Yet for all they shared — culture, language, religion — the marriage was dissolving. How did others from totally different backgrounds work out their problems, Mayer wondered, if he and his wife hadn't been able to manage the task themselves?

Mayer is driven by his passion for Judaism and his hopes for Jewish survival. But he has a deeper impetus as well. He remembers those who were not as lucky as his family, those Jews who perished during the Holocaust. "I do not believe that the so-called Jewish leadership acquitted itself well in the last serious crisis, and I don't believe they are acquitting themselves well now. Left to their own devices, I think American Jewish communal leaders will be as unsuccessful at 'saving' the intermarried as they were unsuccessful at 'saving' the Jews of Europe. I have chosen to see the intermarried, as much as possible, on their own terms, rather than through the lens of historic Jewish communal norms. And I think they are as deserving of the community's collective care and support as any other group. I truly believe that if the community treats them with a welcoming attitude, they are more likely to see themselves as full-fledged members, willingly contributing to the building of a Jewish future." His normally sonorous voice has risen to a shout, which reverberates in his tiny office. "I know, in my life, that I have a tendency to get angrier than is appropriate," he says apologetically. "I don't take pills for it, but sometimes I think I should."

I met plenty of people who had opinions different from Egon's. And, paradoxically, it was one of them, a Conservative rabbi and pugnacious opponent of intermarriage, who nudged me down the road toward converting. His name was Jack Moline, and his uncompromising view of how a congregation or family should deal with interfaith couples was worlds away from Mayer's notion of outreach and inclusion. As I listened to Moline decry the dangers of intermarriage, I felt the blood rising to my face. These outsiders were a threat to the very future of Judaism, of this special civilization.

At first, I saw Mayer and Moline as opposing forces in a primal battle for the soul of Judaism. But over time I saw more and more similarities. Both wanted to foster "Jewish continuity"; both were trying to assure the survival of the American Jewish Community into the twenty-first century. Theirs was a dispute — and a crucial one — over tactics, not goals.

Moline won national attention when the *Wall Street Journal* featured his views against intermarriage in a front-page story —

and prompted hundreds of letters of support. In his sermons for the High Holidays some years ago, he spoke about intermarriage in America as a symptom of Jewish success. To turn the tide against it, he said, families needed to weave Jewish ritual into their lives, to make it "joyously indispensable." Jews had an obligation to marry other Jews, he said, and it was the responsibility of parents to get that message across. "Tell your children: 'I expect you to marry a Jew.'" I read the story with great interest — it was a few years old by the time I saw it — and arranged to meet him at his synagogue. Rabbi Moline is, as my grandmother would say, a "character." A transplanted Chicagoan with the flattened vowels of his native city drawing out every word, he drives a Ford Taurus with the license plate WE 4 CUBS, and wears a Chicago Cubs Swatch. It struck me odd that a guy in his early forties who grew up listening to protest music would have such qualms about those others picked as their mates. Of course, Moline is a Conservative rabbi, and the Conservative movement takes a strong stance against intermarriage; Conservative rabbis are forbidden to perform interfaith weddings. When they do occur, the Conservative rabbinate calls, at the very least, for the conversion of non-Jewish spouses and the conversion of children born to non-Jewish mothers. Most Conservative synagogues do not allow non-Jews to become full members.

When I asked him to explain his tough stand against intermarriage, considering his youth — he looked at me as if I were nuts. "I'm a rabbi!" he shouted, and offered me a Snapple. "Next?" It was hard to keep a straight face, which of course was his point. He had grown up in a traditionally Jewish home, keeping kosher, observing the Sabbath and all Jewish holidays, major and minor. "Shabbat was the most wonderful day of the week," he says. "I felt so lucky to be a Jew, to have that time for reflection and for my family. It was really something special." Ritual bolstered his faith, and he urges his congregants to follow tradition themselves. Keep kosher, he tells them. Mind the Sabbath. He acknowledges that few couples avoid sex during a woman's menstrual period, but he still mentions it. And a lot of his congregants complain. "They say, 'Stop criticizing us. This just isn't important. Stop preaching it to me. I'm doing the best I can. Enough already!' But I can't. This is who I am, and this is the package. It is a divine mandate, and I can't choose to ignore it." As for newfangled notions such as outreach to intermarried couples, Moline guffaws. "Waste of resources," he says. "Marginal Jews" — those Jews who intermarry and make no effort to maintain their ties to the community — are "already gone. Spend that time, that effort, on people who make up the core community."

We met a number of times, and I told him about some of the couples I had talked to. On a hot summer day, he padded around his office in an embroidered yarmulke, sandals, and shorts, white legs a stark contrast to his peeling arms, tanned from a recent trip to Israel. He asked me, point-blank, why I hadn't converted. No one had ever been so blunt about such a personal decision. Well, I stammered. I couldn't come up with an answer right away. I didn't need to, I said. My kids would be fine, I said. He nodded, but his lips betrayed him. They drew into the tight line of a disapproving librarian. I left his office feeling a little unsettled.

I couldn't stop thinking about his question, which was all the more disturbing because it came from someone whose views on inter-marriage I found unacceptable. And naturally I knew why he said what he had: as a rabbi and a committed Jew, he felt it his obliga-tion to ask me about conversion. But still, I wondered, what was holding me back? A Christmas tree, one day a year? I had gone many Christmases without one. What was the point, I wondered, of celebrating a holiday I didn't truly believe in, I didn't truly embrace the meaning of? I was raising my daughter as a Jew; I could raise myself as one, too. I wasn't ambivalent about anything else — politics, music — why this? Long ago, I had decided to cast my lot with the Jews, perhaps before I even realized it. And so I decided: I would convert. The day I made up my mind, Steve and I were preparing dinner for a Polish-Jewish friend who was in town, Kostek Gebert. I blurted out my decision as I cut a lemon. Kostek, a journalist in his forties who is seen as the voice of Poland's remain-ing Jews, embraced me with his customary rib-crushing hug and kissed me on both cheeks. "Mazel tov," he said, eyes brimming with tears. Steve, meanwhile, kept chopping his garlic. "Did you hear me?" I asked, sure that he hadn't. "Yeah," he said. "It's nice." "Nice?" I asked, shocked. I said my words slowly and loudly, as if he spoke English poorly. "You think it's nice that I'm going to convert to Judaism?" He paused, knife aloft. "If I said, 'Darling, I think it's the greatest thing ever,' what would that be saying? That I loved you less before? What do you want me to say? Of course I'm thrilled. I loved you then; I love you now; I'll love you when you're a Jew." He had a point. Either response risked my ire.

A few weeks later, I called a Reform rabbi, Mindy A. Portnoy. She was well known in Washington for her energy and wit, as well as for a book she'd written about being a mother and a rabbi, *Ima on the Bimah: My Mom Is a Rabbi.* I convinced her that, with my background and the book I was writing, I could bypass an introduction-to-Judaism course. She agreed, and I began to study with her privately. I looked forward to our weekly sessions. I felt as if I were in college again, only this time I actually read all the material I was supposed to. Over seven months, I read Hebrew scripture, parts of the Talmud, and many midrashim, the commentaries on the Talmud and the Bible. I learned the Hebrew alphabet. I read the work of Jewish theologians. We talked about being Jewish in a Christian world, raising kids, knotty family problems, everything. Part guide, part sage, part feminist, Rabbi Portnoy was a wonderful teacher. She laughed as I eagerly tackled the Kabbalah, the basic text of the Jewish mystics, and spent hours one night trying to draw explanatory diagrams for myself. (This turned out to be a futile exercise.) There were no term papers, no midterms, just a final: questions by the three rabbis who formed the bet din — Jewish court of law — about my sincerity and knowledge. So, two weeks away from the birth of my second child, Moriah, I climbed into the mikvah with my older daughter, Ilana. We emerged as Jews.

Sometime later, I finally told friends about my conversion. I was shy about it at first, just as I was in ritual. On Friday nights, I was tentative about the blessings over the candles and the challah. At services, I sat in back and fumbled along with the Hebrew prayers. A year after I converted, I read a magazine piece by Stephen Dubner, whose Jewish-born parents had become Catholics. Dubner recounted his return as an adult to his Jewish roots; his words stuck with me for weeks.

"It may be that the transcendent mystery of a religious conversion, like the transcendence of sex, is incommunicable," he wrote. "A conversion is a tangle of loneliness, ambition, fear and, of course, hope. It is never tidy." A memoir written by a convert generally falls into one of two categories, Dubner wrote: the breathless account of an irreversible epiphany — not me for sure — or the story of someone who "pokes around his soul and his mind, yet arrives at no more concrete an explanation than a pressing desire to change the course of his life."[1]

Indeed, after several years of poking around my soul and mind, I found that converting to Judaism was best for me and what I envisioned for my family's future. But it elicited some odd responses. When I told my mother-in-law I was converting, she said, "To what?" Steve told me she was joking, that she didn't want me to think she cared one way or the other. But it took me by surprise.

And if I got that response from her, I could only imagine what my own mother would say. I waited to tell her until I could do so in person, when I was almost finished with my studies. A lump closed my throat as I broached the subject, and she reacted just as I had suspected she would. She was stunned, hurt, and disappointed — my worst, most dreaded childhood fear. "But you said you'd never convert," she said. (I did, I'm sure, but I don't recall saying it.) For my father, a resolute browser of antique stores and a collector of ancient farm implements, the idea of a new twist in his past was more fascinating than threatening. His belief in God was more personal than a connection to any particular denomination. In fact, he had converted to Catholicism some years earlier. His move was made largely because he and my mother do most things together, and the Catholic church is where they found a home after their Episcopal church took a swerve they didn't like. My mother, however, felt very different. Her reaction had nothing to do with my embracing Judaism, she insisted. It was far more essential than that: it had to do with her. My middle sister, Michelle, who had married a Jew, was also converting to Judaism and was raising her kids as Jews. My mother had a lot of questions. If Judaism was a religion as well as a culture, a civilization, how could I, with roots on an Oregon farm, be a part of the latter? Indeed, I had come some distance from my background driving combines and tractors, singing along with Willie Nelson on the radio.

What about *our* traditions, she seemed to be saying. What about what *we* did? What's wrong with *them?* She hadn't worried when I got married, or when my sister did, but this seemed a step too far. Was she losing her daughters? Now that I would no longer share her traditions, wouldn't there be a barrier between us? I didn't think so, but how could I see into the future? She wondered aloud about where she'd gone wrong in not giving us a stronger faith. She had the wrong question, I thought: it was exactly what she had done right, in exposing us to other cultures, in fostering understanding, and in imbuing us with a need for religion that made me seek my own.

My mother's fear is echoed by Jewish parents when their children intermarry — even those who preach tolerance, and who struggle to teach lessons of fairness. Very soon, my mother came around to believing that she had planted the need for religion in our households, regardless of what it was. Still, I can see that it is painful for her not to share elaborate Easter dinners and the festivities she so loves at Christmastime. "Won't you miss Christmas?" she asked once. The first few times I went without a tree — and I did this several years before converting — I had pangs, I must admit. I missed its fresh scent, missed seeing the lights in a darkened room. So I substituted, by putting tiny white lights on one bush outside my house. Surely no one could object to that. It wasn't exactly Jewish, but it didn't seem a proclamation of Christianity, either. Now, our house is the only dark one on the block in December, except for the menorah that glows for a few hours in the windowsill each night during Hanukkah. And I don't, in fact, "miss" Christmas. In America, even a distant bystander — an outsider who has chosen the outside — finds it impossible to "miss" Christmas.

No matter what I say, though, people are bound to doubt my sincerity, my loyalty to Judaism. Converts of any religion face skeptics, those who scorn the ones not born into the faith, those who see it as a birthright to protect. Joe Gold, the born Jew who became a Lutheran, still meets Christians who insist that, forty years after his baptism, he can't really believe in Christ as his savior. There are many converts to Judaism in the Conservative synagogue we joined after a recent move from Washington to New York. In a Hebrew language class I took, seven of the twelve students were Jews by choice — and two were over fifty. Most, I think, try doubly hard to prove their efforts worthy of this civilization they have come to join. But the discomfort is remarkable. When our instructor goodnaturedly scolded us for confusing vowels, one woman said, "What do you expect? Half of us are Italian."

This insecurity is nothing new to those who choose their faiths. Many feel they can't catch up with years of Hebrew or Catholic school or what people picked up through osmosis. I have even heard some arguments for "genetic knowledge." Once in a while, people say odd things. One woman told me she really didn't accept her husband, a convert to Judaism, as "one of us." Someone once sniffed that I could not convert until I learned to read and speak Hebrew fluently. "Do you?" I asked. (She did not.) A mitzvah — good deed — in Judaism is to accept the convert as a true Jew, one who has *chosen*, despite the knowledge of the painful Jewish past, to become a Jew. The Torah instructs Jews to love and respect the convert.

But even the most open-minded people have a way of clamming up when it comes to religion, to heritage, to claims. A Jewish woman I know was terrified of giving her child her husband's Irish surname — the opposite of what Rebecca Schubert felt. Even though the child would clearly be Jewish, she was worried that people would think the child was Irish. "Why?" I asked her. "Is that so bad?" "Yes," she replied. First, she said, she didn't want anyone to think her baby, with such a distinctively Gentile last name, wasn't an authentic Jew; second, the Irish were a bunch of anti-Semites. Did that include her husband? I wondered. On matters of faith, logic has a way of escaping even the most rational minds.

After three years of talking to people in interfaith marriages, I saw and heard some things that helped to tip the scales in my own decision. But I refrain from judging the spiritual dilemmas and solutions that come up for others; enough of them come from elsewhere. I found that in most intermarriages, whether the non-Jewish spouse has converted or maintains his or her ties to an original faith, people are, in fact, knowledgeable about their spouse's religion and traditions. Many of those who intermarry meet their spouses at the workplace or in college, like Maura and Josh. They, too, are intelligent people, whether Catholic or Jew, Hindu or Protestant, Muslim or Buddhist. They, too, have roots and histories, pasts and interests, and, most often, their own relationship with God. Because they have chosen to marry or date a Jew, they may know something about Judaism, Jewish tradition, and Jewish holidays. The world of segregation — Jews in one neighborhood, Christians in another — is for the most part long gone. Educated Americans are well aware of the rituals observed by others. Hanukkah and Passover cards — while not Jewish traditions, they proliferate on stationers' shelves — serve as reminders to the Gentile world that others have holidays as well. Bagels, once the domain of Jewish bakeries, have entered into the American mainstream, as close as your grocer's freezer case or corner Starbucks. Granted, sundried-tomato-and-basil bagels may not exactly fit one's idea of tradition. But in this intermingled culture, where gay fashion dictates what straight people will wear next season, where Protestant Texans say, "Oy vay," where Anglos name their kids after Michael Jordan and Whitney Houston, and where salsa has replaced catsup as the most widely used condiment, it makes perfect sense.

Few Jewish people who choose Gentile spouses do so in a deliberate attempt to vex the Jewish people or to leave Judaism behind. Most have high hopes that they will somehow forge, with their spouses, Jewish children who happen to have Christmas trees. Is this authentic? Only God knows. As a new member of the tribe, I cannot help noting that Jews have survived every imaginable plague and defied every woeful prediction. It is worth keeping in mind.

Glossary

Notes

Glossary

Ashkenazi   Name applied to the Jews of Central and Eastern Europe.

Bar mitzvah (literally, "son of the commandments")   The age at which a boy becomes religiously and ethically responsible for his acts. The service and subsequent party celebrating the achievement of this status are usually held around the boy's thirteenth birthday.

Bat mitzvah (literally, "daughter of the commandments")   The age at which a girl becomes religiously and ethically responsible for her acts. The service and subsequent party celebrating the achievement of this status are usually held around the girl's thirteenth birthday.

Bialy   A flat roll with a depression in the center, usually covered with onion flakes.

Bimah   The platform in the sanctuary from which the Torah is read, and where the rabbi stands while leading services.

B'nai B'rith   Organization of Jewish men, founded in 1843.

Bris   Yiddish for the Hebrew *brit milah*. The ceremony of circumcision, traditionally done eight days after the boy's birth.

Challah   The braided white feast bread.

Dreidel   The four-sided top used to play a game of chance during Hanukkah.

Haggadah   The prayer book for the Passover seder.

Havdalah   The ceremony marking the end of the Sabbath.

Kaddish   One of the most ancient Jewish prayers, recited at the close of synagogue services; also the prayer said every day for a year after the death of an immediate relative, and on the anniversary of that person's death.

Kashrut   The dietary laws of keeping kosher.

Ketubah   The Jewish wedding contract.

Kiddush   The prayer and ceremony that sanctify the Sabbath and other Jewish holidays.

Kiddushin   The first part of the Jewish wedding ceremony.

Macher   Yiddish for someone who arranges or organizes.

Mezuzah   Ritual object containing a scroll inscribed with fifteen verses from the Book of Deuteronomy affixed to the doorjambs of Jewish homes.

Midrash   A collection of rabbinical commentary on the Bible.

Mikvah   Ritual bath used for conversion ceremony.

Mitzvah   Commandment, or good deed.

Mohel   A Jew trained to perform ritual circumcision.

Naming ceremony   The ceremony developed by Jewish feminists in the 1970s to welcome Jewish infant girls into the covenant. The liturgy of the brit milah is modified for the occasion. It can be performed in the home or in a synagogue.

Passover   The eight-day holiday in spring that commemorates the Jews' exodus from Egypt. During the eight days, Jews abstain from all leavened products.

Purim   Festival commemorating the victory of Jews in Persia over Haman, a minister who plotted to kill them, as described in the Book of Esther.

Sandek   Male friend or relative who holds an infant boy during his circumcision. Godfather.

Seder   A ceremonial dinner held on the first and second nights of Passover.

Sephardi Jews who settled in Greece, Turkey, the Middle East, and North Africa after their expulsion from Spain and Portugal.

Shiva The seven days of mourning following the death of an immediate relative.

Shlep Yiddish, to drag.

Shlock Yiddish for a cheaply made article.

Shmegegge Yiddish for a whiner, a jerk.

Shmendrick Yiddish for a nobody, a good-for-nothing.

Shtetl Yiddish for a town or village in Central and Eastern Europe.

Tallis Yiddish for tallit, or prayer shawl.

Talmud The authoritative body of Jewish teaching; commentaries and debates among scholars who for centuries interpreted the Torah (the first five books of the Bible) and applied its lessons to new problems.

Tzedakah The obligation God exacts from Jews to be compassionate and charitable.

Yarmulke Yiddish for skullcap.

Notes

Preface

1. Victoria Redel, *Where the Road Bottoms Out* (New York: Knopf, 1995), pp. 13–25.
2. Elihu Bergman, "The American Jewish Population Erosion," *Midstream* (October 1977), pp. 9–19.
3. Barry Kosmin and Jeffrey Scheckner, "Highlights of the National Jewish Population Survey" (New York: Council of Jewish Federations, 1991), pp. 4–14.
4. *Goy*, Hebrew for "nation," means "non-Jew" in Yiddish. Leo Rosten, in *The Joys of Yinglish* (New York: Plume, 1989), insists that goy is not an "invidious appellation. Goy means gentile — no more, no less. The fact that some Jews pronounce goy with distaste is comparable to the way some gentiles pronounce Jew" (p. 220).

1. That's a Jewish Name, Isn't It?

1. Steven Lowenstein, *The Jews of Oregon, 1850–1950* (Portland: The Jewish Historical Society of Portland, 1987), pp. 89–91.
2. Ibid., pp. 30–31.

4. Double Exposure

1. Kosmin and Scheckner, "Highlights of the National Jewish Population Survey," p. 14.

5. Two Lives

1. Dr. Yehuda Nir, a Manhattan psychiatrist whose practice consists

largely of Holocaust survivors and their children, offered some basic explanations for the desire of those adult children to intermarry. Emphasizing that each case, of course, is different, he said that there are three basic reasons why children of Holocaust survivors choose Gentile mates.

The first, Dr. Nir says, is rebellion. "They are really defiant of their parents. They want to say: 'We're different.' The parents react strongly, even sit shiva in some cases. And in a sense, it works. They *are* breaking away from the past."

Others, he says, may wish to disappear into mainstream culture — something their parents, by and large, were unable to do.

"Finally, they want to merge into the Gentile family, to cut off contacts with the past," Dr. Nir says. "They become immersed in their new environment. They are eager to be accepted — it's their way of saying good-bye to the past. It's almost like leaving the planet. And they really do disappear, for their families and for themselves. It's a self-imposed exile, in a way, a coping mechanism for their parents' past."

Dr. Nir says he often hears the issue of name-identification. To many children of survivors, the idea of camouflaging oneself in a hostile outside world is a great comfort indeed. To appear less vulnerable than their parents is a frequent desire.

Still other children of survivors may want to escape into a world wholly unlike the painful one they know. To many, the Gentile world appears free of the pathos that marks the Jews. To flee into it, Dr. Nir says, represents an escape from the burdens of Jewishness. Since Judaism exacted such a heavy toll on their parents, some feel that moving away from it will ensure them a happier life.

10. Sushi and Gefilte Fish

1. Martin Gilbert, *The Holocaust: A History of the Jews of Europe During the Second World War* (New York: Henry Holt & Co., 1985), p. 84.

11. Chicken Soup

1. In their book on Americans and their religions, *One Nation Under God* (New York: Harmony, 1993), Barry A. Kosmin and Seymour P. Lachman write that about 30 percent of Americans change denominations in their lifetimes. The authors found that the most common reason for

switching is intermarriage, followed by a change in religious conviction or a geographical move. "Most changes to achieve religious consensus in the home usually occur at the time of marriage, at the birth of the first child, or when children reach school age. The push toward religious homogeneity is rooted in the American belief that religious differences between husband and wife are not good either for the marriage or for the children of the marriage. Moreover, it is simpler and more convenient for everyone in the family to belong to the same religious group" (pp. 239–240).

2. Irving Howe, *World of Our Fathers: The Journey of the East European Jews to America and the Life They Found and Made* (New York: Schocken Books, 1989), p. 609.

12. All-American

1. Sara Bershtel and Allen Graubard, *Saving Remnants: Feeling Jewish in America* (Berkeley: University of California Press, 1992), p. 63.

2. According to the National Jewish Population Survey of 1990, only 3 percent of those who said they were born Jewish now identify themselves as converts to another faith (Kosmin and Scheckman, "Highlights of the National Jewish Population Survey," p. 9).

Indeed, under Jewish law, it is technically impossible for a Jew (that is, anyone born to a Jewish mother or anyone who has converted to Judaism) ever to renounce his Judaism. A Jew is a Jew forever, even if he sins. As a sinner he may forfeit some privileges, but he does not lose his basic rights as a Jew; see Alfred J. Kolatch, *The Second Jewish Book of Why* (Middle Village, New York: Jonathan David Publishers, 1985), p. 19.

Epilogue: "Enough Jewish"

1. Stephen Dubner, "Choosing My Religion," *New York Times Magazine,* March 31, 1996.